Implementing Samba 4

Exploit the real power of Samba 4 Server by leveraging the benefits of an Active Directory Domain Controller

Marcelo Leal

[PACKT] PUBLISHING open source community experience distilled

BIRMINGHAM - MUMBAI

Implementing Samba 4

First published: April 2014

Production Reference: 1310314

Published by Packt Publishing Ltd.
Livery Place
35 Livery Street
Birmingham B3 2PB, UK.

ISBN 978-1-78216-658-0

www.packtpub.com

Cover Image by Marcelo Leal (msl@eall.com.br)

Credits

Author
Marcelo Leal

Reviewers
Kai Blin
Henry Gultom
Iulian-Nicu Șerbănoiu
Manikandan Somasundaram

Acquisition Editors
Akram Hussain
Nikhil Karkal

Content Development Editor
Athira Laji

Technical Editors
Manan Badani
Shali Sasidharan

Copy Editors
Tanvi Gaitonde
Aditya Nair
Stuti Srivastava

Project Coordinator
Sanghamitra Deb

Proofreaders
Mario Cecere
Maria Gould
Clyde Jenkins

Indexer
Monica Ajmera Mehta

Graphics
Sheetal Aute
Disha Haria
Yuvraj Mannari

Production Coordinator
Nilesh Bambardekar

Cover Work
Nilesh Bambardekar

Foreword

Shared, networked file and print services are the heart and blood of any office environment. They allow users of a network to store their files reliably, share them with each other, and bridge the gap between multiple places of work, multiple devices and tools, and multiple operating systems.

The latter aspect is key to a modern work environment: integrating the worlds of Unix/Linux and Mac OS X with the traditional Windows PC environment not only allows users of a "foreign" OS to collaborate in a Windows-dominated world, it also enables Windows environments to benefit from the power of Unix/Linux server environments with advanced networking, high availability, backup/recovery, and automation capabilities as well as integration with enterprise-class infrastructure and tools.

When Andrew Tridgell implemented the first version of Samba in 1991, he probably did not foresee the tremendous impact that his software would have on today's office productivity environments and the role it would fill as the bridge between two worlds that couldn't be more different from each other. Yet, this is exactly what makes Samba so fascinating: the power to integrate the Windows world with the Unix/Linux/Mac OS X world, the Rosetta Stone of filesystem protocols.

Wielding this power can be difficult and complicated. In today's hectic world of IT system administration, the pressure to deliver a robust, stable, highly available, and dependable infrastructure at a low cost has never been greater. Modern system administrators frequently don't have the time or training to understand every possible aspect of any given software, especially if it is a complex system that has grown over several decades. They need simple, practical, relevant advice on how to accomplish their day-to-day tasks, enabling them to get the basics of file and print services up and running. They need to do so quickly and efficiently, so they can concentrate on higher-level tasks, knowing that the key underlying infrastructure is in place and running reliably.

I'm very happy to see that Marcelo has accepted the challenge of boiling down heaps of documentation, white papers, and other collateral into a single, concise, practical guide to implementing Samba 4. Marcelo draws from over a decade of experience in running large-scale IT projects, from high-level planning to the nitty-gritty details of command-line options and complex troubleshooting.

And the result is a clear, concise, extremely useful step-by-step guide on how to set up your Samba 4 environment: from basic installation to AD Domain Controller setup and management, migration from an existing Windows server environment, upgrading from Samba 3, running file and print services, LDAP, clustering, and of course scripting. This guide has got you covered.

Of course, no guide can replace the full documentation or address the intricacies of every single corner case. But staying true to the Pareto principle, this is exactly the 20 percent of documentation that you need to read to get 80 percent of your Samba 4 work done. With Marcelo's expertise boiled down into a single book, you can get up and running quickly, then concentrate your energy into those aspects of your installation that are unique to your environment and that warrant your special attention.

IT system administrators often have an aura of "IT wizards" around them, as if they had the power to "heal" a broken computer with the touch of a hand. This "magic" really stems from decades of experience; hard-learned intuition; and the tedious, day-to-day work of getting IT stuff done. I hope that the "virtual Marcelo" distilled into this book can help you become such a "Samba wizard", enabling you to ensure that your organization's productivity is covered, at least from a file and print perspective.

Constantin Gonzalez
IT, Unix and file system survivor

About the Author

Marcelo Leal studied at Unisinos, where he undertook a Bachelor's degree in Computing Science. Having worked in the IT industry for more than 15 years, he has gained experience as a network/system administrator, support manager, Unix/Linux specialist, storage architect, and most recently, as a solutions architect. He was involved in open source projects since the beginning of his career and has developed some open source tools and submitted patches to the GNU/Linux and FreeBSD kernel. In 2005, he was honored for his participation in the Prêmio TI e Governo for the project "Metrópole", Porto Alegre/RS. He was one of the founders of the Porto Alegre OpenSolaris User Group (PoaOSUG) and was a contributor for the Open High Availability Cluster Community (OHAC) within the OpenSolaris Project; he was the first person outside Sun Microsystems to contribute code to the Open Cluster software. He received three prizes at the OpenSolaris innovation awards program (2007-2008), and presented a solution for Storage High Availability using nonshared disks at the first OHAC Summit in San Francisco/California, USA (2009). In 2013, he presented a highly available, scalable, and high performance three-layer storage solution at SNIA SpeedConf, Santa Clara/California, USA, which, besides adding a lot of value to the storage service, provided huge savings in capex and opex costs (millions of dollars in three years). He has led the architecture and development of a distributed Storage Appliance that, in three years, provided more than 1.5 million operations per second (CIFS, NFS, and iSCSI) for almost 10PB in an area available for a diverse range of products. In 2010, he wrote *ZFS -Para usuários OpenSolaris, Windows, Mac e Linux, Brasport*, the first book about ZFS in Brazilian Portuguese and actually one of the few books about ZFS available in a language other than English. He tries to write regularly on his blog at `http://www.eall.com.br/blog`.

Acknowledgments

First, I would like to thank the open source community for all the hackers involved in bringing lines and lines of code, documentation, and knowledge into the world. I would like to specifically thank the Samba project team and community! The Samba 4 software is a huge accomplishment and deserves all our appreciation for the effort taken in delivering such a great product. I would like to thank all the editors and reviewers who worked with me during the journey of this book; I would not have been able to do it without your help and invaluable inputs. I would like to thank my family: Ana, Júnior, Pedro, and Leonardo. It's all for you! Last but not least, a big thank you to my grandmother and my mother, Maria Leal. She is the reason I stand here today.

About the Reviewers

Kai Blin is a computational biologist by trade and an open source developer by passion. As he is more of a network and systems programmer in his spare time, the Samba Team member feels lucky to also be able to work on open source software in his day job. He holds a PhD in Microbiology from the University of Tübingen in Germany and is currently working on his post-doc in Cologne.

Henry Gultom is a Linux consultant for an IT company that operates out of Indonesia, Nigeria, and the Kingdom of Tonga. With more than 10 years' experience in Linux administration, he has acquired a deep technical background in the management, design, assessment, and systems integration of information technologies. Since 2010, he has been helping many IT companies in Indonesia to use Samba 4 and has been successful until now.

Iulian-Nicu Şerbănoiu is a graduate of Politehnica University of Bucharest. He also holds a master's degree in Advanced Computer Architectures from the same institution. He is a senior software engineer, with a specialization in imperative programming languages, such as Java, C++, and Python. He has a passion for free/libre software and always tries to be up to date with the latest technologies. He loves scripting languages and uses them to automate tasks as much as possible.

I would like to thank my family for giving me the opportunity to grow and become what I am today. Thank you very much for your support; without you, I'm nothing.

Manikandan Somasundaram has over three years of experience in the field of Linux administration. He is a BE Computer Science graduate. Being a Linux enthusiast, he has his specialization in RHCE (Red Hat Certified Engineer) and RHCSS (Red Hat Certified Security Specialist). He started his career as a Linux system engineer in a small, Chennai-based start-up company, where he had the freedom to explore/implement the world of open source, so he has migrated a number of software from proprietary to open source, such as the openfire intranet chat server. Then, he moved to SafeScrypt, a business unit part of Sify Technologies Limited, which is the India's first CA (Certificate Authority). Here, he had an opportunity to work with the PKI infrastructure and certification practices that helped him relate his RHCSS studies to reality in a better way. Currently, he is working for MindTree Ltd. as a Linux system administrator and pursuing an MS Software Systems degree from BITS Pilani, India. His main hobby is to provide freelance training on Linux administration, and his other hobbies are yoga, martial arts, gymnastics, and playing the guitar.

I wish to personally thank the following people for their contributions, and for inspiring me and providing me with knowledge and help in reviewing this book:

Well wishers: Prof Vishvanathan, A.V.C. College Of Engineering, Gerald Nathan, Principal Consultant, Corpus Software Pvt Ltd.

My family: Somasundaram (my father), Tamizarasi Somasundaram (my mother), and Durgadevi (my sister).

www.PacktPub.com

Support files, eBooks, discount offers, and more

You might want to visit www.PacktPub.com for support files and downloads related to your book.

Did you know that Packt offers eBook versions of every book published, with PDF and ePub files available? You can upgrade to the eBook version at www.PacktPub.com and as a print book customer, you are entitled to a discount on the eBook copy. Get in touch with us at service@packtpub.com for more details.

At www.PacktPub.com, you can also read a collection of free technical articles, sign up for a range of free newsletters and receive exclusive discounts and offers on Packt books and eBooks.

PACKTLIB®

http://PacktLib.PacktPub.com

Do you need instant solutions to your IT questions? PacktLib is Packt's online digital book library. Here, you can access, read and search across Packt's entire library of books.

Why subscribe?

- Fully searchable across every book published by Packt
- Copy and paste, print and bookmark content
- On demand and accessible via web browser

Free access for Packt account holders

If you have an account with Packt at www.PacktPub.com, you can use this to access PacktLib today and view nine entirely free books. Simply use your login credentials for immediate access.

Table of Contents

Preface

After many years of hard work, coding, and testing, the open source community was presented with the Samba software Version 4 at the end of 2012. Whoever was involved in the Samba project or had participated in the community knows how much this version was awaited. Besides all the new features that the Samba Server Version 4 brings in this important release, the one that stands out unanimously is the Active Directory capabilities. Microsoft Active Directory Services is a very popular technology among different companies, from small or medium size organizations to big enterprises.

With the new Samba 4 software version, users and system administrators will be able to implement an Active Directory Server, file and print services, and deliver a broad range of network services using open source technology. Samba 4 has main built-in capabilities needed for the server side of the Active Directory services, such as the LDAP server, the Kerberos Key Distribution Center, and a simple DNS server.

This book is a practical guide intended to provide easy-to-use, step-by-step procedures to help users and system administrators implement Active Directory services on their networks using the freedom of open source software. We will learn how to use the Samba 4 Server as an Active Directory server, as well as understand the other roles this software can play in the organization environment.

What this book covers

Chapter 1, Installing the Samba 4 Server, provides us with a quick overview of the Debian GNU/Linux installation procedure, and we will learn how to install and configure all the Samba 4 dependencies needed for our Samba 4 use cases. In this chapter, the reader will learn how to validate the Samba 4 installation and how to execute basic tests to make sure that the Samba 4 installation is ready.

Chapter 2, Provisioning Samba 4 as an AD Domain Controller, talks about the basic tasks required to get a proper Samba 4 Active Directory as a Domain Controller configured on the network. This chapter will focus on minimal planning, checklists, and the key points to consider before starting the provisioning. We will learn how to provision the Samba 4 as an Active Directory Server in detail.

Chapter 3, Managing the Samba Active Directory Server, describes the different roles the Samba 4 Server can play on the network, and how to basically manage it using Microsoft Windows machines (for example, Microsoft Windows Server 2008 R2). The reader will learn how to integrate a Debian GNU/Linux client on the Samba 4 domain and to have the authentication and authorization working in this system. Also covered in this chapter are the replication and trust relationship characteristics of an Active Directory Domain Controller when running the Samba 4 Server at the present time.

Chapter 4, Replacing a Microsoft Windows Active Directory Server, intends to show you how to replace a Microsoft Windows Server Active Directory by a Samba 4 Server. We will learn the key consideration points, our example configuration scenario, some backup/recovery and rollback techniques, and in the end, the step-by-step procedure to execute the replacement of our Microsoft Windows Server 2008 R2 with the Samba 4 Server as the Active Directory Domain Controller. We will also learn about some basic tests and validations to make sure that the process is successful and the environment is fully functional.

Chapter 5, Upgrading from Samba Server Version 3, describes the main differences between Samba software Version 3 and Version 4 and the considerations before planning a successful upgrade. We will also learn about the plan, tests, validations, as well as a step-by-step procedure to execute the upgrade and all the commands and scripts that are needed to go from a Samba 3 Primary Domain Controller to a Samba 4 fully functional Active Directory Domain Controller.

Chapter 6, Printing and File Services, covers the file and printing services for the Samba 4 Server. We will learn about some differences between the file and printing capabilities of Samba Server Version 3 and Version 4. We will learn about the SMB/CIFS protocol versions of Samba 4, the Samba 4 file and print server daemons, Microsoft Windows print driver Version 3 and Version 4. We will learn how to configure a printer on the Samba 4 Server host using CUPS and how to share the printer on a Microsoft Active Directory network using Samba. We have introduced Microsoft Windows Point and Print Samba Server configuration and basic File sharing with Samba 4.

Chapter 7, Extending the Active Directory Schema Using Samba 4, describes how to extend the default Active Directory schema for some specific applications when using a built-in Samba 4 as the Active Directory Domain Controller.

Chapter 8, Implementing a Highly Available Distributed File Server, focuses on how to implement a highly available and distributed file server using Samba 4 Server, GlusterFS, and CTDB.

Chapter 9, The Samba 4 Python Scripting Interface, describes some basics about the Samba 4 internals, going through some code snippets and understanding the open source development and collaborative work. This chapter also provides us with an introduction to the Samba 4 Python bindings, teaches us how to explore and start using the new Python interface of the Samba 4 Server, and describes a practical example using the combined power of Python and Samba 4.

Appendix, References, provides the links for the references used in the book.

What you need for this book

This book is focused on the Samba 4 software and its installation on a Debian GNU/Linux operating system. So, the reader will need an Internet connection to download and install both the software and a CD/DVD with the respective software that is available. The procedure to install the Debian GNU/Linux system is specific, but it should be simple or adequate to other GNU/Linux distributions (the shell scripts are written in bash, and should be similar in any GNU/Linux distribution).

All code and procedures presented through this book must not be used in production; so, a test environment with the machines needed for each lab needs to be created. It's highly important that the step-by-step procedures be executed in an isolated environment where the reader can stress test all the code and configuration examples provided. A good option is to use a virtualized environment, and if that is the choice for the readers, any virtualized solution that supports the Microsoft Windows Servers and GNU/Linux needed by the customer can be used.

Who this book is for

People who will benefit the most from this book should fit into one of these two categories: they should have good knowledge of Microsoft Windows and basic knowledge of GNU/Linux systems or they should have good experience with GNU/Linux systems and basic knowledge of Microsoft Windows Operating System. Both groups need to manage and integrate a heterogeneous environment, where GNU/Linux and Microsoft Windows Servers and workstations need to have a centralized authentication and authorization service, file and print sharing, configuration management, and so on.

The expected audience will have specific needs and should seek pragmatic solutions such as replacing a Microsoft Windows Active Directory Server with a Samba 4 Server when the administrator does not have much experience with GNU/Linux, or implementing an Active Directory Server in an environment where the majority of the systems are GNU/Linux operating systems, while still having to support and integrate Microsoft Windows machines.

Conventions

In this book, you will find a number of styles of text that distinguish between different kinds of information. Here are some examples of these styles, and an explanation of their meaning.

Code words in text are shown as follows: "We just need to install the `kerberos config` file in its right directory, and to do that, we just need to issue the following command:"

Any command-line input or output is written as follows:

```
leal@debian7:~$ sudo /usr/local/samba/sbin/samba -i -M single
Password:
```

A block of code is set as follows:

```
[DEVCODDS]
    comment = DEV COD DS
    path = /var/lib/samba/devcodds
    read only = No
```

New terms and **important words** are shown in bold. Words that you see on the screen, in menus or dialog boxes for example, appear in the text like this: "We can connect to our snapshot directly by issuing the following command at the **Start** | **Run** menu:".

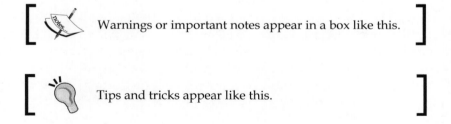

> Warnings or important notes appear in a box like this.

> Tips and tricks appear like this.

Reader feedback

Feedback from our readers is always welcome. Let us know what you think about this book—what you liked or may have disliked. Reader feedback is important for us to develop titles that you really get the most out of.

To send us general feedback, simply send an e-mail to `feedback@packtpub.com`, and mention the book title via the subject of your message.

If there is a topic that you have expertise in and you are interested in either writing or contributing to a book, see our author guide on `www.packtpub.com/authors`.

Customer support

Now that you are the proud owner of a Packt book, we have a number of things to help you to get the most from your purchase.

Downloading the example code

You can download the example code files for all Packt books you have purchased from your account at `http://www.packtpub.com`. If you purchased this book elsewhere, you can visit `http://www.packtpub.com/support` and register to have the files e-mailed directly to you.

Errata

Although we have taken every care to ensure the accuracy of our content, mistakes do happen. If you find a mistake in one of our books—maybe a mistake in the text or the code—we would be grateful if you would report this to us. By doing so, you can save other readers from frustration and help us improve subsequent versions of this book. If you find any errata, please report them by visiting `http://www.packtpub.com/submit-errata`, selecting your book, clicking on the **errata submission form** link, and entering the details of your errata. Once your errata are verified, your submission will be accepted and the errata will be uploaded on our website, or added to any list of existing errata, under the Errata section of that title. Any existing errata can be viewed by selecting your title from `http://www.packtpub.com/support`.

Piracy

Piracy of copyright material on the Internet is an ongoing problem across all media. At Packt, we take the protection of our copyright and licenses very seriously. If you come across any illegal copies of our works, in any form, on the Internet, please provide us with the location address or website name immediately so that we can pursue a remedy.

Please contact us at `copyright@packtpub.com` with a link to the suspected pirated material.

We appreciate your help in protecting our authors, and our ability to bring you valuable content.

Questions

You can contact us at `questions@packtpub.com` if you are having a problem with any aspect of the book, and we will do our best to address it.

1

Installing the Samba 4 Server

In this chapter, we will begin with the GNU/Linux distribution, which we will use as the base **operating system** (**OS**) to run the Samba 4 software. We will install packages and execute some basic and fundamental configurations on the system. We will cover the following subtopics:

- A quick overview of the installation process of the GNU/Linux distribution Debian 7.0 (Wheezy). This OS installation procedure will not be covered in much detail, because it should be really straightforward for the reader. Also, there are many excellent resources available online for further reading in case of any doubts regarding the installation process of GNU/Linux.
- How to install and configure all the dependencies needed for a proper Samba 4 installation.
- Step-by-step procedures and explicit command line examples to install the Samba 4 software.
- How to use the Debian's official packages and repositories for all the dependencies.
- How to install the Samba 4 Server using the source code (stable branch) from the official **GIT** repository of the project.
- How to perform basic validations of the Samba 4 Server installation to be sure that the environment is ready for configuration and to provide a full range of the network services for which it's intended.

It's really important to have a sane environment on which the user can rely on and be sure that any issues faced later at the production phase are not caused by an unmet dependency, misconfiguration of one of the needed core parts of the OS, or even caused upon an auxiliary service (for example, the `dhcp` server) that is not properly configured or enabled.

Installing Debian 7.0 (Wheezy)

To get started with our Samba environment, we need to install the OS, and for that, the first task must be to choose of the right installation media. To install the Debian 7.0/Wheezy, released in May 04, 2013, we will use the network-installed **ISO** image. The installation is a very simple and quick process where we will go through using all the default configuration options. You can download the latest ISO (net install) 32-bit image file from the following link (for example, `debian-7.0.0-i386-netinst.iso` at the time of this writing):

`http://cdimage.debian.org/mirror/cdimage/release/current/i386/iso-cd/`

Take a look at the proper hardware architecture for the system that you will install, and then choose the right ISO image file accordingly for your system's hardware. The Debian GNU/Linux distribution is available for many different platforms (`amd64`, `ia64`, `powerpc`, and `sparc`, just to name a few). We did choose `i386`, because our hardware is 32-bit.

We will run the `dhcp`, `ntp`, and Samba 4 Servers on the same system. Our Samba 4 Server will be the default gateway for our Microsoft Windows and GNU/Linux systems that will rely on our AD services. Therefore, it will perform **Network Address Translation** (**NAT**) for our clients, as in our example network our clients do not have direct access to the Internet; they will have Internet access using our Samba 4 Server as an intermediate machine. For this configuration, our Samba 4 Server will have two network cards—one in our private network (`eth1`) with IP 192.168.1.1 and another with Internet access (`eth0`).

It's really important for any environment to have all systems with the time properly synchronized. Because Samba 4 uses Kerberos as the authentication mechanism, it's even more important to have the system time in sync, so we will configure the `ntp` services on our server. The `dhcp` server provides us with a powerful solution to manage the IPs on the network, integrate them with **DNS** services, and also automatically register their hostnames (another essential feature for **AD** services). If you already have a `dhcp` server on your network, you don't need to configure this service again on the Samba 4 Server.

If you already have an installed OS where you intend to install the Samba 4 Server, you can directly go to the installation and configuration phases of the dependencies and auxiliary software sections in this chapter. In the book, we will assume a configuration where `dhcp` and Samba 4 Servers will run on the same system and will provide the basic configuration files for all these services. Another important service that is crucial for the Samba 4 Server deployment is DNS. Samba 4 itself provides a basic but sufficient DNS server for most installations, and that's why we'll use it. As in the case of the `dhcp` service, if you already have DNS servers on your network, you can continue using them instead.

Just after you boot the system with your chosen installation CD, you will receive a screenshot similar to the following (this one is from the `netinst` ISO image) one:

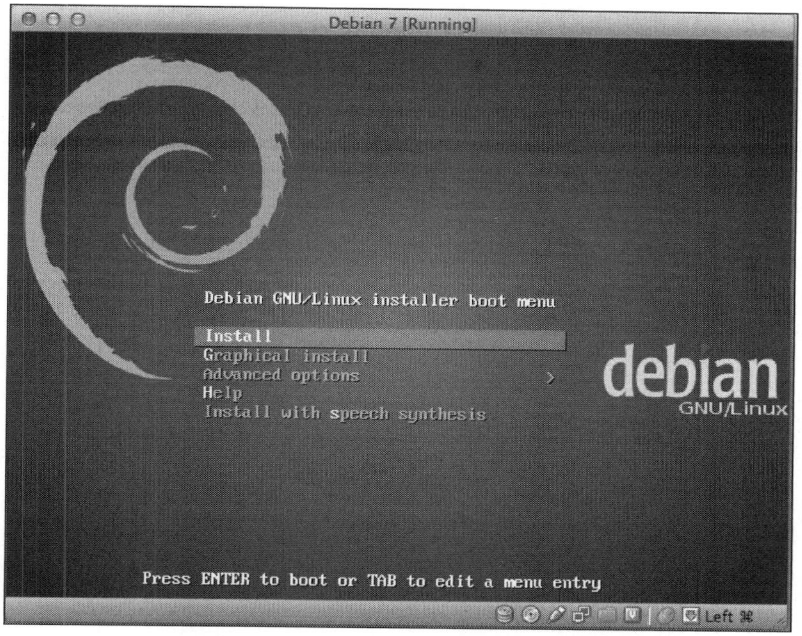

You just need to follow the screens as the default options should be sufficient for most installations. When the installation is completed, don't forget to update and upgrade the OS:

```
leal@debian7:~$ sudo apt-get update && sudo apt-get upgrade
```

This is an important point, and will guarantee that you will be working with all the security patches that are available up to this point, and your running system will not start production with any known security flaws.

Installing and configuring Samba 4 Server's dependencies

With our system up, running, and up to date, we can start installing and configuring the Samba 4 Server's dependencies. Working with all the dependencies provided directly by the GNU/Linux distribution gives us all the support from the Debian community to maintain our system that is patched against security issues. It also saves a large number of working hours as we can install ready binaries for our system. All we need to do is issue the following command at the terminal:

```
leal@debian7:~$ su - root
Password:
root@debian7:~# apt-get install build-essential python-dev pkg-config
libcups2-dev cups krb5-user docbook-xsl libldap2-dev libattr1-dev
libacl1-dev libgnutls-dev attr python-dnspython libreadline-dev
libbsd-dev libblkid-dev libpopt-dev cups git acl gdb xsltproc
libsasl2-dev libaio-dev libpam-dev valgrind resolvconf autoconf ldap
utils ntp isc-dhcp-server && echo OK
...
OK
root@debian7:~# exit
leal@debian7:~$
```

It's recommended and is a best practice to just use the root account as needed, and to use `su` or `sudo` to execute the commands that need super user privileges (for example, to install the software). So, if you want to follow the `sudo` approach, you need to have it installed and configured, and in case of using `su`, don't forget to leave the root shell after the needed administration task is performed. We will use both approaches as examples throughout the book.

The previous command will install some auxiliary components, such as Kerberos, `dhcp` server, cups (for printing services), and many libraries and other packages, which are needed to compile the Samba 4 Server. We just listed the main packages that we want to install on the command line as the GNU/Linux distribution will take care of and install all the other dependencies that are needed by these packages, in order to properly install them in the server. This is a powerful feature of the Debian package management system and saves a lot of time, as you see that many other packages are required to fulfill the installation command that we discussed previously.

While the installation of these packages is running, we only need to provide some information for the Kerberos configuration. If you have provided your domain information during the installation of the system, the Default Realm will already be filled with the right information. If not, you can do it now and add the information about the Realm and Administrative Server in the dialog box that `apt-get` install will bring up while installing `krb5-user`:

```
Default Realm: EALL.COM.BR
Realm: 127.0.0.1
Administrative Server: 127.0.0.1
```

> It's crucial to write the Kerberos Default Realm (FQDN) in uppercase.

If you have installed Debian 7.0 with the default options, it has been configured with the ext4 filesystem. So, let's just make sure that we have availability for all that we need in terms of filesystem features for a proper Samba 4 installation. To do that, we will inspect the kernel's config file placed in the /boot directory.

In a standard Debian installation, we can check the availability of the features of filesystems we need just by issuing the following script on the command-line prompt:

```
leal@debian7:~$ grep CONFIG_EXT4_FS /boot/config-`uname -r`
```

> If you have a custom kernel and have the config file in a different location, change the file's path at the previous command to adjust it to your settings.

The output for that command must be like the following:

```
CONFIG_EXT4_FS=m
CONFIG_EXT4_FS_XATTR=y
CONFIG_EXT4_FS_POSIX_ACL=y
CONFIG_EXT4_FS_SECURITY=y
```

What the previous output tells us is that the ext4 filesystem was configured as a dynamically loadable module and the features of xattr (extended file attributes), posix_acl (access control lists), and security have been built on it.

> You can use a script such as grep CONFIG_EXT\[2-4\]_FS /boot/config-`uname -r` to check ext2, ext3 and ext4 filesystems' features on your kernel.

All these extensions are needed by the Samba 4 Server for its proper execution, as it's needed by the Samba 4 AD/DC functions (for example, ACLs are required to handle Microsoft Windows OS permissions properly). With all these features available, we are in good shape and ready to proceed.

Now we will edit the fstab file of the OS to configure our system, thus enabling that features on our ext4 filesystem and providing them to the Samba 4 Server later on. Remember that any misconfiguration on your fstab file can make your system unbootable. So, after any changes on it, take a closer look at the edited fstab file to check if everything is as it should be.

First, it's a good practice to create a backup of the `fstab` file before editing:

```
leal@debian7:~$ su - root
Password:
root@debian7:~# cp -pRf /etc/fstab /etc/fstab-bkp && echo "OK"
OK
root@debian7:~# exit
leal@debian7:~$
```

The output of the preceding command must be `OK` as it is a confirmation that our original `fstab` file has a backup copy to restore the file in case of any issues. After that, the following one-line script will handle the edition task of `fstab` for us:

```
leal@debian7:~$ su - root
Password:
root@debian7:~# FFILE=/etc/fstab; cp -pRf $FFILE $FFILE-`date
'+%m%d%Y'` && sed -e 's/^UUID.* \/ .*errors=remount-
ro/&,user_xattr,acl,barrier=1/' $FFILE > $FFILE-new && mv $FFILE-new
$FFILE && echo "$FFILE edited OK."
/etc/fstab edited OK.
root@debian7:~# exit
leal@debian7:~$
```

The output must be like the following code:

```
/etc/fstab edited OK.
```

If the result is not like the output, as mentioned in the preceding code, check the special characters that we have on the script, because that can be a common source of mistakes. Any errors found on the script execution must not change anything on your original `fstab` file. Anyway, if the output suggests an error, take a look at the original file and in case of doubt, restore it from the backup we did before the patch (for example, `/etc/fstab-bkp`).

What the preceding one-liner script does is that it replaces any line in the `fstab` file that starts with UUID and has the pattern `errors=remount-ro` (characteristic for an `ext3` or `ext4` filesystems line) with a patched version that includes the needed directives—`xattr` and `acl`. Even if you have any customized partition scheme (for example, a separated `/usr/` partition), it will work, and all the lines will be patched. Take a closer look at it before you go to the next step.

Another important OS configuration is the network interfaces' file (as they are configured as dynamic by default), our domain, and DNS servers. We will configure our Samba 4 Server for the `192.168.1.0/24` IP on the `eth1` interface of our system. So, this is the configuration that we need in our `/etc/network/interfaces` file for our `eth1` card:

```
iface eth1 inet static
address 192.168.1.1
netmask 255.255.255.0
dns-search eall.com.br
dns-domain eall.com.br
dns-nameservers 192.168.1.1
```

> Don't forget to add the second interface (`eth1`) to the `allow-hotplug` directive, and the right configuration for your `eth0` interface (the one with Internet access and a default gateway).

The configuration specified in the preceding code creates our interface `eth1 static`, sets the IP and netmask addresses, and configures our domain. Remember to change the domain in the previous example with your domain. We will work with the examples in this book with the `EALL.COM.BR` domain.

Note that `dns-nameservers` is configured to be this server itself; this is because we will soon configure the Samba 4 Server, and it has a built-in DNS server. We can perform some final checks on the edited files, and if everything is good, we will restart our server:

```
leal@debian7:~$ sudo shutdown -r now
```

After the restart, we can continue with our configuration, and the next step is the configuration of two auxiliary packages that we mentioned earlier. We need this for a proper Samba 4 Server execution of `ntp` and `dhcp`. We already have both of them installed since our previous dependencies' installation phase; we just need to configure and enable them.

Let's start with the **Network Time Protocol** (**NTP**) configuration (`/etc/ntp.conf`). Just add the following lines to the standard Debian NTP configuration file:

```
#Implementing Samba 4
ntpsigndsocket /usr/local/samba/var/lib/ntp_signd/
restrict default mssntp
```

The first line in the preceding code is a comment, and it's always a good idea to add descriptive information about what and why something is being changed, added, or removed in any configuration (for example, you should replace the comment in the preceding example with something more descriptive). Another good practice is to add your name and date close to the change that makes everything easier when we need to understand what has been changed and why something is not working as it should. The next two lines are for the configurations that are needed for signed `ntp` and `ms-sntp` (authentication extensions).

The **Dynamic Host Configuration Protocol (DHCP)** configuration is not complex; we just need to add a few more lines to it. In a terminal window, just edit the `/etc/dhcp/dhcpd.conf` file, and replace all its content with the following lines:

```
# Implementing Samba 4
ddns-updates on;
option domain-name "eall.com.br";
option domain-name-servers 192.168.1.1, 192.168.1.1;
option netbios-name-servers 192.168.1.1;
option ntp-servers 192.168.1.1;
default-lease-time 600;
max-lease-time 7200;
log-facility local7;
subnet 192.168.1.0 netmask 255.255.255.0 {
range 192.168.1.10 192.168.1.30;
option routers 192.168.1.1; }
```

> If you use the `vi` editor, you can replace the whole content of the file (just after the file is opened), issuing: `dGi`. After that, just add the lines in the preceding command and close and save the file, issuing: `Esc:x`.

In some of the configuration lines in the preceding code, it is important to get a detailed explanation as they are directly involved in Samba 4's server operations. After the comment line (the first one, starting with the # character), we have `ddns-updates on`. This is the directive that tells the `dhcp` server to update the DNS server about the new IP releases and register the client's hostname. All the `option` lines are information that the `dhcp` server will forward to its client's OSes when they get a `dhcp` lease. So, they will have a proper domain name server, netbios name server, `ntp`, and router information.

Before starting the `dhcp` server, the last step is to edit the `/etc/default/isc-dhcp-server` file and configure the interface on which the `dhcp` server will listen:

```
INTERFACES="eth1"
```

Now we are ready to start the `dhcp` server, as the installation process has already added it to `init.d runlevel` in order to start it at the server's boot time. To start the `dhcp` server now, just issue the following command:

```
leal@debian7:~$ su - root
Password:
root@debian7:~# /etc/init.d/isc-dhcp-server start
```

The output of this command must be like the following:

```
[ ok ] Starting ISC DHCP server: dhcpd.
```

Installing Samba 4 Server step by step

For the installation of the Samba 4 software, we will use GIT. So, we should start creating a workspace (for example, directory) to download the sources of the Samba 4 Server stable branch into it. In a terminal window, just execute the following command:

```
leal@debian7:~$ mkdir ~/workspace; cd ~/workspace && echo "OK"
```

We must receive an `OK` output in our terminal, and that is sufficient to be aware that the workspace was created successfully and we are already inside it. Now, let's download the Samba 4 source code and continue our installation process.

> The previous command will create the workspace directly on our home directory.

Now, we will clone the Samba 4 stable branch from the official project's repository, configure it, and compile the software:

```
leal@debian7:~$ git clone -b v4-0-stable
git://git.samba.org/samba.git samba4
```

This command will take some time to complete as all the Samba 4 source code will need to be downloaded (the total time will vary depending on your Internet connection). Next, note the use of the `--enable-self test` option it the following configure command, as we will need the features added by this option in a later phase:

```
leal@debian7:~$ cd samba4
leal@debian7:~$ ./configure --enable-debug --enable-selftest
leal@debian7:~$ make && echo "OK"
```

This command will take some time to actually compile all the sources of the Samba 4 Server, and at the end, the output must be `OK` (the total time will vary depending on your system's resources). Here, you can see the last lines of the compilation process that I got on my system, along with the final successful result and the total elapsed time:

```
Waf: Leaving directory '/home/leal/workspace/samba4/bin'
'build' finished successfully (13m0.539s)
OK
leal@debian7:~/workspace/samba4$
```

We will not install it on its definitive place in our system just yet. First, we will execute some validations to make sure that our resulted binaries are fully operational.

Basic validations of the Samba's installation

We need to have automated deployments, and that includes automated tests. It's really important to have proper tests for all of our deployments, because that is the guarantee that everything is the way we are used to and the way we expect it to be. I'm used to saying that in IT, everything needs to be an "Automated beast" and not a "Masterpiece". With that in mind, we do not stand in front of the servers to draw like Da Vinci (even if we could). However, we need to have everything automated (scripted), so it can be easily reproduced, and we can create, destroy, and recreate the whole environment without any effort.

The Samba 4 project helps us a lot with its built-in test suite, which is a great starting point for our environment's validation. Just issue the following command:

```
leal@debian7:~$ sudo make quicktest
```

We will receive a verbose output that will report the execution of many invaluable tests to verify whether our Samba 4 Server's installation is fully working. Pay close attention to each line as you'll be able to follow the status of each test that is being executed.

In case of any failure, we will need to review all of our installation and configuration steps to see what point was not executed properly. We need to pass this step cleanly to actually proceed to our Samba 4 Server configuration. The following is an excerpt of an example execution of the test suite:

```
[250/310 in 43m52s] samba4.raw.write(dc)
[251/310 in 43m53s] samba4.raw.rename(dc)
[252/310 in 43m55s] samba4.raw.qfsinfo(dc)
[253/310 in 43m55s] samba4.raw.qfileinfo(dc)
[254/310 in 43m56s] samba4.raw.close(dc)
[255/310 in 43m56s] samba4.raw.mkdir(dc)
[256/310 in 43m56s] samba4.raw.ioctl(dc)
[257/310 in 43m56s] samba4.raw.seek(dc)
[258/310 in 43m57s] samba4.raw.eas(dc)
[259/310 in 43m57s] samba4.raw.qfileinfo.ipc(dc)
[260/310 in 43m57s] samba4.ntvfs.cifs.krb5.base.delete(dc)
...
ALL OK (2061 tests in 310 testsuites)
```

A summary with detailed information can be found in:

```
./st/summary
'testonly' finished successfully (50m11.201s)
```

All tests must pass `OK`, as you can see in the preceding code so we can perform the installation of the binaries into their final destination (`/usr/local/`).

You can do this by issuing the following command:

```
leal@debian7:~$ sudo make install
```

This command will copy all the required files to their final destination on our filesystem. So, we will have the Samba 4 Server properly installed and ready to be configured and provide our network services.

Summary

In this chapter, we were introduced to the GNU/Linux distribution that we will work on as a base throughout the book. We got a quick overview of the Debian installation process and some specific operating system configurations that are needed to prepare it for the Samba 4 network services. In the next chapter, we will learn how to provide the Samba 4 Server we just installed as **Active Directory Domain Controller** for our network. So, we can start to use some of the many features with which Samba 4 software provides us.

2

Provisioning Samba 4 as an AD Domain Controller

In this chapter, the user will learn about the basic tasks that are required to get a proper Samba 4 Active Directory configured as the Domain Controller for the network. We will cover the following topics in this chapter:

- The minimal planning needed to deploy a Samba 4 Active Directory as the Domain Controller (for example, domain, network topology/addresses, and services required) as well as the basic concepts involved in the Domain Controller service configuration.
- The network topology with which we will work through our example configuration in the book, with basic planning techniques and checklists to show the user how to prepare and have at hand all the information needed for the provisioning setup of Samba 4 at hand.
- The deployment of the Samba 4 Server and the services needed for a proper Samba 4 configuration through explicit command-line examples.
- Other important aspects of any Active Directory Domain Controller network services such as the availability, performance, and replication considerations. We will look at these characteristics in our specific example scenario, explain what our assumptions were, and discuss some general ideas about how you should approach a real-world situation.
- The provisioning of Samba 4 as an AD Domain Controller will be described in detail, and at the end of the chapter, the reader will learn how to perform basic validations of the Samba 4 configuration setup. This is a very important task in order to have a sane environment that the administrators can rely on to have a fully functioning Samba 4 Active Directory Domain Controller.

Highlighting the planning points for an AD service

The most important task that we need to focus on before any other task, when planning for Active Directory Domain Controller, is to our network services' topology. For our Active Directory services to provide a resilient service, we need to be effective in creating a simple (yet descriptive) and scalable architecture that will fit our environment's needs and requirements.

Active Directory Domain Controller can provide us with a centralized management point for our network devices and thus gives us full control over a large number of objects (for example, users and machines). This is the key to achieving a lower cost in administrative tasks, resource control, and security (authentication and authorization) management in a specific network. To organize users and resources in a way that is simple to manage and is scalable (for example, facilitates delegation) is the key. On top of that, there is no reason to have a Domain Controller in our network if the applications are not able to integrate themselves with it. Thus, we cannot use all the features and facilities that an AD/DC can provide. Designing the proper architecture for a specific site is a complex and extensive task and is outside the scope of this book. However, we will discuss some general points and show you an example configuration and topology, so that you can use it as a base for future installations. As in any installation, the administrator needs to think about users, machines, organizational units, domains, forests, and services.

We will present a simple but effective architecture to the user for the `EALL.COM.BR` domain, with a structure that will help him/her understand important concepts and serve as a starting point for the readers to work upon and evolve to more complex environments. General advice is to focus on your specific topology and requirements, extract the essential concepts, and work similar structures in your design that fit your organization environment. Do not copy some **Master Architectural Design** from the Internet thinking that it will fit your network out of the box just because it handles all departments or definitions possible in the software. If you do not need that level of complexity, do not use it. I could see many sites that were designed based on general rules that were not intended to be used in that particular case but provide a simple and scalable environment instead; they also create a network environment that is too complex and really inefficient from the most basic administrative perspective. This is the exact opposite of what a well-planned Active Directory Domain controller should be.

One analogy for such an inefficient architecture can be, for example, a file system directory structure. Sometimes, we are compelled to create a really complex directory hierarchy with many subdirectories and a nested, and deep tree that, in the end, just keeps us away from the right file instead of helping us access it in a fast and simple way.

Just because we can create a lot of directories inside one another, it does not mean that we need to do it for every object or create a structure using hundreds of subdirectories that will just add to the complexity. In such situations, we need to think about the following points:

- How many files will we need to handle?
- What we want to achieve—fast placement of files, fast access to the files, (or both)?
- Is it a directory structure that will be used directly by a person or an application?
- Do we have an intelligent name for the files that we will be storing?
- If not, do we have the control to change the name of the files in order for them to have an intelligent name?
- Do we need to manage different/specific users and groups for each directory or file?
- Will the structure help us delegate the administrative task to some directories for specific users and/or departments?

You might think that creating a directory structure is supposed to be a simple thing. However, as you start to think about it and look at the previously discussed questions, you realize that it can be a tricky task and if the answers for the above questions are not the right ones, the simple task can become a big problem in the near future. In my experience, I have come across many solutions with performance or scalability problems (and even security problems) just because the architect of that solution did not think about these questions.

Similar design questions will come up when planning for Active Directory services in your network. The questions about a simple task as a file system directory structure can be eye opening to help us make the right architectural decisions in different design problems. Systems that are well designed share the same principles and are based on the same well-known characteristics of scalability, performance, security, and simple administration.

Let's get back to the Active Directory services and their architecture. What we need to have in mind at the highest level are these three basic concepts: forests, domains, and organizational units. Forests are the top level of abstraction on the Active Directory service. They provide us with security boundaries and contain one or more domains inside it.

Domains are divisions (or partitions) inside a forest, and they have one or more **Organizational Units** (**OU**) inside them. Organizational Units are entities that group different objects (for example, users and/or machines) to help the administration of these elements in a specific and scalable way (for example, making it easy to delegate the administration).

So, following a general definition from Microsoft Active Directory Documentation, forests are mainly there to implement a security control (boundary) on our Active Directory environment. Domains provide us with an administrative point where we can control the replication, thus establishing trust relationships. Organizational Units are an administrative point to delegate administration, thereby providing us with an invaluable resource to divide administrative responsibilities across the entire organization (source: `http://technet.microsoft.com/en-us/library/cc756901(v=ws.10).aspx`). This is an important aspect of scalability, as people (for example, administrators) are an essential asset for any company and are the most expensive resource to scale. The architecture needs to take this into consideration from the very beginning.

Our example configuration will use a simple forest model, as it is the simplest model with the lowest administrative overhead and will fit our requirement perfectly. There are situations where you may need to have multiple forest models, so you should plan to design such models instead. However, a single forest model is preferred if your organization does not have complex requirements (for example, totally autonomous divisions).

The forest root domain in our implementation will be `MSDCBRZ.EALL.COM.BR`, and we will work with just one location (child domain) named `POA.MSDCBRZ.EALL.COM.BR`. There are a lot of different approaches to organize the organizational units within a site, and many administrators have a different view of the structure as each organization has different needs.

We will start with 10 organizational units, following a model that basically separates the workstations, services, and users. These are the three important objects that we need to maintain on any directory services, and they will make the administration and implementation of specific policies in the future easier.

> **Downloading the example code**
>
> You can download the example code files for all Packt books you have purchased from your account at `http://www.packtpub.com`. If you purchased this book elsewhere, you can visit `http://www.packtpub.com/`support and register to have the files e-mailed directly to you.

The structure will have three top level OUs, which are workstations, services, and users. The workstations' OU has the different type of devices that we plan to manage for our users, such as laptops and desktops. This is a crucial separation as we need to identify and handle the mobility of our users as they have specific security concerns. This depends on whether the users are using our corporate network every time or whether they are using laptops on the go. Our service's OU starts with three services and can actually grow as we install others—terminal servers, print servers, and SQL servers. Remember, if our network services are not integrated and cannot use the directory features, there is no big advantage of having a directory service with a centralized management.

Our last top level OU is for our users (**People**) and has two organizational units inside it—standard users and power users. This is a simple division and is a good base to leverage our user's administration.

In the following diagram, we can see our Active Directory's structure:

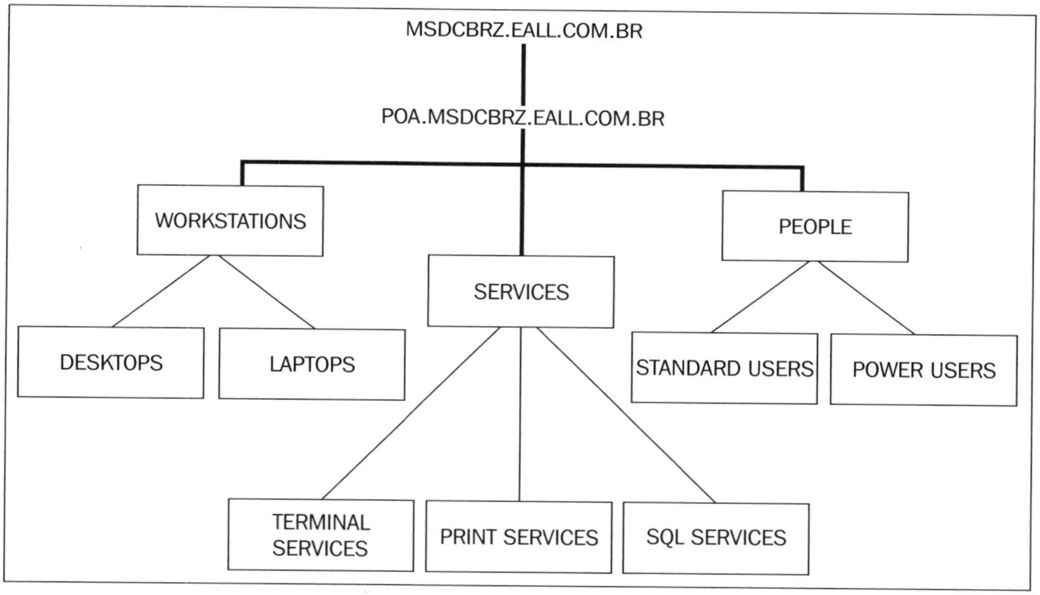

Acquiring information for deploying an AD service

To facilitate the understanding of this concept and help us have at hand all the information that we need to deploy the Active Directory services on our network, we will create a checklist with all the information that we need prior to the deployment of an AD service. Based on our last topic, we know exactly what we need, how we have defined the topology, and how our network will be implemented. So, we are able to create a document with the information we need, and this will help us identify any missing points about our design. In the following table, we can see all the information we need prior to the implementation of Samba 4 Active Directory. This is organized in a table for ease of understanding and referencing during the configuration phase. To have such information at hand, it is vital that we have a clean and straightforward process; feel free to add as much information as you have when planning for your AD services. The following is a table that can be of help as a starting point to organize the data:

Samba 4 Active Directory configuration checklist	
Question/Parameter	`Answer/Value`
Role	`Domain Controller`
DNS Infrastructure already in-place	`( x ) Yes (   ) No`
Active Directory IP Address/interface	`192.168.1.1 (eth1)`
How many Organization Units	`10`
Locations/Physical Sites	`1`
How many Domain Controllers	`1`
Domain	`POA.MSDCBRZ.EALL.COM.BR`
DNS Resolver Configuration	`Forwarding (IP: 8.8.8.8)`
DHCP Server IP Address	`192.168.1.1`
Default Router IP Address	`192.168.1.1`
How many users	`50`

As we saw in the first chapter, the Samba 4 Active Directory services rely on some other essential services to be able to fully provide its services. It has already a vital built-in service, DNS, which is well suited for many installations; we will use it as our configuration's base. However, we also need **Network Time Protocol** (**NTP**), as the time for all systems on the network needs to be in sync. This is even more important for the authentication of Kerberos. **DHCP** is another service that is highly necessary to provide the network administrators with a simple way to dynamically set up a new machine on the network (for example, assign it a new IP address) as well as register this new system on the DNS server (essential to the AD services). All the services mentioned in the table are already configured in our Debian 7 server as their configuration was part of our installation procedure for the Samba 4 services.

Availability, performance, and replication for the network service

When planning for any network service, we need to think about its availability and performance from the beginning as a service that does not have any of these two characteristics is useless. This is no different for an Active Directory Domain Controller, as it provides core services to the whole domain underneath it. If the server is not available, the result will be that the users will not be able to connect to the network, servers will not be able to resolve names, and so on. The checklist that we built has high-level information that will help us in getting answers to some important questions regarding availability and performance. This is why it is so important to have a documented plan as it makes things much easier. The sizing and architecture of the Active Directory services to a specific site is outside the scope of this book, and there are many articles on the Internet that discuss different aspects of a scalable, highly available, and high performance design. Some attention points on our checklist that need to be taken into consideration when thinking about performance and replication are as follows:

- The number of users
- The number of domains
- The location/physical sites

These points are just some examples of parameters that will have a huge impact on the load of our **Active Directory Server** but there are others examples as well. The more information you gather to add to your plan, the easier will it be to plan for the resources that are needed to provide the right performance for your site.

A good example of another kind of information that we can have on our checklist is provided by our Active Directory diagram. The services that we intend to have in our domain and ones that will interact with our AD, will generate load (DNS queries, authentication, and so on), so they too are performance factors that we need to take into account. Our example scenario has a few users and a few services and one server is sufficient to handle the load. We just have one site (location) and one domain, so there are no concerns about the link's performance in order to replicate the AD database. When we talk about availability, there is no small setup and we just cannot afford to not have redundancy (high availability) in our services. In *Chapter 4, Replacing a Microsoft Windows Active Directory Server*, we will see how we can add redundancy to our setup and how we can have high availability in the Active Directory services.

Setting up Samba 4 as an AD Domain Controller

One important configuration that will make our lives a lot easier is adding the Samba 4 installation path to our `bash_profile` file so that we have all the Samba tools in our search path and we don't need to work with full (absolute) paths. To do this in a `sh` or `bash` shell environment, just run the following command in your prompt:

```
leal@debian7:~$sudo echo 'export PATH=/usr/local/samba/bin:\
/usr/local/samba/sbin:$PATH' >> /root/.bash_profile && echo OK
```

The preceding command must give just the `OK` output. This is the signal that we have configured our `bash_profile` file in the Samba 4 software's binary path (for example, tools), so for future shell instances, we will have the search path ready.

After we have all the requisites for the Samba 4 environment fulfilled and our software installation validated, setting up a Samba 4 Server as an Active Directory Domain Controller is a simple task. We just need to execute the following command in the command line prompt and we are ready to go:

```
leal@debian7:~$ sudo samba-tool domain provision --
realm=POA.MSDCBRZ.EALL.COM.BR --domain=POA --adminpass='w1ndow$$!' --
server-role='domain controller'
```

The previous `samba-tool` command can be executed interactively by just passing the `domain provision` argument and answering the questions one by one (for example, `domain`, `adminpass`, and so on). One of the objectives of this book is to provide the readers with as many automated procedures and simple scripts as possible. We invoked the `samba-tool` command with all the commands and arguments directly in one shot; this will execute the whole Samba 4 Server provisioning without further interaction.

> If you want to re-execute the provisioning command, you will need to remove the `smb.conf` file prior to the new execution or you will receive an error and the execution will be aborted (for example, `sudo rm /usr/local/samba/etc/smb.conf`).

So, let's take a look at the previous command line and explain each of the arguments that were used; then, the reader can understand all the options and tweak them as appropriate. The arguments are described as follows:

- `samba-tool`: This is the main Samba administrative tool.
- `domain provision`: This is the argument where the domain is the subcommand on `samba-tool` that handles the domain's management tasks, and provision is the subcommand that actually performs a provision of a domain. This is the main part of our command as it provides us with the provisioning of the domain.
- `--realm`: This is the realm's name.
- `--domain`: This is the argument where we set our domain name.
- `--adminpass`: This is the administrative password, (if we do not provide one, Samba will create a random password), which is an important point in the configuration of Samba 4 as there is a strict policy for passwords in the Active Directory services (**Microsoft Windows Password Policies**). If we provide a password that is not strong enough, we will receive an error and will need to execute the command again. The password used in this book is a simple password that respects that policy but is *not* intended to be used in production.

The `--server-role` argument tells you that you must choose a secret and strong password for your installation. We are provisioning an Active Directory Domain Controller, so we will use `domain controller` as our `server role`. However, there are other options such as `dc`, `member server`, `member`, and `standalone`. The default `server-role`, if not provided by the user, is `dc`.

> You can take a look at all available options which issue the `samba-tool` command without any options, or access the main page (for example, man `samba-tool`).

Just after we issue the preceding command to set up Samba 4 Server as an Active Directory Domain Controller, we can follow the output to be sure that everything was okay in the execution. We can take a look at an example output in the following command:

```
Looking up IPv4 addresses
More than one IPv4 address found. Using 192.168.1.1
Looking up IPv6 addresses
No IPv6 address will be assigned
Setting up share.ldb
Setting up secrets.ldb
Setting up the registry
Setting up the privileges database
Setting up idmap db
Setting up SAM db
Setting up sam.ldb partitions and settings
Setting up sam.ldb rootDSE
Pre-loading the Samba 4 and AD schema
Adding DomainDN: DC=poa,DC=msdcbrz,DC=eall,DC=com,DC=br
Adding configuration container
Setting up sam.ldb schema
Setting up sam.ldb configuration data
Setting up display specifiers
Modifying display specifiers
Adding users container
Modifying users container
Adding computers container
Modifying computers container
Setting up sam.ldb data
Setting up well known security principals
Setting up sam.ldb users and groups
Setting up self join
Adding DNS accounts
Creating CN=MicrosoftDNS,CN=System,DC=poa,DC=msdcbrz,DC=eall,\
C=com,DC=br
Creating DomainDnsZones and ForestDnsZones partitions
Populating DomainDnsZones and ForestDnsZones partitions
```

```
Setting up sam.ldb rootDSE marking as synchronized
Fixing provision GUIDs
A Kerberos configuration suitable for Samba 4 has been generated
 at /usr/local/samba/private/krb5.conf
Once the above files are installed, your Samba 4 server will be
 ready to use
Server Role:        active directory domain controller
Hostname:           debian7
NetBIOS Domain:     POA
DNS Domain:         poa.msdcbrz.eall.com.br
DOMAIN SID:         S-1-5-21-1069074877-2280341390-3609431641
```

The output in the preceding command has some information about each step of the provisioning of the Samba 4 Server, so we can see messages about setting up some resources, creating some default containers, users, groups, as well as some DNS setups.

The last lines have some useful information; they give us the Domain Name and SID; they also give us an important hint about the Kerberos configuration file that was automatically generated for us, and we need to use it to finish the Samba 4 Server configuration. We just need to install the `kerberos config` file in its right directory, and to do that, we just need to issue the following command:

```
leal@debian7:~$ su - root
Password:
root@debian7:~# cp -pRf /usr/local/samba/private/krb5.conf /etc/ && echo
OK
OK
root@debian7:~# exit
leal@debian7:~$
```

If the output for the previous command is `OK`, it means that our Kerberos configuration file is installed in the right location and we are almost there. Now, we need to edit the `smb.conf` file and configure our DNS server, which Samba will use to forward any Domain Name resolution queries that are outside its authoritative zone. In this example, we will use the Google DNS open servers, but you should use the addresses for your DNS servers. Just take a look at the `smb.conf` file before editing it as the right DNS forwarded IP address could be configured automatically by the `samba-tool` script, so you don't need to change anything.

The following script should do that for us:

```
leal@debian7:~$ sudo cp -pRf /usr/local/samba/etc/smb.conf
/usr/local/samba/etc/smb.conf-bkp && sed -e 's/dns forwarder =.*$/dns
 forwarder = 8.8.8.8/g' /usr/local/samba/etc/smb.conf >
 /usr/local/samba/etc/smb.conf-new && mv
 /usr/local/samba/etc/smb.conf-new /usr/local/samba/etc/smb.conf &&
 echo OK
OK
leal@debian7:~$ sudo cp -pRf /usr/local/samba/etc/smb.conf \
    /usr/local/samba/etc/smb.conf-bkp && \
    sed -e 's/dns forwarder =.*$/dns forwarder = 8.8.8.8/g'
    /usr/local/samba/etc/smb.conf > /usr/local/samba/etc/smb.conf-new
 && \
     mv /usr/local/samba/etc/smb.conf-new
/usr/local/samba/etc/smb.conf && \
    echo OK
OK
leal@debian7:~$
```

If the output is `OK`, it means that our `smb.conf` file was edited fine and we are ready to start the Samba 4 Server. In case we receive any error, we should not change any line of our original Samba configuration file. If any change was made and we received an error that means that the editing was not successful, we will get a backup file that contains the original content of our `smb.conf` file, as the first command issued in our script created a copy of the Samba configuration file. So, we have a `smb.conf-bkp` file with our original configurations and we can just restore it.

Now, we will start our Samba 4 Server to have it running in the foreground. It should be single-threaded to be able to identify any errors or warnings the software can raise as in the next topic, we will execute a series of tests and validations to verify that our configuration is ready to enter production. In a terminal window, issue the following command:

```
leal@debian7:~$ sudo /usr/local/samba/sbin/samba -i -M single
Password:
```

If everything was fine with our installation and configuration process, we should receive the following output:

```
samba version 4.0.5 started.
Copyright Andrew Tridgell and the Samba Team 1992-2012
samba: using 'single' process model
```

```
Attempting to autogenerate TLS self-signed keys for https for
 hostname 'DEBIAN7.poa.msdcbrz.eall.com.br'

TLS self-signed keys generated OK
```

You will notice that the Samba process remains attached to your shell, as it has not forked. The message indicates the 'single' option as our process model, as we started the daemon with the -M single option. This is to make our life easier while debugging and searching for any error messages, as we have just one process to handle our Active Directory services; there's no risk of losing the message involved as we are looking at the right process.

Validating the Samba 4 configuration

Now that we have our Samba 4 Server installed and configured, we execute some basic validations to guarantee us that our environment is ready to go live. These tests will cover DNS queries, Kerberos authentication, and some basic request/response capabilities of our brand new server.

As we stated in the first chapter and will do in others throughout the book, it's always important to have an automated test procedure to validate our environment. So, it's highly recommended that you start creating scripts to test your Samba 4 configuration for future installations, upgrades, or maintaining the database. Creating a battery of tests and validations is the key to help us with any changes in the environment and can identify problems before you go live, providing you with the option to rollback the modifications and go back to the planning board.

Let's start with the DNS tests as the Domain Name resolution is essential for the proper working of Active Directory [13]. If we have any issues with our configuration, we will face trouble ahead. The Active Directory uses the **SRV** record to locate domain controllers, as this resource record is used to identify servers that provide specific services. Two SRV records need to be created for any Active Directory Domain Controller: _kerberos and _ldap. So, we need to validate that our systems have these records, so clients will be able to communicate and find our services on the network. Issue the following commands on a new shell:

```
leal@debian7:~$ host -t SRV _kerberos._udp.poa.msdcbrz.eall\
.com.br

_kerberos._udp.poa.msdcbrz.eall.com.br has SRV record 0 100 88 debian7.
poa.msdcbrz.eall.com.br.


leal@debian7:~$ host -t SRV _ldap._tcp.poa.msdcbrz.eall.com.br

_ldap._tcp.poa.msdcbrz.eall.com.br has SRV record 0 100 389 debian7.poa.
msdcbrz.eall.com.br.
```

```
leal@debian7:~$ host -t A poa.msdcbrz.eall.com.br
poa.msdcbrz.eall.com.br has address 192.168.1.1
```

The output for the preceding commands should be similar in your environment. In case you receive an error stating that the entries were not found, you need to review the configuration process to make sure that every step was properly executed. As we can see from the output for both the preceding commands, our SRV records for `_ldap` and `_kerberos` are configured `OK`.

Another important point about our DNS setup is the forwarding configuration, so the ability to resolve names that our Active Directory is not authoritative. We can test this by trying to check some well-known sites. The steps to test the same are as follows:

1. Execute the following command:

   ```
   leal@debian7:~$ host www.amazon.com
   ```

   The output should be something like the following command:

   ```
   www.amazon.com hashas''''''' address 72.21.215.232
   ```

2. We can try to resolve the MX record for the `amazon.com` domain. For that, just issue the following command at one terminal:

   ```
   leal@debian7:~$ host -t mx amazon.com
   ```

   The output for that command should be something similar to the following command:

   ```
   amazon.com mail is handled by 5 amazon-smtp.amazon.com.
   amazon.com mail is handled by 10 smtp-fw-4101.amazon.com.
   amazon.com mail is handled by 10 smtp-fw-9101.amazon.com.
   amazon.com mail is handled by 10 smtp-fw-31001.amazon.com.
   amazon.com mail is handled by 10 smtp-fw-33001.amazon.com.
   amazon.com mail is handled by 15 smtp-fw-2101.amazon.com.
   ```

   So, with these tests, we are sure that our Active Directory's built-in DNS server is working just fine, resolving DNS names for our domain (`poa.msdcbrz.eall.com.br`) and forwarding the requests for the other domains. We also validated the `_kerberos` and `_ldap` SRV records and are able to proceed to test the Kerberos authentication mechanism.

3. To test the kerberos authentication, we can use the `kinit` command. Kinit is a utility to obtain and cache the Kerberos ticket-granting ticket (see `man kinit`). The simplest form to invoke `kinit` and test our Samba 4 configuration is by executing the following command:

   ```
   leal@debian7:~$ kinit administrator@POA.MSDCBRZ.EALL.COM.BR
   ```

4. You should receive the following prompt:

```
Password for administrator@POA.MSDCBRZ.EALL.COM.BR:
```

5. So, you must enter the administrator password and press *Enter*. The output should be a warning like the following command:

```
Warning: Your password will expire in 41 days on Sat Jul 13
19:22:46 2013
```

6. Now, we can use the `klist` command to verify that we have actually received a ticket and Kerberos is working fine:

```
leal@debian7:~$ klist
```

7. The output for the `klist` command in the preceding command should be something like the following command:

```
Ticket cache: FILE:/tmp/krb5cc_1000
Default principal: administrator@POA.MSDCBRZ.EALL.COM.BR
Valid starting     Expires           Service principal
06/02/13 02:09:59  06/02/13 12:09:59  krbtgt/POA.MSDCBRZ.EALL.\
COM.BR@POA.MSDCBRZ.EALL.COM.BR
renew until 06/03/13 02:09:54
```

If you receive an output similar to the `klist` command execution, it means that the Kerberos authentication mechanism is working fine.

The next validation will be the `ldap` backend of our Samba 4 Active Directory Domain Controller. We can use the `ldapsearch` utility to perform queries on our AD and verify that it is working as it should. The first query can be the following command:

```
leal@debian7:~$ ldapsearch -x -h localhost -s base -D
 cn=administrator,cn=Users,dc=poa,dc=msdcbrz,dc=eall,dc=com,dc=br -W
```

You will be prompted to provide the administrator password and after that, you should receive a verbose output. For brevity, we will reproduce just the last few lines here:

```
namingContexts:
DC=DomainDnsZones,DC=poa,DC=msdcbrz,DC=eall,DC=com,DC=br
namingContexts:
DC=ForestDnsZones,DC=poa,DC=msdcbrz,DC=eall,DC=com,DC=br
supportedSASLMechanisms: GSS-SPNEGO
supportedSASLMechanisms: GSSAPI
supportedSASLMechanisms: NTLM
highestCommittedUSN: 3723
domainFunctionality: 2
```

```
forestFunctionality: 2
domainControllerFunctionality: 4
isGlobalCatalogReady: TRUE

# search result
search: 2
result: 0 Success

# numResponses: 2
# numEntries: 1
```

If you have received a similar output in response to the previous `ldap search` query, it means that our Active Directory `ldap` backend should be working fine.

The last test is the most important one as we will actually test Microsoft Windows Machine and try to add it to our brand new domain. We will use a Windows Server 2008 R2 operating system, and after the machine has joined the domain, we will use it to create the organizational units on our Active Directory Domain Controller.

Just after the installation of the Microsoft Windows 2008 Server, we can check if our system could get an IP address from our DHCP server; do execute a quick reachability test (for example, ping) just to make sure that everything is fine with our network's setup. Using PowerShell, we can issue the following command to look at our network configurations (`IPv4 Address`, `DNS Servers`, `Default Gateway`, and and so on):

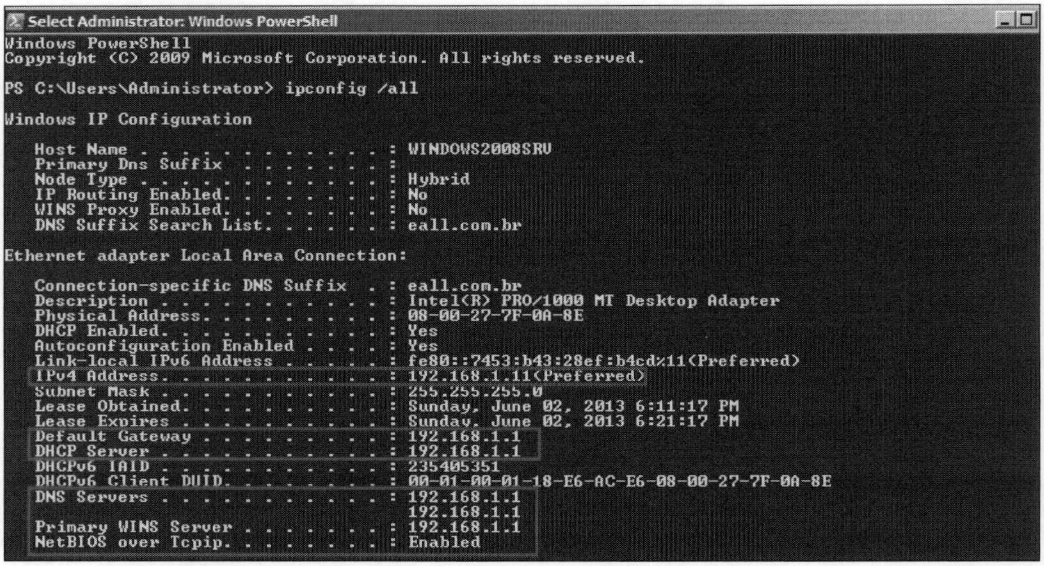

We can see from the preceding screenshot that the Windows 2008 Server could get an IP address (`192.168.1.11`). We have `DHCP Server`, `IPv4 Address`, `Primary WINS Server`, `DNS Servers` and `Default Gateway`—all pointing to our Active Directory Domain Controller, `192.168.1.1`.

To make sure that our system is able to reach our Active Directory (Samba 4 Server), let's execute a quick `Ping` test:

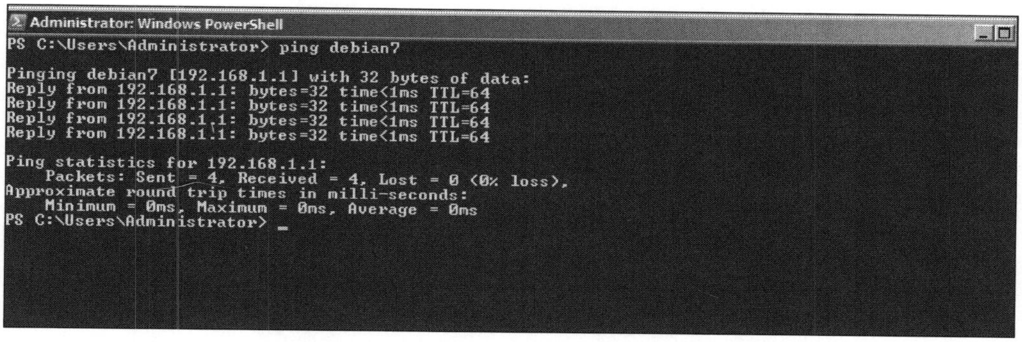
Administrator: Windows PowerShell
PS C:\Users\Administrator> ping debian7
Pinging debian7 [192.168.1.1] with 32 bytes of data:
Reply from 192.168.1.1: bytes=32 time<1ms TTL=64
Reply from 192.168.1.1: bytes=32 time<1ms TTL=64
Reply from 192.168.1.1: bytes=32 time<1ms TTL=64
Reply from 192.168.1.1: bytes=32 time<1ms TTL=64
Ping statistics for 192.168.1.1:
Packets: Sent = 4, Received = 4, Lost = 0 (0% loss),
Approximate round trip times in milli-seconds:
Minimum = 0ms, Maximum = 0ms, Average = 0ms
PS C:\Users\Administrator>

As we can see in the preceding screenshot, no problems are pinging our Active Directory Server (Debian 7), and this test performed an indirect test as it validated our DNS configuration and also tested the ability of this Windows 2008 Server to access our DNS Server (Debian 7) and resolve names.

Before we execute the procedure to actually join the `POA.MSDCBRZ.EALL.COM.BR` domain, we can do a last check to make sure that the Windows Server clock is right. We can check this by looking at the time shown at the desktop dock (bar at the bottom of the screen) or issuing the `date` command in the PowerShell prompt. In case we identify that our server's date or time is not right, we need to adjust it before moving on to the next step. To adjust the hour, just double click on the clock at the dock and click on **Change date and time settings...**:

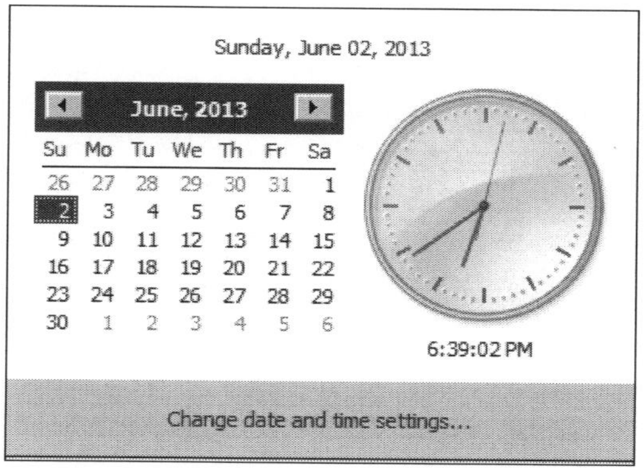
Sunday, June 02, 2013
June, 2013
Su Mo Tu We Th Fr Sa
6:39:02 PM
Change date and time settings...

Now that we have finished the preliminary checks to make sure that our Active Directory and Microsoft Windows 2008 server are well configured and are ready to communicate with each other, we can execute the procedure to join the Windows 2008 Server to the Active Directory Domain.

The procedure to join a machine to a domain can be executed in the Windows 2008 Server following a quick and simple procedure. First, we click on the **Start** button and right-click on **Computer**. In the context menu, click on **Properties**.

The following screenshot shows us the procedure:

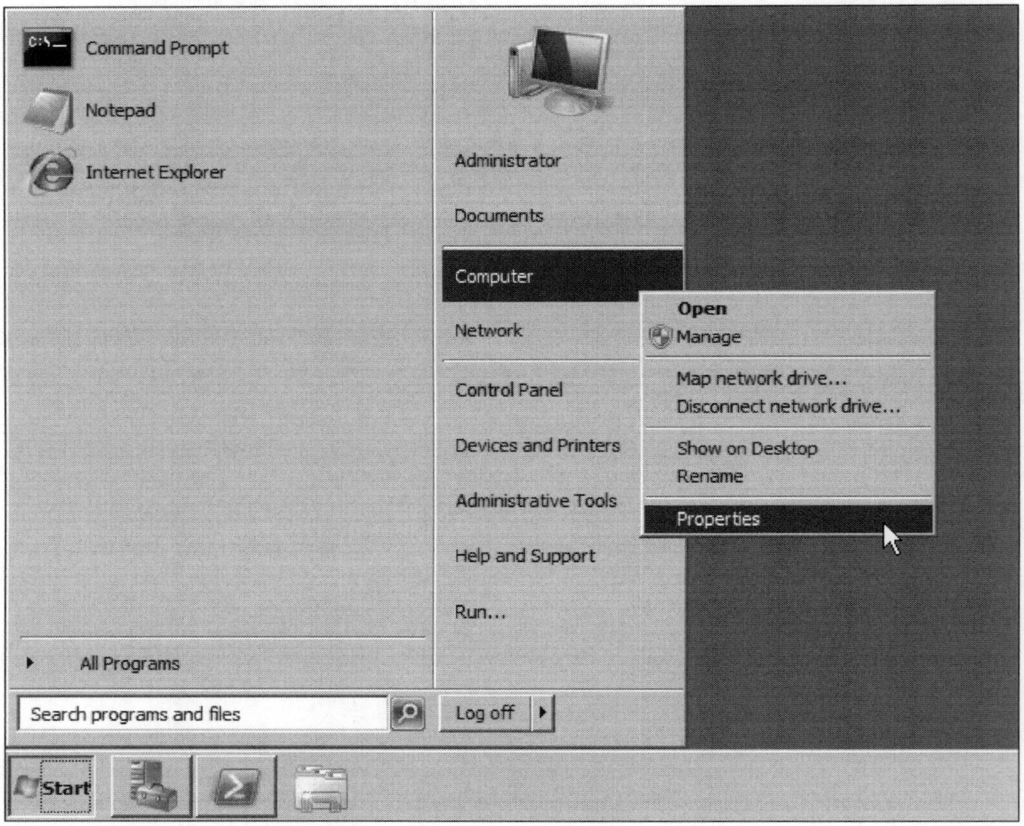

In the next screenshot, we will navigate to **Control panel** | **System and Security** | **System** and will be able to see information about our system. Next to the middle of the screen, we will have information about the computer's name, domain, and workgroup settings. In this section, we will see the **Change Settings** option, and that is the option we need to click. Take a look at the following screenshot:

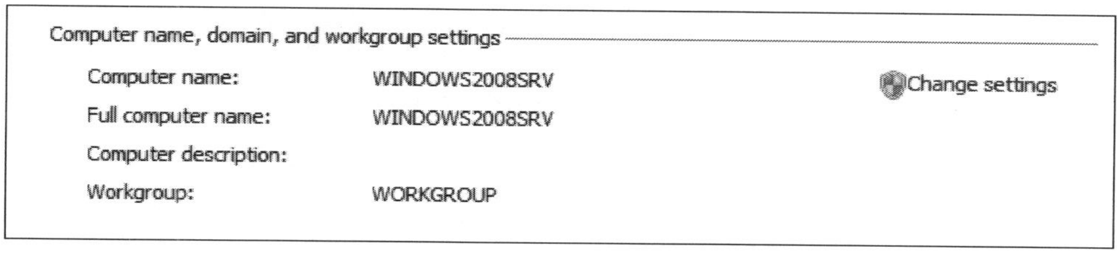

The screen that we will be presented with will have a button named **Change** next to this text: **To rename this computer or change its domain or workgroup, click Change**. We need to click on the button as shown in the following screenshot:

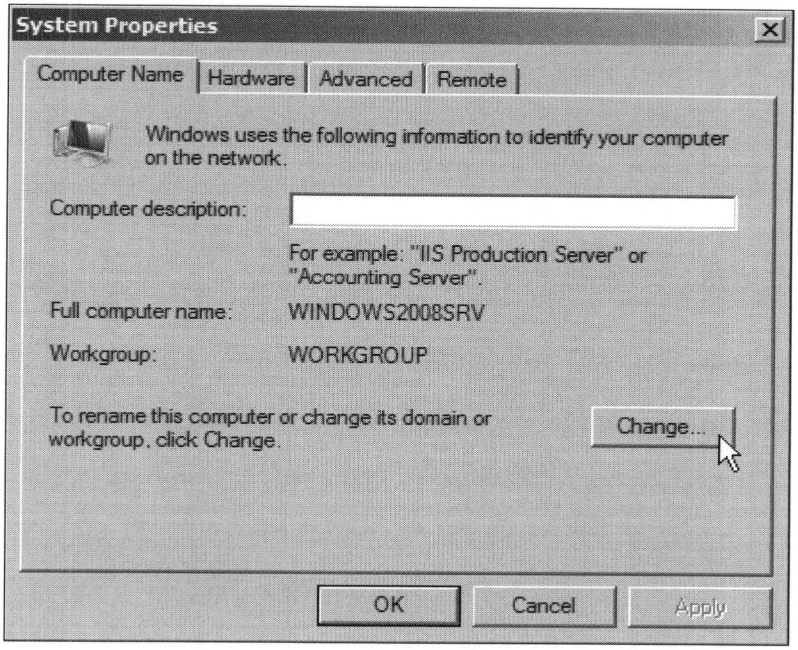

The next screenshot will provide us with a selection of an option to join a domain, and we just need to fill it with our domain's name as `POA`. The following screenshot shows us exactly how we did the configuration for our domain:

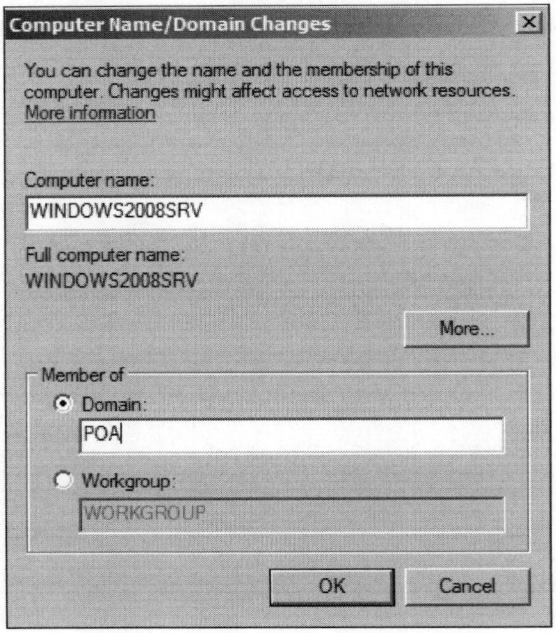

After filling the name for our domain, we just need to click on the **OK** button and fill our administration credentials. Here is what the dialog screen looks like:

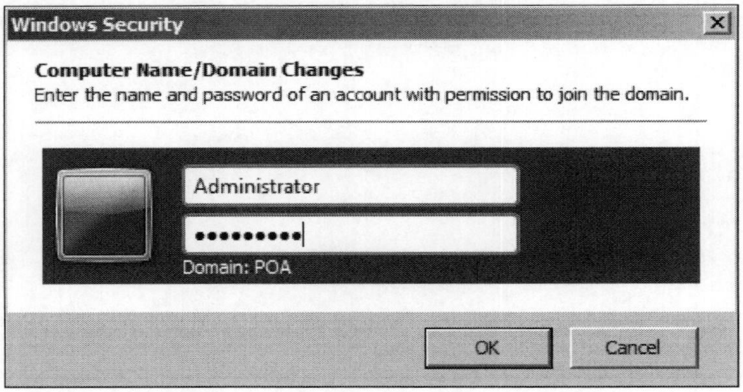

If everything went just fine, after a couple of seconds, we should see the dialogue box with the message **Welcome to the POA domain**, as shown in the following screenshot:

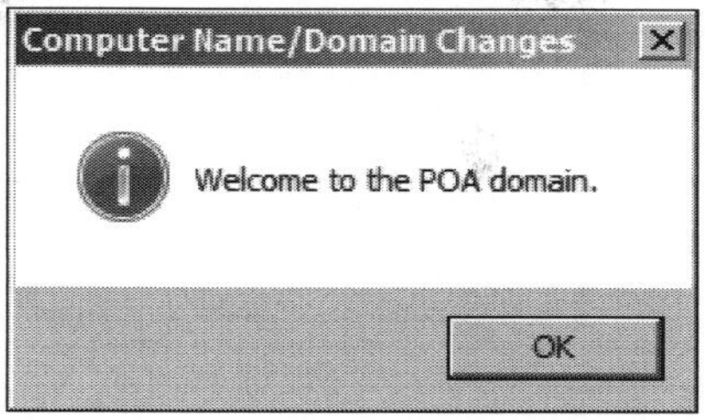

Just after we click on the **OK** button in the dialog box shown in the preceding screenshot, we will see another dialog box with a message stating that we need to restart the operating system so that the changes take effect. The following screenshot shows the message stating that if you have any open files, make sure you close and save them before restarting your system:

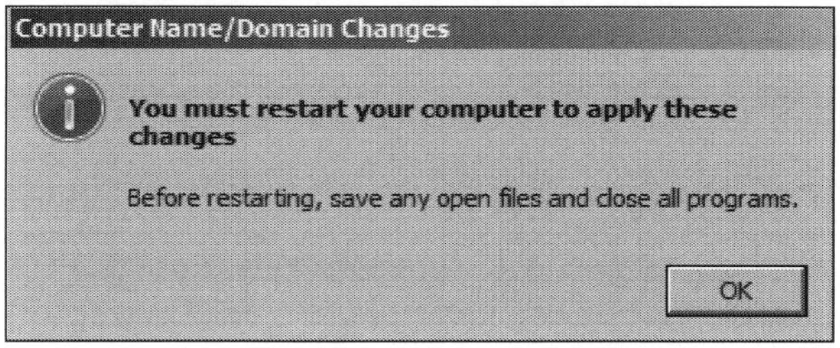

Now, we can safely click on **OK**, and Windows Server 2008 will restart after we click on the button shown in the following screenshot:

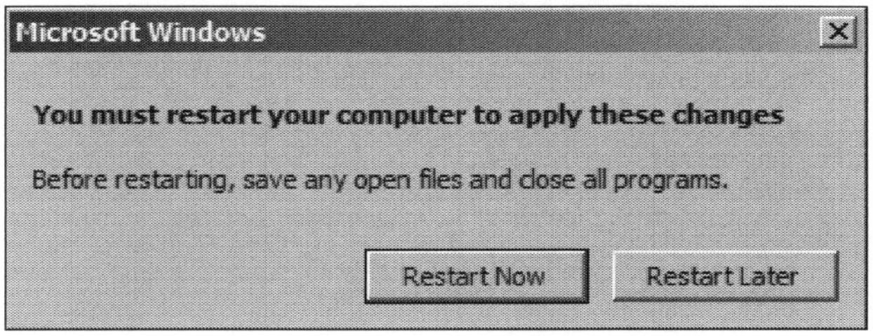

It's important to take a closer look at the log in screen the next time the server starts. If we do not pay attention to it, it may seem like we have the same options and the default option is to log in as the last user we did last time (which is the local **Administrator**). In contrast to other Microsoft Windows versions that offer an option to choose a user-friendly domain to log into, we need to use the direct log-in method using the **DOMAIN\User** option.

In the next screenshot, we see an example of how to log in to the POA domain that we just joined (remember to use the password for the POA domain's administrator):

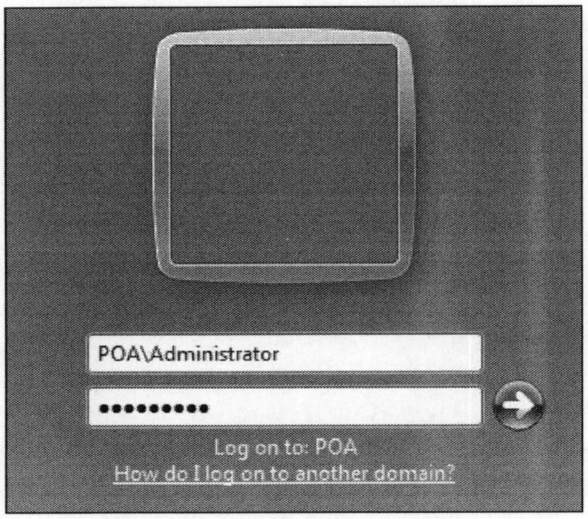

After we press *Enter*, we should log in to our new domain, and we will see that we have the Microsoft Windows Server 2008 R2 totally configured in the Samba 4 Active Directory POA domain. This is the final test and validation that our configuration is fully functional and our domain controller is ready to go live!

As we have this test machine ready and integrated with our domain, we will use it to create our organizational structure on our Active Directory. In our example, we have 10 OUs to create our structure and have it ready for production. This is an important procedure as we have some default configurations that we can use to test this machine to prepare our environment. We will not discuss many changes in detail, but I do recommend that you use this procedure of any Active Directory configuration to make all the changes you need to set up your environment as closely as possible to your needs.

To remotely manage our Samba 4 Active Directory Domain Controller using our Microsoft Windows 2008 R2 Server, we don't need to install extra software or download anything as in other Microsoft Windows versions, but we do need to configure (that is, enable) some features in the Server Manager that are not enabled by default.

> We can manage our Samba 4 Server using other versions of Microsoft Windows, such as Microsoft Windows 2003, Microsoft Windows XP, and Microsoft Windows 7.

For that, start the **Server Manager** tool. To do that, you just need to click on the **Start** menu button, choose **Run**, type `ServerManager.msc` in the input field, and press *Enter*. It's important to note that you actually need to write the extension `(.msc)`. If you do not, the file explorer (**Windows** | **System32** | **ServerManager**) will be opened instead. Alternatively, we can start the **Server Manager** by clicking on the link in the **Start** menu button.

Now, on the **Server Manager** screen, we need to click on the **Features** option in the left panel, and in the right panel, we need to click on the **Add Features** button. Look at the following screenshot where we show the **Features** option in the left panel highlighted, and the **Add Features** option on the right panel:

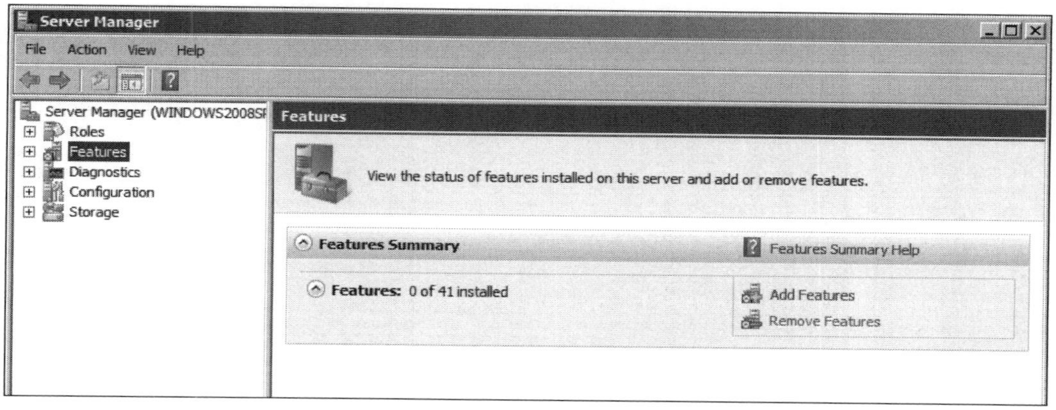

There are many Snap-Ins which we can enable in the **Add Features** menu, many needing the installation of the Microsoft .NET Framework (for example, the Active Directory Administrative Center), but for now, we will add just the following:

`AD DS Snap-Ins and Command-Line Tools`

`AD LDS Snap-Ins and Command-Line Tools`

Using both the preceding Snap-Ins should be sufficient to run the `dsa.msc` tool and so, we can start creating our Domain's OUs. The following screenshot shows what the **Add Features Wizard** screen looks like:

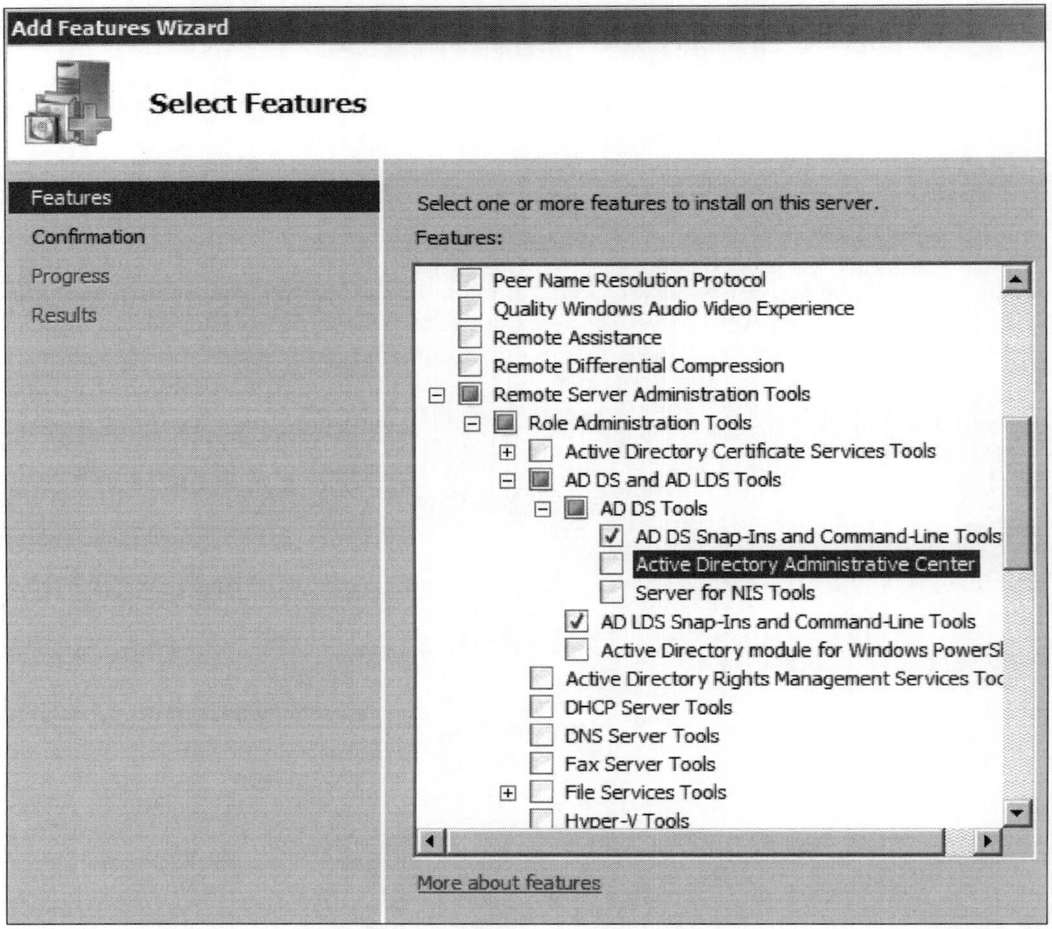

Just click on **Next** and perform a final check of the right panel to confirm that you have selected the right options. If everything is as it should be, we can go ahead and click on the **Install** button, as shown in the following screenshot:

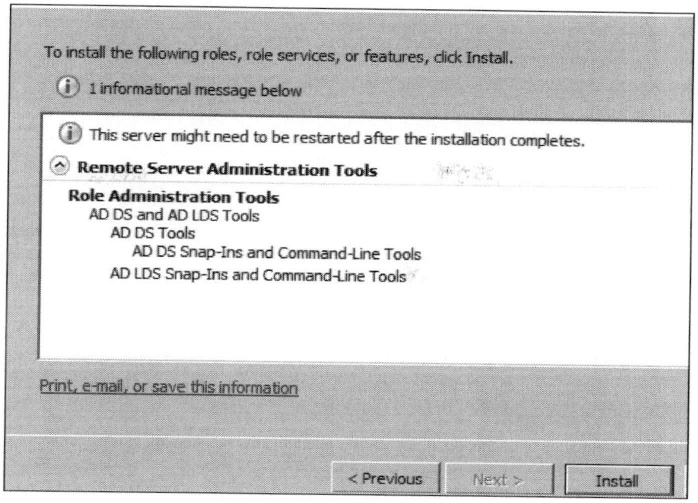

If you have not enabled the automatic update option on the Windows Server, you will receive a warning informing you that you should turn on Windows Update. Just check whether or not the installation process was completed without any error and the AD, DS, and LDS tools were successfully installed, and we can go on to the next step. Just click on the **Close** button on the **Add Features** installation screen, and we can close the Server Manager tool.

Now we can click the **Start** menu button, choose **Run**, and execute `dsa.msc`. After this, we should see a window on our screen like that shown in the following screenshot:

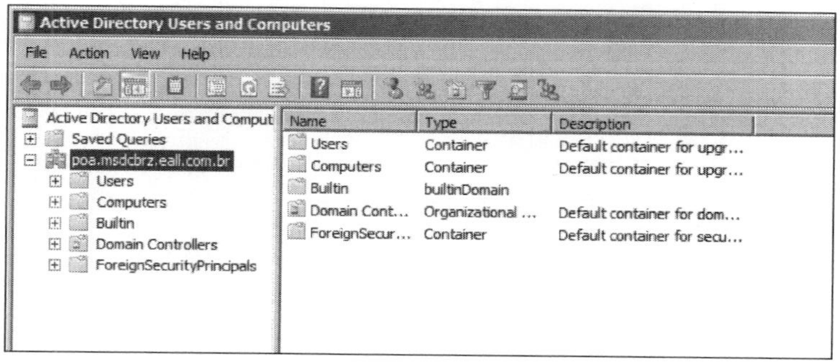

In the preceding screenshot, we have just selected our Active Directory domain `POA.MSDCBRZ.EALL.COM.BR` in the left pane, and to the right, we can see the default objects that are created when we perform the provisioning of a Samba 4 Domain Controller.

With this tool, we can create our OUs and create our structure to accommodate our objects the way we planned. In the following screenshot, we can see how to create the first top-level OU—`Workstations` (In the following screenshot, behind the first dialog box, we can see that our domain has been selected; this means that our new OU has been created under the domain):

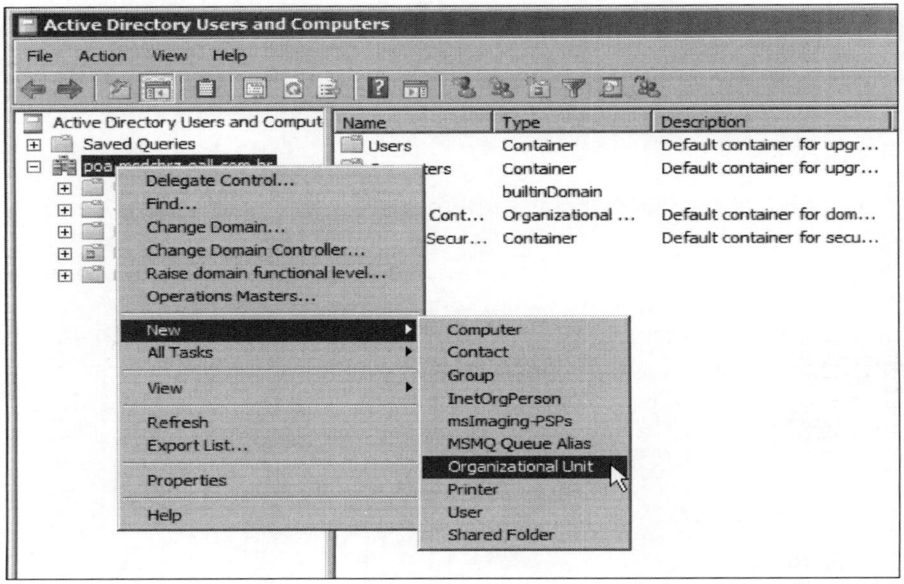

In the following screenshot, when we are asked to enter a name for the OU, we just need to enter the name of the new OU, we want to create, in the text field, and click on **OK**.

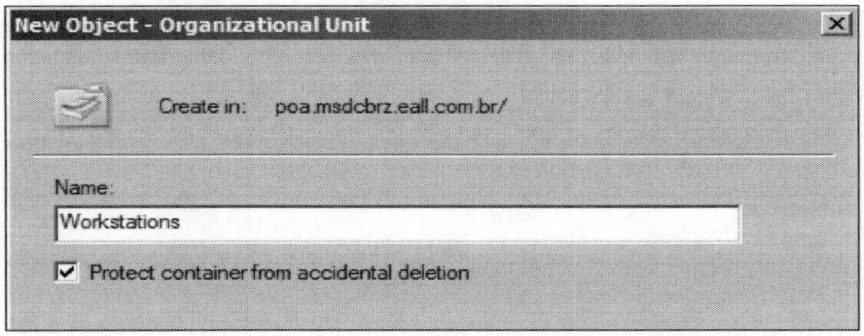

Now, we can repeat the same procedure to create the remaining nine Organizational Units we planned for our AD. The remaining nine OUs are as follows:

- **Desktops**
- **Laptops**
- **Services**
- **Terminal Servers**
- **Print Servers**
- **SQL Servers**
- **People**
- **Standard Users**
- **Power Users**

When every OU has been created, our Active Directory structure will look as shown in the following screenshot:

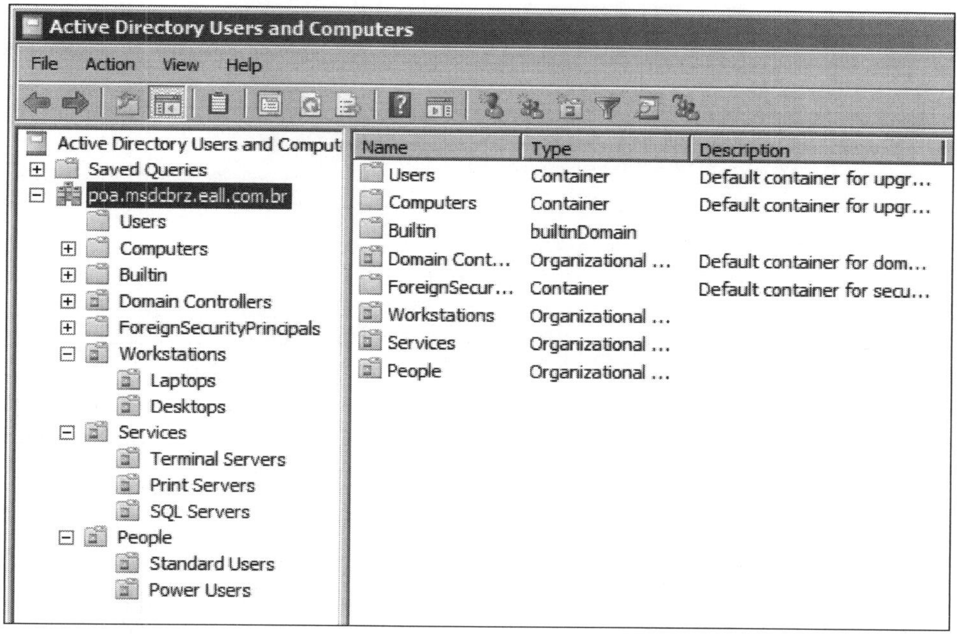

Once we have our Active Directory structure finished, we can close the `dsa.msc` tool and log out from our Windows 2008 R2 Server. Now, we go back to our Samba 4 Server where we will create our 50 users (47 **Standard Users** and 3 **Power Users**). With the bundle of scripts from the book's repository, we have a tool to create all our users in the appropriate OU and with all the relevant attributes. The initial password will be the same for all users (**Standard Users**), and in the first log-in, the users will need to register a personal password. For creating a user, just open a terminal shell and execute the following command:

```
leal@debian7:~$ cd ~/workspace/implementing_samba4/ &&
./createusers.sh -h
```

The previous command's output should be something like the following:

```
+--------------------------------------------------------------+
| Simple script to create users on the AD/DC (Samba 4 Server) |
|                                        Implementing Samba 4 |
|                                                              |
|                               Copyright(c) 2013 Marcelo Leal |
+--------------------------------------------------------------+
 Usage:

 "-h" for this help message
 "-c" creates users (silently).
 "-v" creates users (verbosely),
             showing the actual add user commands.
```

To create the users, the script uses a file named `users.txt`, which needs to be in the current directory.

```
Error Codes:   (0)OK,
      (1)Wrong Options,
      (2)At least one user creation error,
      (3) Could not open users.txt file.
```

First, we will create the Standard Users using the names provided in the `users.txt` file, and the script that we will use is intended to create users in the `People/Standard Users` OU only.

The file `users.txt` is very simple and is just a list of users with the name and surname. All the other attributes are handled by the `createusers.sh` script (for example, username and initials). The following is an excerpt of our `users.txt` file:

```
Vincent Vega
Jules Winnfield
Bruce Coolidge
Mia Wallace
Marsellus Wallace
Jimmie Dimmick
Phil Marvin
```

So next, we need to execute the following command in the Samba 4 Server prompt:

```
leal@debian7:~$ sudo ./createusers.sh -c
```

The output will show one line for each user created, indicating whether or not the user was created successfully or we faced any error. The following lines show the execution result for our file `users.txt`:

```
User: jajonnes created  OK.
User: zojarratt created  OK.
User: sahill created  OK.
User: qumichael created  OK.
User: rojohnson created  OK.
User: jabrown created  OK.
User: legecko created  OK.
-------------------------
Total Users Created..: 47
Total Creation Errors: 0
Total Users Processed: 47
-------------------------
```

At the end of the preceding output, we can see that we have processed 47 users and no errors were reported. All users were created without any issue, and we should have them all in our `Standard Users` OU.

Now we can take a look at our Active Directory tree again and see in the graphical user interface, all the users we have just created, as shown in the following screenshot:

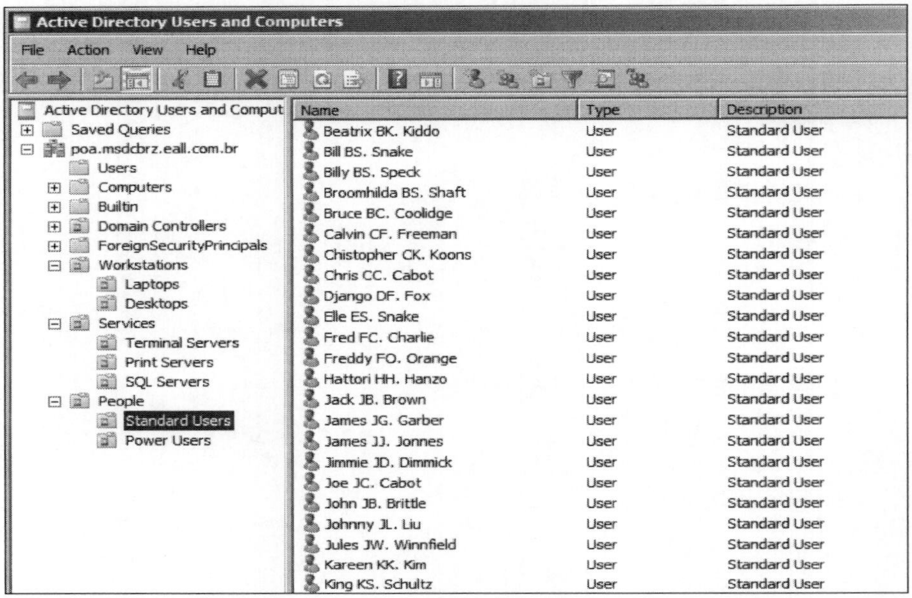

Summary

In this chapter, we saw in detail how to perform the provisioning of the Samba 4 Server as an Active directory Domain Controller, went through the initial phases of planning the network topology, structured the Active Directory, and created a checklist to help us organize information.

At the end of the chapter, we executed a series of tests and validations of important parts of the Active Directory server and thus, touched upon the subsystems that provide the core functionality of the Samba 4 AD/DC services. The last test was actually for joining a test server (Microsoft Windows 2008 R2 Server) to our POA Domain. We learned how to manage the Samba 4 Server from the Windows 2008 server, using the features that needed to be enabled on this Windows server's version.

Using our test machine, we tested the creation of custom OUs in our Active Directory, and so we could create our planned structure; and with the help of prebuilt scripts, we populated the AD/DC with 47 (nonPower) users.

In the next chapter, we will learn about the tools we can use to manage the Samba 4 Server, the basics of Group Policies management, and we will also cover authentication and authorization among other important GNU/Linux Systems features.

3

Managing the Samba Active Directory Server

In this chapter, we will present the different possible roles for the Samba 4 Server in the network, and learn how to manage it in the Active Directory Domain Controller role using a Microsoft Windows Server 2008 machine. In this chapter, we will cover the following points:

- The tools that are needed to manage the Samba 4 Server, the process to install them, and some basics about how to implement centralized change and configuration management for users and machines using **Group Policy Objects** (**GPO**). We will also learn how to create a custom management console to have every management tool quickly accessible and organized.
- Implementing authentication and authorization working on Samba 4 for GNU/Linux Systems (for example, the Debian 7 client) using the Samba software. We will also learn how to implement the standard subsystems from the GNU/Linux operating system for the authentication and name resolution, **Pluggable Authentication Modules** (**PAM**), and the **Name Service Switch** (**NSS**).
- Automating the managing tasks on the Samba 4 Server as well as on the GNU/Linux operating system.
- The replication and trust relationship characteristic of Active Directory Domain Controller when running the Samba 4 Server.

At the end of the chapter, we should have a good knowledge of the Samba 4 Server usecases and strengths, its roles, and how to obtain the best from the software. We will have plenty of command-line examples and step-by-step procedures to help the understanding of each configuration directive, so the reader will know exactly what each setting does (or does not) for each specific case.

Understanding the possible roles of the Samba 4 Server on the network

When we are planning to implement a Samba 4 Server, one point to have in mind is to determine the role that this new server will play on our network. Samba 4 has many server roles, and these roles are tied to one of these two options:

- The NT4-like domain operation mode from Samba 3
- The Active Directory Services mode from new Samba 4

Looking at the documentation of the Samba 4 software, we can have a detailed explanation of each role, and we will briefly describe it in the following list:

- **Auto**: This is the default, and if we use this option (`server role = auto`) at the command-line tool (for example, `samba-tool`), we are actually telling Samba to follow the configuration specified on the `security` setting of the `smb.conf` file (for example, `/usr/local/samba/etc/smb.conf`).
- **Standalone**: This is an operation mode that can be selected in the following two ways:
    - Explicitly using `server role = standalone` on the command line
    - Leaving `server role` (command line) and the `security` directive (for example, `/usr/local/samba/etc/smb.conf` file) untouched

  In this configuration, the Samba 4 Server will run as a simple (standalone) file/printer server, and the clients will need to authenticate (encrypted username/password by default) directly on it to gain access. So, the Samba 4 Server in this mode of operation will not be connected to a particular domain.

- **Member Server**: This is the server role configuration that will make Samba 4 operate as a server that is a member of one domain. Then, the authentication (username/password) will be validated by a **Domain Controller** (**DC**) on the network. The Samba 4 Server will forward the authentication/authorization task to a DC so it expects the **encrypted passwords** option to be configured to **yes**. We need to have in mind that this machine needs to be part of a Windows Domain (for example, it should have joined a valid Windows Domain). Another important point stated on the manual page is the fact that there is a need to still have valid Unix accounts to map file access and not just the accounts on the DC (Samba provides us with the Winbind service for this purpose).

- **Classic Primary Domain Controller**: This is one mode of the NT4-like domain operation, and in this mode, Samba 4 will provide logon services to the clients who have successfully joined the domain (for example, a single LAN/NetBIOS scope). We can have just one **Primary Domain Controller (PDC)** for each NetBIOS scope that is different from the next server role.
- **Netbios Backup Domain Controller**: As a **Netbios Backup Domain Controller (NBDC)**, the Samba 4 Server will add redundancy and resiliency to an NT4-like domain logon service, as adding servers in this role will add a fault tolerance to our network service. As we can have just one server as the Classic Primary Domain Controller for each NetBIOS scope, the ability to have multiple NBDCs is vital for the availability of the NT4-like domain logon services.
- **Active Directory Domain Controller**: This is brand new functionality and a great feature of the Samba 4 Server. This server role gives us the ability to run the Samba 4 Server as an Active Directory Domain Controller (AD DC) on the network, providing us with a multitude of services (for example, logon, configuration management, and so on) as well as great administrative power for system administrators. In the previous chapter, we had gone through all the steps required to successfully deploy a Samba 4 Server in this role, and had a close look at the procedure required to set up a Samba 4 Server as an AD DC.

Implementing the AD authentication and authorization for GNU/Linux systems

When we start to talk about GNU/Linux operating systems' authentication and authorization mechanisms, we need to understand more about two important subsystems of this environment: PAM and NSS.

Pluggable Authentication Modules (PAM) is a modern system that relies on specific libraries to provide us with authentication services. As a general **Application Programming Interface (API)**, all applications that are PAM-aware (for example, builds supporting PAM) can be integrated by the system administrator and can be authenticated using any authentication method that the PAM is configured to. This gives a lot of flexibility to the system administrators and also provides a centralized point to handle the users' authentication very effectively.

In an example scenario where an application is built to use PAM for authentication and the PAM subsystem is configured to authenticate users accessing local files (for example, `/etc/passwd`), switch the authentication mechanism for that application to authenticate in a LDAP server; for example, all we need to do is to reconfigure PAM to authenticate it on the LDAP server instead of reconfiguring this specific application. A more important point is that any other application that is configured to use the same PAM configuration will automatically be able to authenticate itself on the LDAP server too.

The **Name Service Switch** (**NSS**), on the other hand, is a scheme that will provide the name resolution for different services for the operating system when looking for specific database sources such as users, groups, hosts, networks, mail aliases, and so on. The NSS works by implementing specific services to access the different databases through separated modules. This is similar to the pluggable module approach by PAM, but very different in its purposes and the kind of services provided to the operating system.

As an example, in the case of users and groups, the operating system needs to map UID/GID for authorization to grant or deny access. The same application that had authenticated the user (for example, using PAM) will call functions from the NSS subsystem to inquire about the operating system to get such credentials (for example, `getent(1)`). GNU/Linux systems use both (PAM and NSS) facilities to provide us with the authentication/authorization, and we will learn how to configure them both to get our Debian GNU/Linux client fully integrated on our Active Directory network.

Now that we know about the subsystems that are involved in the authentication and name resolution of the operating system, we need to take a look at the applications that will integrate with these facilities, so we can have our GNU/Linux system work seamlessly within our Active Directory environment.

The GNU/Linux world as an open source environment is full of flexibility. So, we have many options to accomplish its integration with the AD DC, but we will focus on the pure Samba 4 approach. Using the same method through which we were able to integrate a Microsoft Windows machine with just a few configurations and without the complexity of many pieces of different software, the Samba 4 Project integrates all the features that are needed by the Samba software to facilitate the adoption and operation of the system administrators.

So, the program that integrates Samba with the PAM and NSS subsystems is called Winbind. The daemon (`winbindd`) is responsible for answering the inquiries from PAM (for the authentication requests); it is also responsible for answering specific requests from the operating system's NSS (for example, users and groups UID/GID). Winbind is part of the Samba Project and is fully integrated with the underlying protocols used by the Active Directory (for example, Kerberos).

To start our configuration tasks on PAM, NSS, and Winbind, we need Samba 4 installed on our Debian 7 GNU/Linux client machine. To make things easier, we can follow the instructions from *Chapter 1, Installing the Samba 4 Server*, to install the dependencies and the Samba 4 software itself. The only difference is that we don't need packages such as `dhcp-server`. With the help of the Samba 4 configuration commands, the default for the `ads` security support is described as `auto`, and with the LDAP libraries and all dependencies properly installed on the system, we will have no issues and don't need to explicitly use the options `--with-ads` during the Samba 4 installation.

> ADS support is needed for our configuration, and if it's not available in our Samba 4 build, we need to take a look at our Samba 4 installation instructions before trying to explicitly enable it, in *Chapter 1, Installing the Samba 4 Server*, and fixing the issues as it should be enabled automatically.

After the `configure phase`, `make`, and `make install` processes are done, we can go ahead and integrate our system into our Active Directory environment. In this procedure, we will also learn how to deploy a GNU/Linux system as a Domain Member Server, as we will join it into the Active Directory Domain. Let's get started!

As we already know, Kerberos is a central point for the Active Directory services. So, task number 1 is to make sure that the time and date are fine and our DNS resolver is configured to be our Active Directory Domain Controller. In our example system, the Debian GNU/Linux system is configured to get all the network configurations through DHCP (for example, our AD DC).

In our network, just the Domain Controller has access to the Internet; because of that, to install the dependencies and clone the Samba 4 software, we have our AD DC providing **Network Address Translation** (**NAT**) for our LAN. This configuration can be quite handy, so here is a simple command-line procedure example to accomplish this (remember that it needs to be persisted if you want a permanent configuration):

```
leal@debian7:~$ sudo su
[sudo] password for leal:
root@debian7:~# sysctl -w net.ipv4.conf.all.forwarding=1
root@debian7:~# iptables -t nat -A POSTROUTING -s 192.168.1.0/24 -o eth0
-j MASQUERADE
root@debian7:~# iptables -A FORWARD -s 192.168.1.0/24 -i eth1 -j ACCEPT
root@debian7:~# exit
leal@debian7:~$
```

> In the previous example, eth0 is the Internet interface.

When time, date, and DNS are checked, we can configure and test Kerberos. To do that, we'll just copy our Kerberos configuration from our AD DC (/etc/krb5.conf):

```
[libdefaults]
default_realm = POA.MSDCBRZ.EALL.COM.BR
dns_lookup_realm = false
dns_lookup_kdc = true
```

Task done, we can test it:

```
leal@debianclt:~$ kinit administrator@POA.MSDCBRZ.EALL.COM.BR
Password for administrator@POA.MSDCBRZ.EALL.COM.BR:
Warning: Your password will expire in 22 days on Sun Jul 14 17:55:04 2013
leal@debianclt:~$ klist
Ticket cache: FILE:/tmp/krb5cc_1000
Default principal: administrator@POA.MSDCBRZ.EALL.COM.BR

Valid starting     Expires            Service principal
22/06/2013 12:53  22/06/2013 22:53  krbtgt/POA.MSDCBRZ.EALL.COM.BR@POA.
MSDCBRZ.EALL.COM.BR
renew until 23/06/2013 12:53
```

The result of the previous commands confirms that our Kerberos configuration is okay, and we can move on to the next steps. As we will need to configure our **PAM** and **NSS** system files to use specific modules, it's a good idea to have these libraries in place before such configuration. This is crucial because if we do the configuration without having the libraries configured, we can leave the system in an unresolved situation and many parts of the operating system (login included) might stop working.

Configuring the PAM and NSS libraries

The Samba 4 software that we compiled and installed has the PAM and NSS libraries that we need to use. The standard place for the PAM modules on Debian 7 (i386) is: /lib/i386-linux-gnu/security/. If we list the content of that directory, we will see many files following the same pattern such as pam_* (for example, pam_unix.so). The PAM module provided by the Samba 4 software has the same pattern and is located in /usr/local/samba/lib/security/ with the name: pam_winbind.so.

We will not mix the Debian 7 distribution files and programs with the Samba 4 software we installed (not using the distribution official packages), so we will just add a link on the standard location to reference our PAM Winbind module in our Samba 4 installation directory.

Let's just execute the following command at the Debian GNU/Linux client:

```
leal@debianclt:~$ ls /usr/local/samba/lib/security/pam_winbind.so
/usr/local/samba/lib/security/pam_winbind.so
leal@debianclt:~$
```

If the output of the previous command is the `pam_winbind.so` PAM module, we are good to go. If the result is `No such file or directory` or any other error, we need to review our Samba installation procedure from *Chapter 1, Installing the Samba 4 Server*, and check if all the dependencies described in that chapter were properly installed prior to our Samba 4 installation. Just go ahead to continue the configuration after the PAM module is ready and available on the system.

With the PAM module ready, we can inform the system of its presence. Just execute the following commands at one terminal at the Debian GNU/Linux client machine (in this example, we are listing the 32 bit library version):

```
leal@debianclt:~$ cd /lib/i386-linux-gnu/security/
leal@debianclt:~$ sudo ln -s /usr/local/samba/lib/security/\
pam_winbind.so
[sudo] password for leal:
leal@debianclt:~$ ls -l pam_winbind.so
lrwxrwxrwx 1 root root 44 Jun 21 08:33 pam_winbind.so -> /usr/local/
samba/lib/security/pam_winbind.so
leal@debianclt:~$
```

Double-check the output of the preceding code to make sure that the link is pointing to the right location. If you have changed the default Samba 4 installation directory (for example, using a specific location with the `--` prefix), you will need to change the previous command to reflect your setup.

After the PAM module link is created, we can create the link for the NSS. The standard location for the NSS libraries on the Debian 7 GNU/Linux is `/lib` (for example, `/lib/x86_64-linux-gnu` for 64 bit systems), and the name pattern is `libnss_*`. We should have the `libnss_winbind.so` library in the Samba 4 installation directory, `/usr/local/samba/lib/`, so we will do a similar procedure to validate our Samba 4 installation before creating the link.

In one terminal window, just issue the following command:

```
leal@debianclt:~$ ls -l /usr/local/samba/lib/libnss_winbind*
lrwxrwxrwx 1 root staff    19 Jun 22 02:03 /usr/local/samba/lib/libnss_
winbind.so -> libnss_winbind.so.2
-rwxr-xr-x 1 root staff 34223 Jun 22 00:04 /usr/local/samba/lib/libnss_
winbind.so.2
leal@debianclt:~$
```

Notice the two lines that we have in the preceding output. One is for the `libnss_winbind.so.2` file (the library itself), and the other is for compatibility/noversion purposes (`libnss_winbind.so`). Again, it is important to make sure that these two lines are present in the output of the previous command before moving on to the next steps. If we see any errors or the absence of any of the lines of the preceding code, we need to review our Samba 4 installation based on the procedure of *Chapter 1, Installing the Samba 4 Server*, and make sure that all the dependencies are properly installed on the system.

If everything is just fine, we can create the links for the NSS libraries—a procedure that is similar to the one we did for the PAM modules. We can do this by issuing the following commands:

```
leal@debianclt:~$ cd /lib/
leal@debianclt:~$ sudo ln -s /usr/local/samba/lib/\
libnss_winbind.so* /lib/
[sudo] password for leal:
leal@debianclt:~$ ls -l libnss_winbind.so*
lrwxrwxrwx 1 root root 38 Jun 21 08:33 libnss_winbind.so -> /usr/local/
samba/lib/libnss_winbind.so
lrwxrwxrwx 1 root root 40 Jun 21 08:33 libnss_winbind.so.2 -> /usr/local/
samba/lib/libnss_winbind.so.2
leal@debianclt:~$
```

Once again, it is important to double-check whether the links are right in place before going to the next phase of the OS configuration. As we confirm that the libraries for PAM and NSS are available on the system, we can configure the files to make use of them. Before that, we will create a minimal `smb.conf` file to configure our Samba 4 software and join Debian 7 GNU/Linux into our Active Directory Domain.

Here, we have a simple and fully functional `smb.conf` file to work with:

```
[global]
workgroup = POA
```

```
security = ADS
realm = POA.MSDCBRZ.EALL.COM.BR
encrypt passwords = yes
template shell = /bin/bash

idmap config *:backend  = rid
idmap config *:range = 100000-200000

winbind use default domain = yes
winbind enum users  = yes
winbind enum groups = yes
```

The workgroup and realm are the same as our AD DC. Note that the `encrypt passwords` option is configured to `yes` as we mentioned it as a requirement when configuring a Samba 4 Server as a Domain Member Server. We have a general `template` configuration for the login shell configured to `/bin/bash`. Without this configuration, our users will not be able to log in, as the `login shell` attribute will be translated by the Samba 4 Server to the default value `/bin/false`.

> In our configuration, we have a Samba 4 Server in the AD role, but we can join Samba 4 as a member server of Microsoft Windows AD Domain Controller too.

Next, we have two lines starting with the directive `idmap`. As we mentioned at the beginning of this topic, there are many ways to integrate GNU/Linux into an Active Directory Domain, and one of the options is related to the approach of handling the users and groups IDs. Samba controls these options through the directive `idmap config` backend, and in this example, we are using `rid`. The reasons for this choice are basically related to the following three `rid` backend characteristics that we want for our environment:

- **Simple**: With this backend, Winbind doesn't need to maintain a local database to persist the users' and group's ID translations. This is a great feature as we want to add more GNU/Linux systems to our Active Directory Domain, but to maintain all the systems with the DBs in sync is not a task we want. This is why we have an AD DC in the first place.
- **Deterministic**: The translation of the users' and groups' IDs is deterministic; by these means, it follows a formula to actually have the translation consistent between different GNU/Linux Domain Member Servers. The translation is made on the fly and cached locally, not needing a local `idmap` database as a point of failure and an administration headache.

- **No need to manage UID/GID on the AD DC**: Another great advantage of this backend is that we don't need to populate the UID and GID numbers in our Active Directory Schema. As the translation is made following a formula on the fly, we don't have to worry about creating UID or GID during the creation of the user and group, and we don't need to handle complexities such as collision.

Every solution is based on trade-offs and features that system administrators may or may not want (or need) for their environments. This is why Samba provides us with many options, and flexibility is the mother of all good software. The second `idmap config` line is the range that the `rid` backend will utilize in its formula to generate the user and group IDs. From the Samba Project Documentation [1], this is the formula for the `rid` backend UID/GID translation:

```
UNIX ID for a RID:
ID = RID - BASE_RID + LOW_RANGE_ID

RID from a UNIX ID:
RID = ID + BASE_RID - LOW_RANGE_ID
```

> We gave a 100,000 ID range for the `rid` backend utilization of the translations.

The last three lines are Winbind directives and the first one (`use default domain = yes`) is a configuration option that lets the users be referenced using just the username (for example. striping the domain part). As our environment is one domain only, we can use it without any problem. If we were deploying a multidomain solution, we probably would not be able to use this feature as we could potentially have username collisions.

The `enum users` and `enum groups` options are needed, so Winbind is able to enumerate domain users and/or groups. This is an important feature and is crucial for the operating system to work properly (for example, Name Service Switch), to obtain detailed information about users and/or groups.

As we can see, our configuration file is very practical and simple; we have used the excellent Samba project's documentation to understand the features that we need and use them. However, there are many other options that we can use in the future, but that is a case-by-case analysis and the important point is to use what is needed and keep the configuration simple, just adding features or restrictions that are really needed for the environment. Many installations (for example, sites) have options and configurations in many systems that nobody knows why. This can be a security risk and a useless complexity for sure. Keep in mind that we need to know and understand every option we have in any configuration file, for any system under our management.

Joining the Debian 7 GNU/Linux into our Active Directory Domain

Now we can join our Debian 7 GNU/Linux system into our Active Directory Domain with the following command:

```
leal@debianclt:~$ sudo net ads join -U administrator
Enter administrator's password:
```

> We need to remember to add the `/usr/local/samba/sbin` and `/usr/local/samba/bin` directories to our `PATH` variable, or we will need to use the absolute pathnames for commands such as the preceding one.

After providing our Domain administrator's password at the prompt, we would receive the following output after a few moments:

```
Using short domain name -- POA
Joined 'DEBIANCLT' to dns domain 'poa.msdcbrz.eall.com.br'
```

After this, our system becomes part of the Active Directory Domain as a Member Server, and we can start the `winbindd` daemon and perform some tests before going further and configuring the system files for the PAM and NSS. As soon as we validate that the Winbind is fully working, we will move on to the final tasks.

Just issue the following commands at the Debian 7 GNU/Linux client machine:

```
leal@debianclt:~$ sudo winbindd
[sudo] password for leal:
leal@debianclt:~$ wbinfo -u | head -9
mawallace
brshaft
```

```
chkoons
mawhitaker
juwinnfield
qumichael
spbennett
brcoolidge
cafreeman
```

The first of the preceding commands starts the Samba 4 Winbind daemon (`winbindd`), and if you are following our procedure in a lab and using our same users, you should see a similar output that shows you the first 10 users of our domain after the second command. In case you are implementing in a test environment (for example, a clone subset of your production), you should see the first nine users of your domain.

Let's try to enumerate our domain groups now:

```
leal@debianclt:~$ /usr/local/samba/bin/wbinfo -g | head
allowed rodc password replication group
enterprise read-only domain controllers
denied rodc password replication group
read-only domain controllers
group policy creator owners
ras and ias servers
domain controllers
enterprise admins
domain computers
cert publishers
```

With the output of the preceding commands, we confirm that our environment is in good shape and we can go ahead and configure the operating system to be aware of the AD DC users and groups, so as to be able to authenticate and authorize them onto our system.

> Before starting the configuration of the PAM and NSS subsystems, it is a good idea to have more than one root shell on the machine (for example, the Debian 7 GNU/Linux client). So, in the case of any mistakes, we can use the other root shells to fix it or rollback the configuration.

To configure NSS, we need to edit the `/etc/nsswitch.conf` file. For that, we just need to add the `winbind` keyword after the `compat` directive in three lines, just like the following example:

```
# /etc/nsswitch.conf
#
# Example configuration of GNU Name Service Switch functionality.
# If you have the `glibc-doc-reference' and `info' packages installed, try:
# `info libc "Name Service Switch"' for information about this file.

passwd:         compat winbind
group:          compat winbind
shadow:         compat winbind
```

The PAM architecture was created to provide us with a pluggable model for the authentication and for other tasks such as setting the password, managing the account and session; it also has some control flags (for example, required, optional, sufficient [2]). So, the different GNU/Linux distributions organize the files and configurations in a very specific way. For our Debian 7 system, we have four common files used by the majority of applications (for example, Secure Shell/SSH): `common-auth`, `common-account`, `common-password`, and `common-session`. All files are located in the directory: `/etc/pam.d/`.

Starting with the `common-auth` file, we need to add the following line before the standard authentication line that uses the `pam_unix.so` module:

```
auth    sufficient                      pam_winbind.so
auth    [success=1 default=ignore] pam_unix.so\
nullok_secure use_first_pass
```

Notice that we added an option to the `auth` line for `pam_unix.so` (`use_first_pass`) in the preceding commands. This is an option to actually use the same password that the user provided in the first interaction; in the others, authentication options are configured. Another important point is the flag `sufficient` we have used on our `pam_winbind.so` line from the PAM RFC.

With this flag, if the module succeeds, the PAM framework immediately returns `success` to the application without trying any other modules.

This is the behavior we need as we are saying, "If the user has the right credentials on our AD Domain Controller (for example, username/password), let him/her pass to the next PAM's validation on the stack."

For the common-password file, we add the following command (again, just before the pam_unix.so line):

```
password sufficient                     pam_winbind.so
password [success=1 default=ignore]     pam_unix.so obscure sha512
```

This time, we don't add any options to the pam_unix.so line, and we are using the same sufficient flag. We do the same for the common-account file:

```
account sufficient           pam_winbind.so
account [success=1 new_authtok_reqd=done default=ignore] pam_unix.so
```

The only file we will need to add to the two lines is in the common-session file. As we are not creating the users on our GNU/Linux systems, we do not have the home directories created beforehand. So, for our users to be able to log in, we need to make sure that he/she will have a home directory before allowing them to access the system. Notice that we use the following required flag for the pam_mkhomedir.so PAM module:

```
session required   pam_mkhomedir.so skel=/etc/skel/ umask=0022
session required   pam_winbind.so
session required   pam_unix.so
```

If we have a problem creating the user home directory, then that module will return an error code. As the flag is required, PAM will understand that one step of the authorization process was broken (one that is required), and will deny the access.

Here is an excerpt about PAM RFC [2]: With this flag, the module failure results in the PAM framework that returns the error to the caller _after_ executing all other modules on the stack.

PAM is a powerful authentication framework and to cover it all is outside the scope of this book. However, there are many great sources of real good content on the Internet, apart from entire books about the subject. You can take a look at the manual page of your GNU/Linux distribution (for example, man PAM), as it's a very good starting point.

We have just edited important system files, and if anything is wrong, we can get stuck without being able to authenticate in our machine. So, it's important to validate and check that everything is right before leaving our root shell. It's a good advice to actually use a root shell and not sudo vi to do these tasks because if we did something wrong, maybe we will not be able to authenticate it again to fix it.

So, let's see if we are still able to log in to the system using our local user account (for example, leal), and become root:

```
leal@debianclt:~$ ssh localhost
leal@localhost's password:
Linux debianclt 3.2.0-4-686-pae #1 SMP Debian 3.2.46-1 i686
The programs included with the Debian GNU/Linux system are free software;
the exact distribution terms for each program are described in the
individual files in /usr/share/doc/*/copyright.

Debian GNU/Linux comes with ABSOLUTELY NO WARRANTY, to the extent
permitted by applicable law.
You have new mail.
Last login: Sat Jun 22 02:10:05 2013 from debian7.local
leal@debianclt:~$ sudo su
[sudo] password for leal:
root@debianclt:/home/leal#
```

Excellent! Now, we can perform some tests to validate whether our system can recognize our Domain users and groups, and after that, try to log in to the system using one of our Domain users. In a terminal in the Debian 7 GNU/Linux client machine, issue the following command:

```
leal@debianclt:~$ for x in `wbinfo -u`; do echo -n "User: $x `id
$x`"; echo ""; done
```

We should see a long list with all our 50 users and some standard AD users (for example, guest). But we are actually listing the Unix information for them, and so let's see an excerpt of that output:

```
User: mawallace uid=101191(mawallace) gid=100513(domain users)
 groups=100513(domain users)
User: brshaft uid=101220(brshaft) gid=100513(domain users)
 groups=100513(domain users)
User: chkoons uid=101196(chkoons) gid=100513(domain users)
 groups=100513(domain users)
User: mawhitaker uid=101199(mawhitaker) gid=100513(domain users)
 groups=100513(domain users)
User: juwinnfield uid=101188(juwinnfield) gid=100513(domain users)
 groups=100513(domain users)
```

We can see the first five users, with their respective UIDs and GIDs, in the output of the preceding commands. As we know the formula that the `idmap` uses to do the translation of the IDs, let's take a look at the first one and see if it makes sense. Just type the following command in a terminal window:

```
leal@debianclt:~$ wbinfo -n mawallace
leal@debianclt:~$ S-1-5-21-721742975-1223580478-3920759553-1191\
SID_USER (1)
```

The `idmap` formulae is:

- $ID = RID - BASE\_RID + LOW\_RANGE\_ID$
- $ID = 1191 - 0 + 100000$
- $ID = 101191$

> `BASE_RID` is `0` by default and deprecated [1].

So far so good; now, let's look at a proper `passwd` entry (for example, `getent`), and see the NSS in action. Just type the following command at the terminal to see how Marsellus Wallace looks like:

```
leal@debianclt:~$ getent passwd mawallace
mawallace:*:101191:100513:Marsellus MW. Wallace:/home/POA/mawallace:\
/bin/bash
leal@debianclt:~$
```

This is exactly how a `passwd` structure should be, and Marsellus Wallace could now try to access the Debian 7 GNU/Linux client system, but before that, let's just take a look at the end of the `passwd` line of the preceding code. Notice that the home directory is defined as `/home/POA` at a high level, and we do not have the top-level directory for our Domain users just yet. So, before the user is actually able to access the system, we need to create the `/home/POA` top directory. We can issue the following command:

```
leal@debianclt:~$ sudo su -
Password:
root@debianclt:~# mkdir /home/POA && echo OK
OK
root@debianclt:~# exit
leal@debianclt:~$
```

Remember that we don't need to create the user's home directory (for example, `mawallace`) because our PAM stack at the session phase will use the `pam_mkhomedir.so` module to do that for us, if needed. So, Marsellus Wallace can now try to access the system using SSH:

```
leal@debianclt:~$ ssh localhost -l mawallace
mawallace@localhost's password:
You need to change your password now
Creating directory '/home/POA/mawallace'.
Linux debianclt 3.2.0-4-686-pae #1 SMP Debian 3.2.46-1 i686
The programs included with the Debian GNU/Linux system are free software;
the exact distribution terms for each program are described in the
individual files in /usr/share/doc/*/copyright.
Debian GNU/Linux comes with ABSOLUTELY NO WARRANTY, to the extent
permitted by applicable law.
WARNING: Your password has expired.
You must change your password now and login again!
Changing password for mawallace
(current) NT password:
Enter new NT password:
Retype new NT password:
passwd: password updated successfully
Connection to localhost closed.
leal@debianclt:~$
```

Perfect! Now we can see that the user was forced to change his/her password as it was the first login and we created all our users with the password expiration flag enabled. After the user was logged out automatically, let's see if the home directory was created with the right credentials:

```
leal@debianclt:~$ ls -ld /home/POA/mawallace
drwxr-xr-x 2 mawallace domain users 4096 Jun 22 17:35
 /home/POA/mawallace
leal@debianclt:~$
```

> Take a look at the UMASK for the home directory creation in the `common-session` PAM configuration file, and you can configure it according to your domain's security standards/policies.

Let's see what happens if the user tries to log in again:

```
leal@debianclt:~$ ssh localhost -l mawallace
mawallace@localhost's password:
Linux debianclt 3.2.0-4-686-pae #1 SMP Debian 3.2.46-1 i686

The programs included with the Debian GNU/Linux system are free software;
the exact distribution terms for each program are described in the
individual files in /usr/share/doc/*/copyright.

Debian GNU/Linux comes with ABSOLUTELY NO WARRANTY, to the extent
permitted by applicable law.
Last login: Sat Jun 22 17:35:14 2013 from localhost
mawallace@debianclt:~$ pwd
/home/POA/mawallace
mawallace@debianclt:~$
```

As we can see, with this procedure, it is really simple to quickly integrate a GNU/Linux system into an Active Directory Domain, as in a few minutes we had a Member Server ready to be authenticated without any hurdle. In the rest of the chapters, we will learn how to create a highly available file server in more detail so that we can host our home directories in a central server and provide mobility and consistency to our users, when accessing different GNU/Linux machines.

Starting with the basic concepts for Group Policies on Samba 4

System administrators are always looking for ways to do more for their IT environment while spending as few of the organization's resources (for example, money and time) as possible. The main concern when we need to do any work is about the time we will spend on it, so we need to be efficient and effective in our actions to accomplish the right task at the right and minimum time. So, in the systems administration task, this challenge is more real than ever as there is a need to be efficient while managing dozens or thousands of users and at the same time controlling one or thousands of servers with the same level of availability and service features that our customers expect.

Any company's environment is a moving and evolving live organism where computers, services, and people have relationships that can quickly become highly complex. At the same time, the management of these assets needs to be scalable enough to provide and sustain these relationships, as they are a vital part of any organization. Samba 4 with its compliant Active Directory Domain Controller implementation, provides a central tool for configuration and change management for system administrators and managers to cope with demanding characteristics like the ones we just presented in the Group Policies.

Group Policies Objects (GPO) are settings or a set of rules that are applied for a group of users and computers, from logon/logoff scripts to shutdown/start up routines. The objective of this book is not to be an exhaustive guide about all the GPO features or the Active Directory functionalities, as there are whole other books for these specific subjects. However, it must provide you with a good starting point to understand its general characteristics while also trying to help you understand how the powerful Samba 4 Server becomes integrated with these features.

The implementation of Group Policies is very site dependent with regards to all the security rules and policies for each organization, the structure of the Active Directory implemented, and the experience of the system administrators. This is because GPOs are applied to users and/or computers and linked to the OUs, affecting all users and/or computers within one or more specific OUs. We will use some general examples and our Microsoft Windows 2008 machine to execute the administration tasks and create the GPOs at our Samba 4 Active Directory Domain Controller.

In the last chapter, we showed how to install the tool to manage the Active Directory users and computers, and here, we have used it to create the organizational units that we planned for our environment. Now we will add another important feature to our Active Directory management kit in the previously configured Microsoft Windows Server, which will give us the ability to perform the Group Policy management:

1. Log in to our Microsoft Windows 2008 machine, open the Server Manager, and choose the **to add features** option. Then, we check the **Group Policy Management** box as shown in the following screenshot:

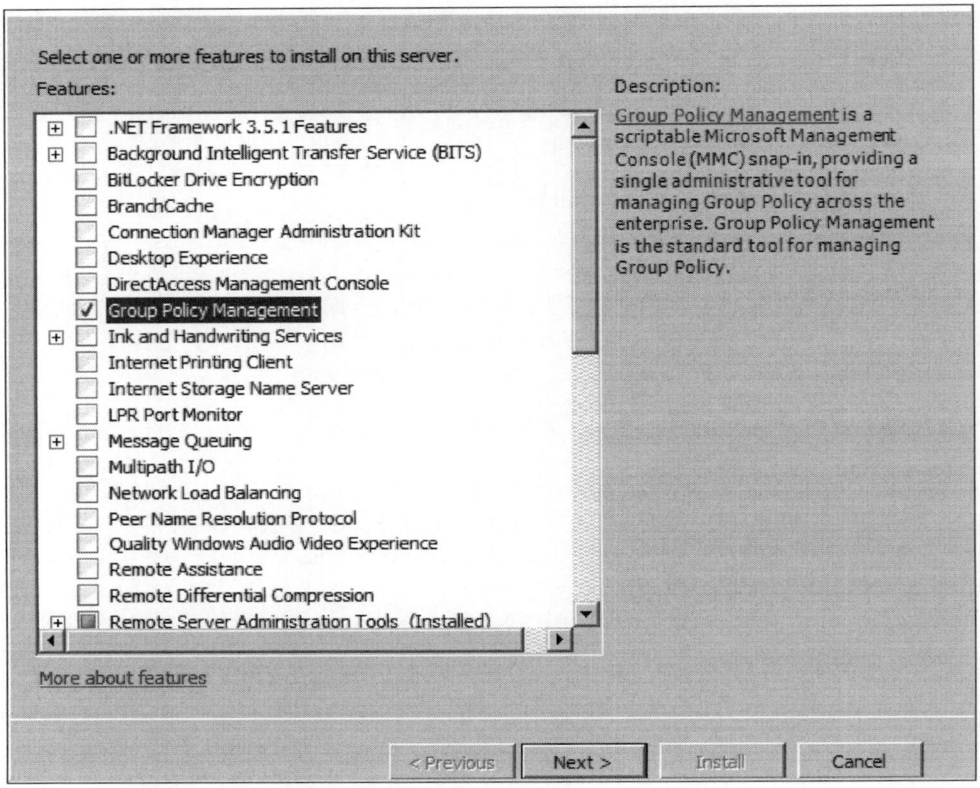

2. As we can see from the description displayed on the left side of the preceding screenshot, this is the standard tool to manage the Group Policy Framework. Just click on the **Next** button and then click on **Install** (note that the machine will need to be restarted to finish the installation).
3. After the restart, we can navigate to **Start** | **Administrative Tools** | **Group Policy Management** to open the tool. Take a look at the following screenshot:

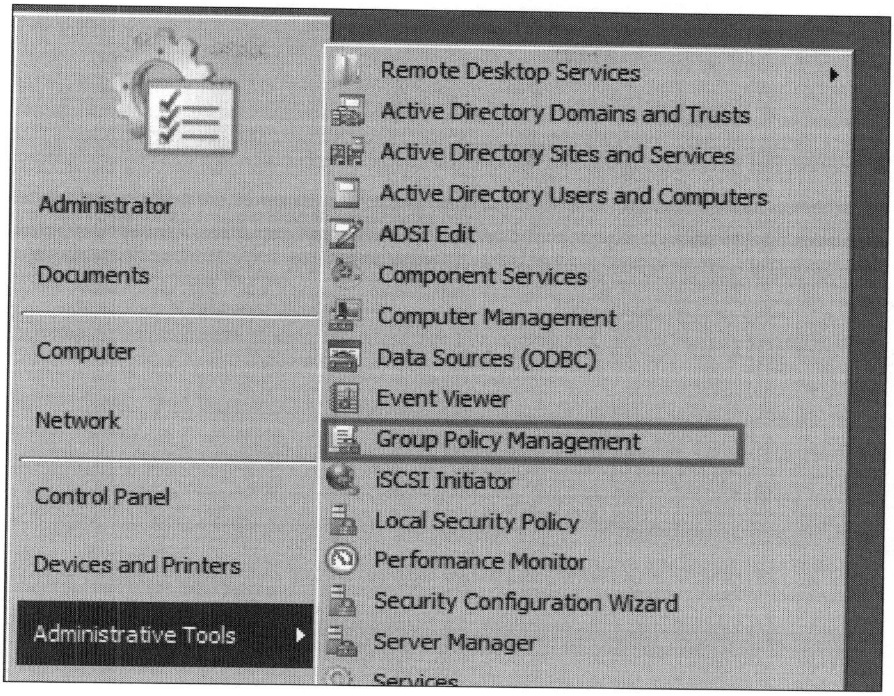

4. To facilitate our management work, to have all the tools we need in one place, and to have quick access to them, we will execute another procedure before we start working on the GPO. We will create a console with the two snap-ins that we have installed: **Active Directory Users and Computers** and **Group Policy Management.** Just press the **Start** button, click on **Run**, and execute the `mmc` console:

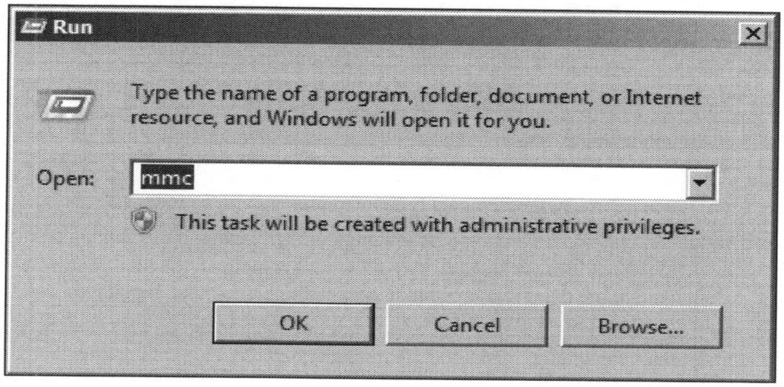

5. The console root will show up, and we can navigate to **File | Add/Remove Snap-in...** (or the shortcut *Ctrl + M*) to start creating our customized administration console. In the following screenshot, we can see these steps:

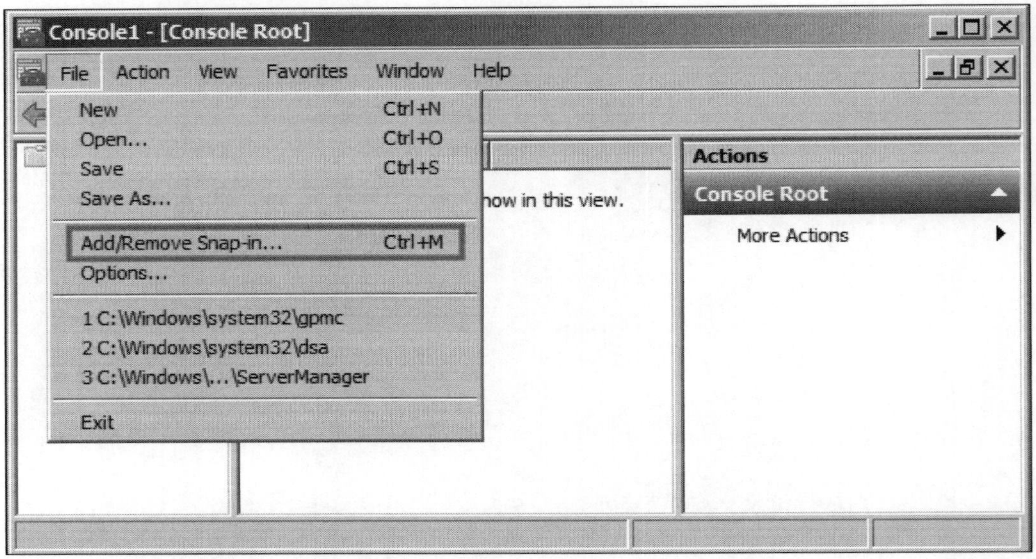

6. In the following screenshot, we will have the available features installed on our machine to add to our custom console. Let's first add the `Users and Computers` snap-in:

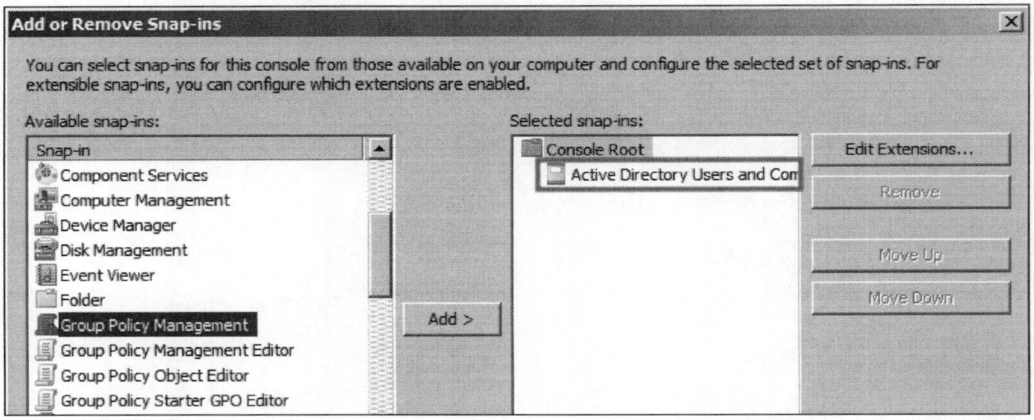

7. After this, we add the **Group Policy Management** snap-in:

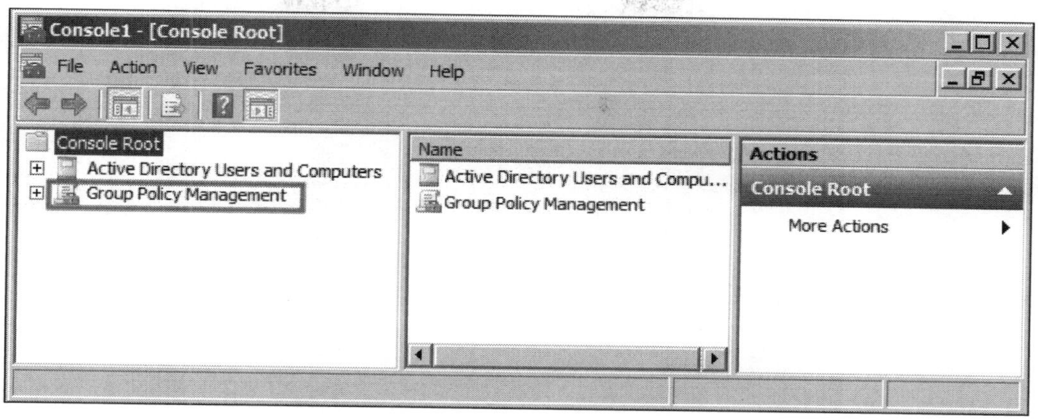

8. Now all we need to do is navigate to **File** | **Save as** and choose the destination of our custom console for quick access. In our example, we saved the custom console to the desktop, as shown in the following screenshot:

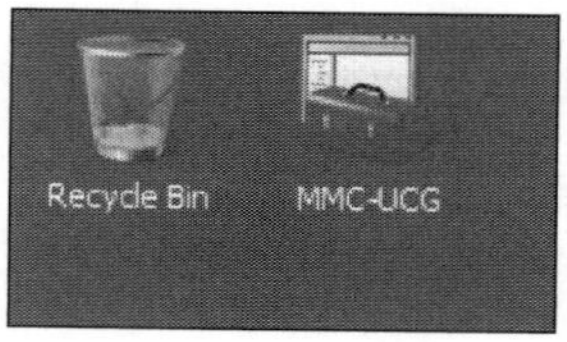

With this procedure, we have just created a custom console with our two main administrative tools that we need for now. Hold this process to use it later and save time switching applications, with all the management tools organized and quickly accessible. We can create as many customized consoles as we want, and as we add more snap-ins or features to our system, we can change our settings and save a newer version.

[If we want, we can access all the different administrative tools separately through the **Administrative Tools** menu.]

Let's launch our customized console and start the Group Policy management tool, so just double-click on the **MMC-UCG** icon from where you have saved it:

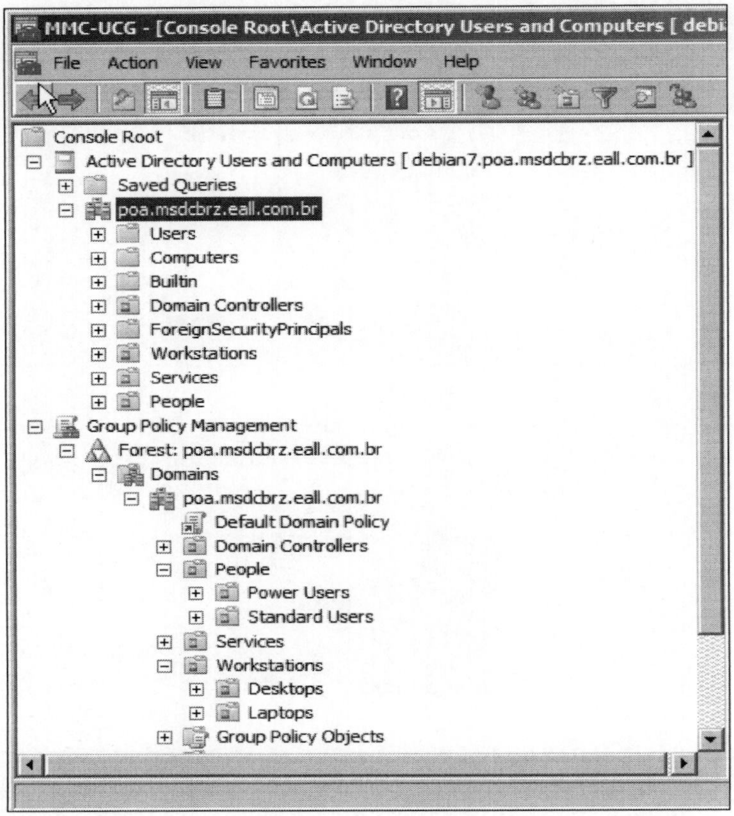

In the previous example, we have just expanded **Active Directory Users and Computers** and **Group Policy Management** as well as the **Forest** and **Domain** trees to show you the structure that we will work on. Notice that we have expanded our People OU and we are able to see these OUs: Power Users and Standard Users. Our objective is to separate one system administrator from the `Standard Users` OU (Django Fox), and move him to `Power Users`. So, we can give him administrative powers (for example, delegate him the Group Policies management on the `Standard Users` OU).

Allowing a user to create Group Policies

This task is divided into two procedures; first, we will add the permission for the user to create GPOs and after that, we will allow him to link them to the `Standard Users` OU. The user Django Fox (username: `djfox`) can open the Group Policy Management Console, but as we can see in the following screenshot, he is not able to create Group Policies:

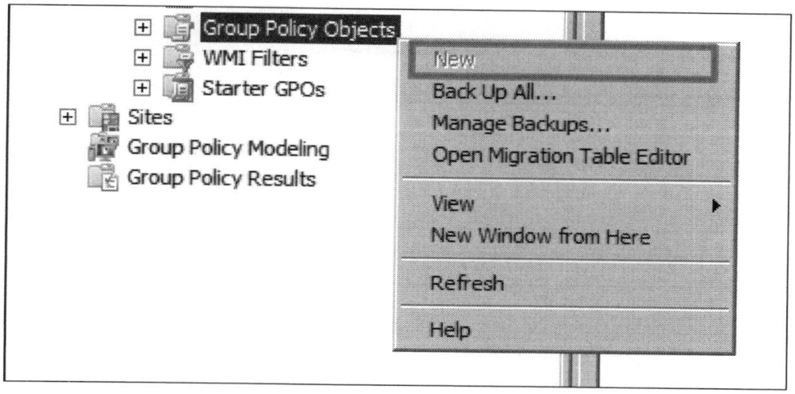

Use the following steps to gain permissions to create Group Policies:

1. In the preceding screenshot, we can see that the **New** option that would be used to create a new GPO is disabled for this user. So, what we need to do is log in as the Domain Administrator and give Django Fox the right permissions. Just open the `MMC-UCG` customized console and click on **Group Policy Objects** as shown in the following screenshot:

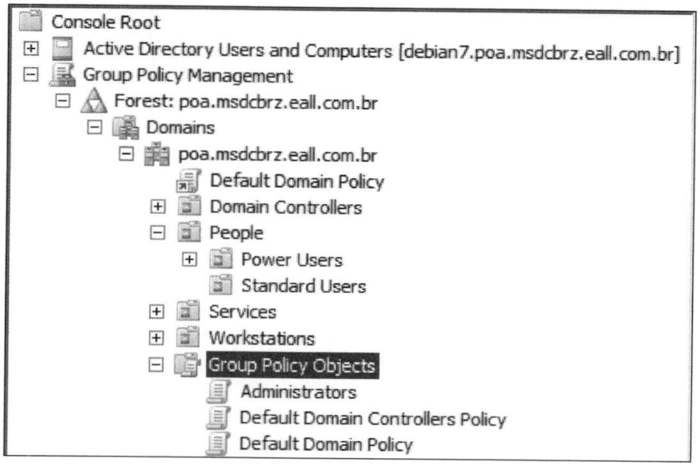

2. After it is selected, look at the right pane and click on the **Delegation** tab. We should see a screen like the one shown in the following screenshot:

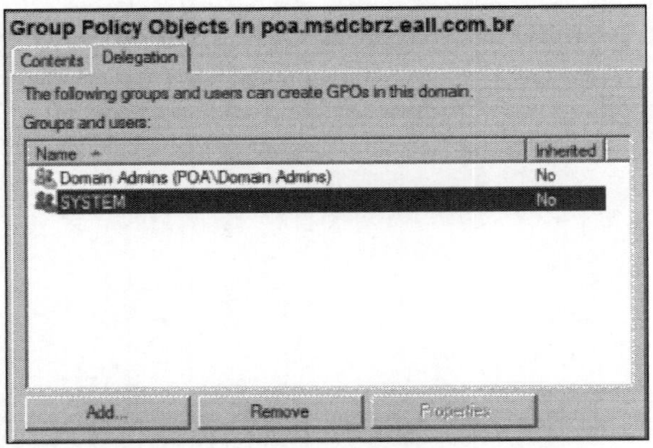

As we can see from the preceding screenshot, we have two groups that can create the GPOs in our Domain. We could do the same and create a group to manage our specific users that we plan to delegate a GPO creation to, but in this example, we will follow a different path as a learning opportunity.

3. To add our user `djfox` to that list, we just click on the **Add...** button at the bottom of the previous screen, and before we fill the username, let's click on the **Object Types** option. Take a look at the following screenshot:

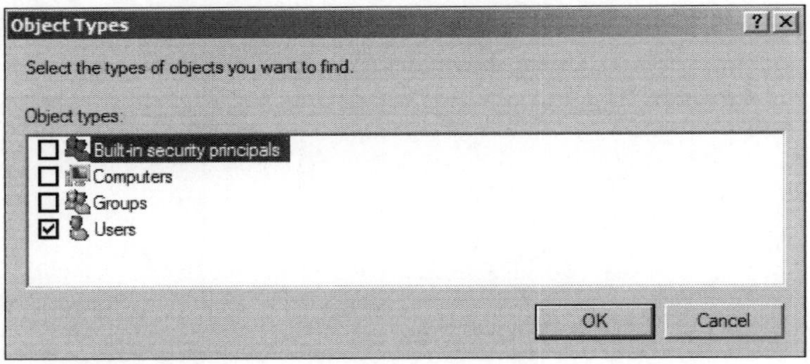

4. In the previous example, we checked just the **Users** box. In the following dialog box, we will write the username of our user and click on the **Check Names** button. We can see the result in the following screenshot:

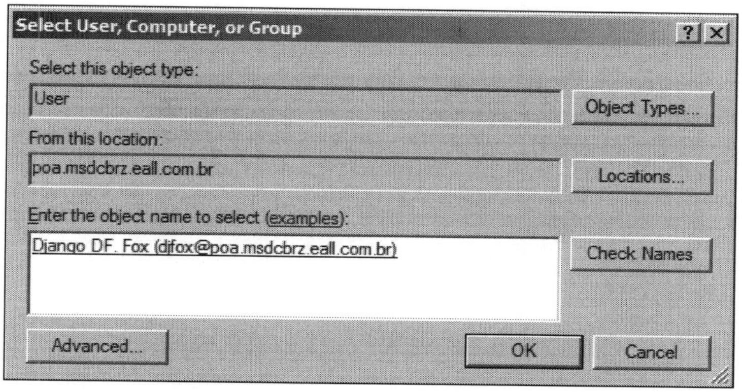

5. Automatically, the system will fill the full name and the location (for example, the domain) of our user. Just click on **OK** and the delegation screen for the GPO will be shown, now with the user Django Fox listed together with the prior two groups:

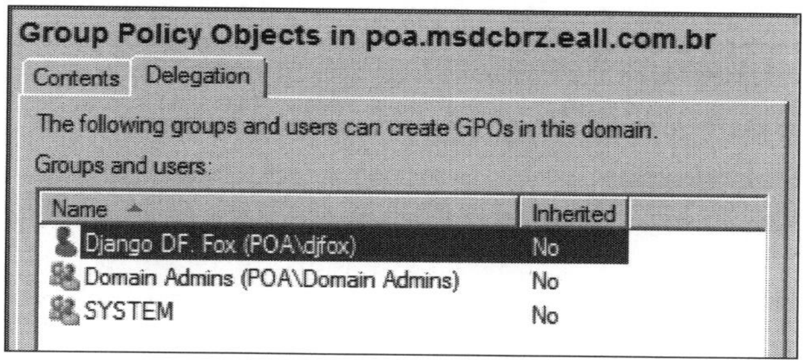

6. Now, the `djfox` user has the permission to create Group Policies in our domain. If the user `djfox` logs in and tries to create a GPO, the **New** option will now be enabled:

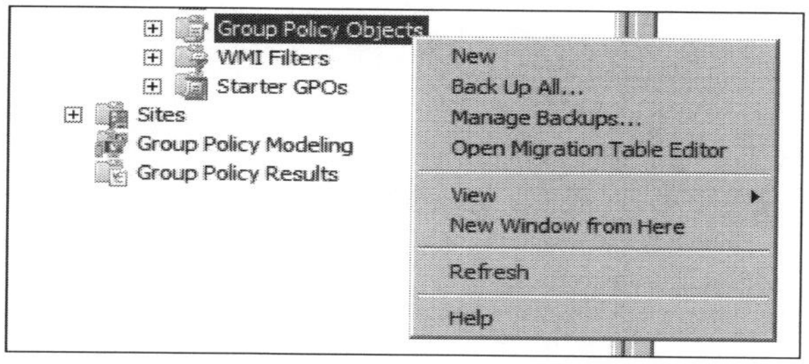

However, this permission is not sufficient, as shown in the following screenshot. To be effective, the user needs the ability to link the GPOs to one or more OUs. In our use case, we want him to be able to manage the GPOs for the `Standard Users` OU.

Notice what happens when the user `djfox` tries to right-click on the **Standard Users** OU to see what administrative options are available to him:

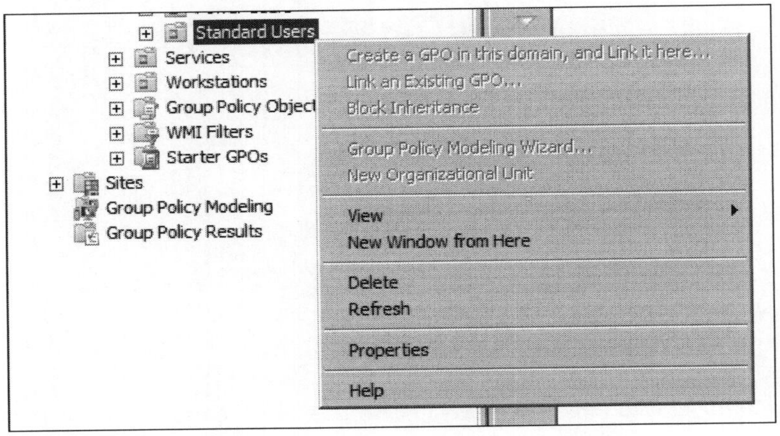

In the preceding screenshot, we can see that the **Link an Existing GPO...** option is disabled (the first option is disabled too because the first option is to create and link to this OU).

Allowing a user to link Group Policies to OUs

Back in our Domain Administrator's session, we can select the `Standard Users` OU. Take a look at the right pane (**Delegation** tab) of the following screenshot for the link GPOs permission:

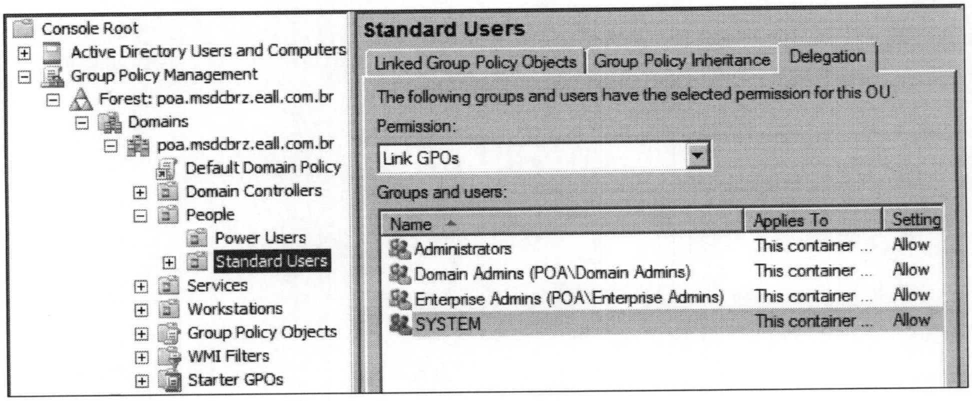

So, we need to add our user to the **Delegation** list, and we do so by clicking on the bottom of the screen in the **Add...** button. Fill the username `djfox` and click on **Check Names**. After our user's full name appears, we can click on **OK**, select **This container and all child containers**, and click on **OK** again:

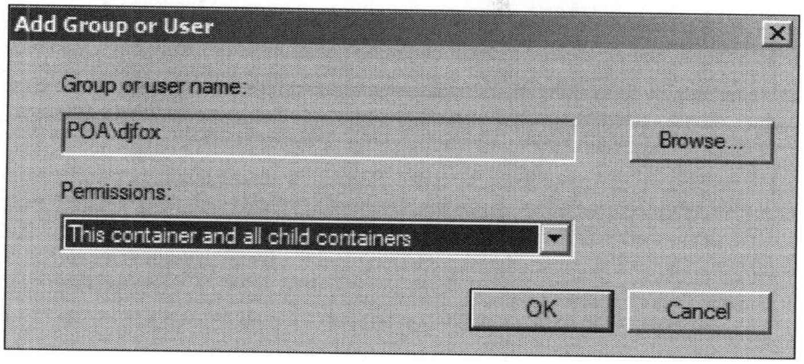

After this, we will be able to see our user in the listing of the `Standard Users` delegation, for linking the GPOs to this OU:

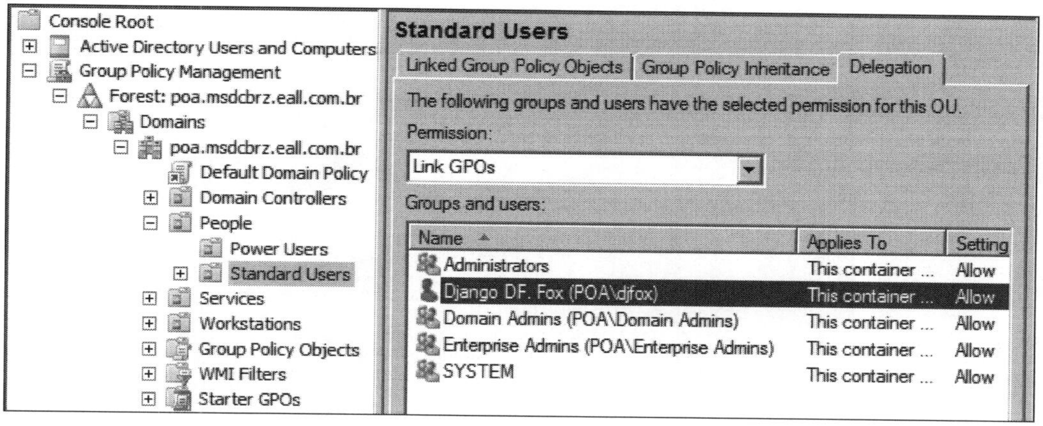

Let's see this time what happens when the user, Django Fox, logs in and tries to check his administrative options at the OU of `Standard Users` again. We can check this in the following screenshot:

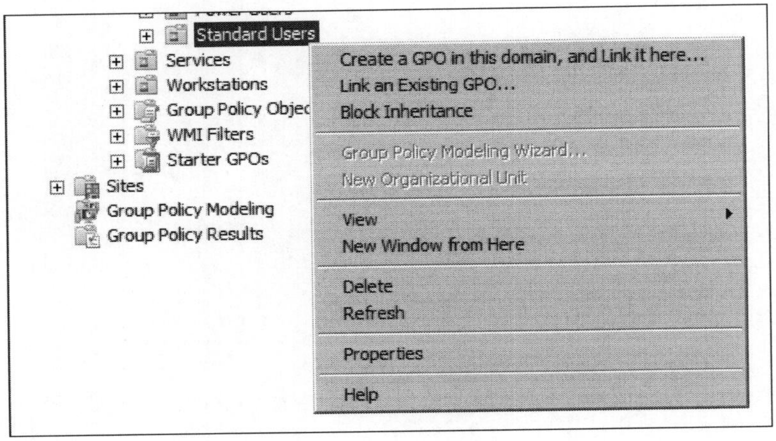

As we can see in the previous screenshot, the task is done. We can also see that now the user, Django Fox, can link GPOs to the Standard Users OU. Before we actually click on the first option and start to create a GPO, let's take a look at the **Start** menu for the user, Hattori Hanzo, (username: `hahanzo`) to see how it looks:

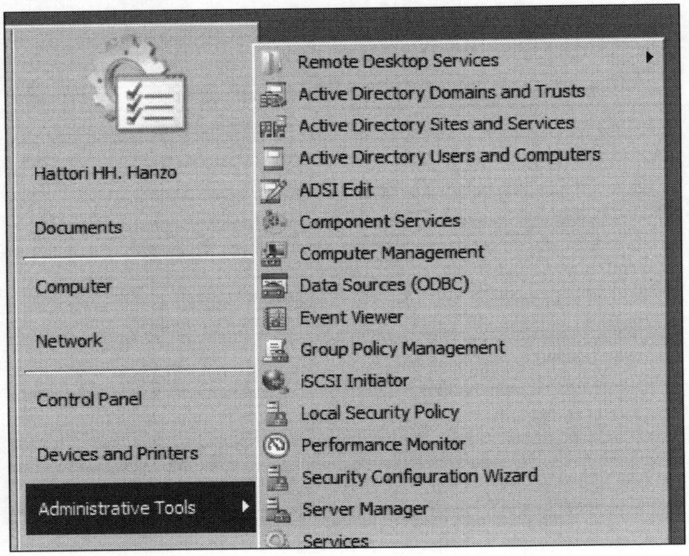

As we can see, the **Administrative tools** menu option is available, so all the tools are listed for the one user who is not an administrator and is on the `Standard Users` OU.

Creating a Group Policy

So, back in the Django Fox session, let's click on the first option, **Create a GPO in this domain**, and then click on **Link it here...** and create a Group Policy for the `Standard Users` OU. The GPO that the `djfox` user will create will be called **Block Administrative Menu**, so all users on the `Standard Users` OU will have the **Administrative Tools** menu hidden. Take a look at the following screenshot:

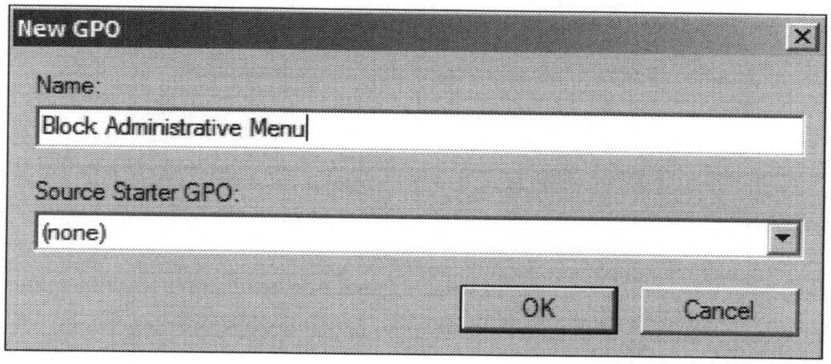

After we click on **OK**, we select the **Linked Group Policy Objects** tab on the right pane of the following screenshot and see that our brand new GPO is listed and enabled:

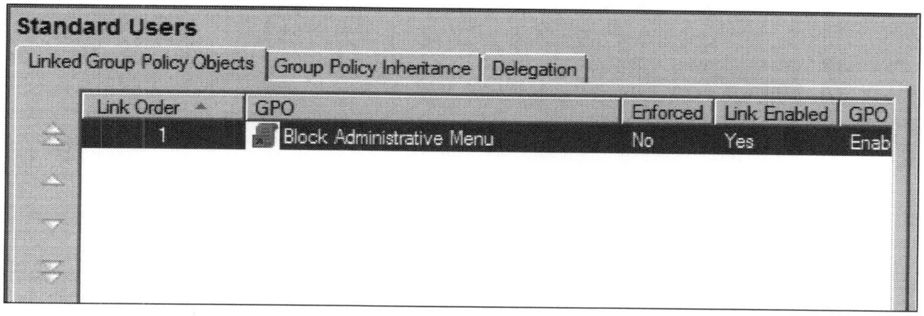

Right-click on it and click on **Edit**. The Group Policy Management Editor will open, and on the right pane, we navigate to **User Configuration** | **Preferences** | **Control Panel**. Right-click on the last item, **Start Menu**, and navigate to **New** | **Start Menu**. The following screenshot shows you these selections:

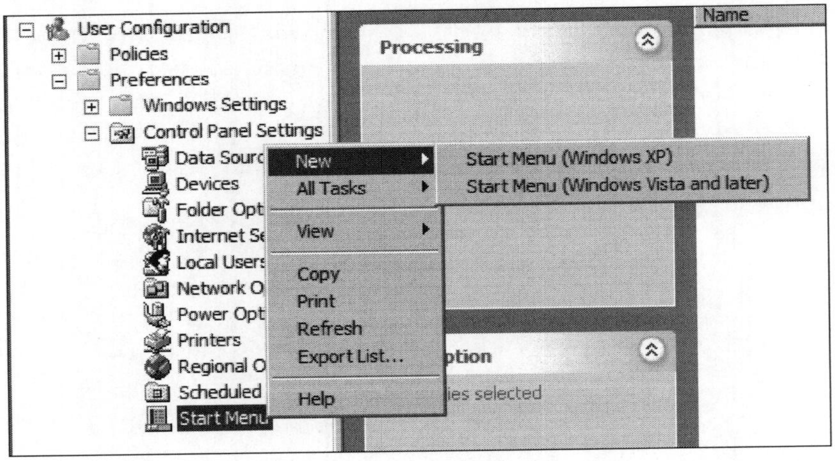

The following screenshot will be a dialog box that displays the properties of the **Start Menu** menu under the **New** tab. At the end of the list of **Start menu items**, we will see one item named **System administrative tools**. We need to check the **Don't display this item** option if it is not checked already. Take a look at the following screenshot to see how it must be configured:

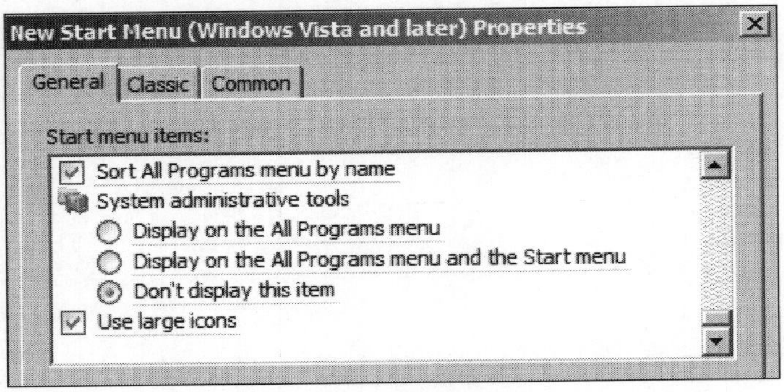

Just click on **OK** and we should have a new **Start Menu** menu in our GPO. Now we can close the editor and test our user again from the `Standard Users` OU (for example, `hahanzo`) to see if the administrative tools are still present or not. The following screenshot shows you a screenshot of the `hahanzo` user's desktop, where we can see that the **Administration Tools** menu option is absent:

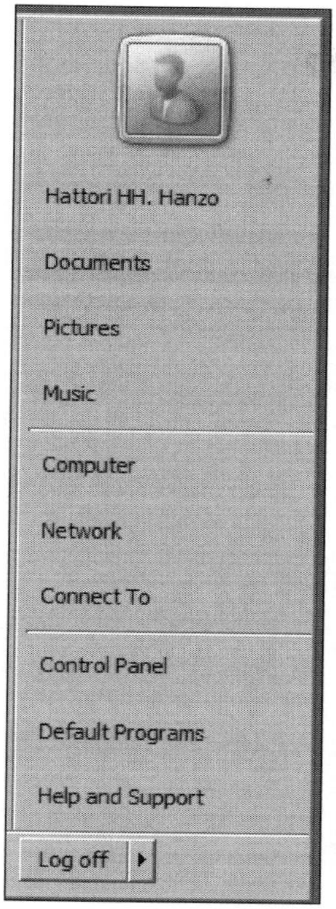

Remember that Group Policies are complex subjects, and to actually prevent unauthorized users to have access to the administrative tools, we need to make more adjustments for the system and enhance our GPOs to make sure that we cover all the possibilities (for example, the customization of our user's menu) to actually have our policy fully applied.

Trust relationships and replication with Samba 4

Samba 4 is a brand new software that was released in 2013 and is already pretty stable and as we are learning, full of features. However, as this is a new release, there are many challenges and some of its components need to evolve. At the time of writing this book, the `SysVol` share has no replication currently implemented [3], and a workaround needs to be used to replicate the changes [4]. Trust relationships are not fully implemented, and as a result, Samba 4 can be trusted but it cannot trust [4].

All the directory replications are already implemented and fully functional. We will add another Domain Controller to our Debian 7 GNU/Linux Samba 4 Server AD DC, and verify if the replication of users, groups, and our GPO is properly synced.

> The Samba 4 status for many different parts of the code can be checked at the following site:
>
> `https://wiki.samba.org/index.php/Samba4/Status`

To add our Microsoft Windows Server 2008 as an additional Domain Controller, we just need to log in as a Domain Administrator and execute the `dcpromo` utility; just navigate to **Start** | **Run and execute dcpromo**. If the Active Directory Service binaries are not already installed in the system, we should be presented with a screen similar to the one shown in the following screenshot:

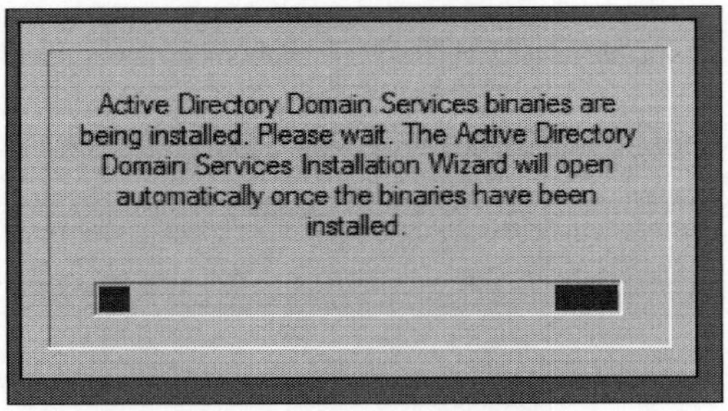

The preceding screenshot shows you that the operating system automatically installs the needed components and after that, it will start the AD DC installation wizard. When that process is finished, we will actually be presented with the wizard and the following message will be displayed: **This wizard helps you install Active Directory Domain Services (AD DS) on this server, making the server an Active Directory domain controller. To continue, click Next**. So we just need to click on **Next** twice, and we will be able to see the following screenshot:

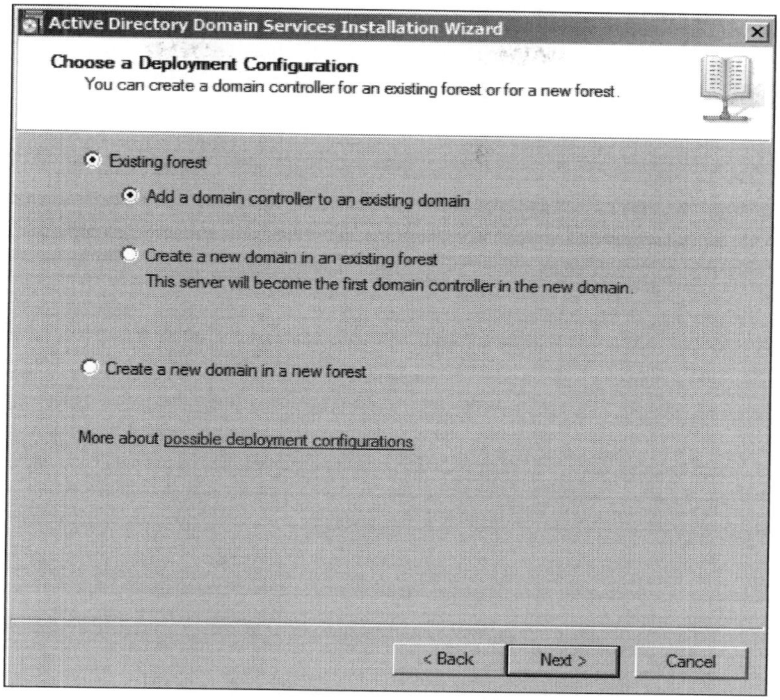

As we will add this new Domain Controller in an existing forest and to an existing domain, we choose the first option and click on **Next**. The following screen will ask for the credentials and confirm the domain that we want to join, so we just click on **Next**:

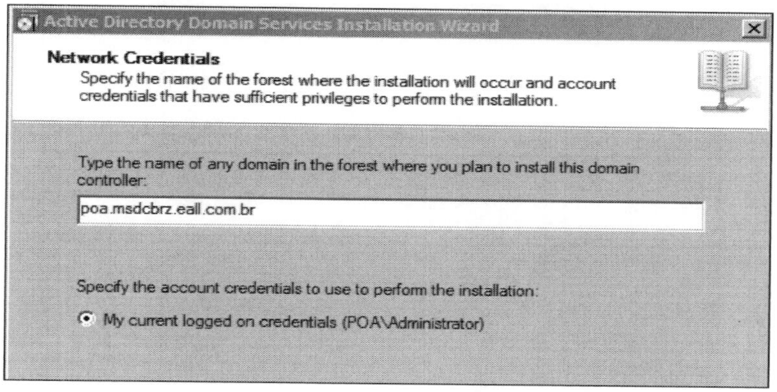

In the following two screenshots, we will just need to confirm our domain and site (we can click on **Next** twice without changing any option). Following this screen, we will be presented with the **Additional Domain Controller Options** screen:

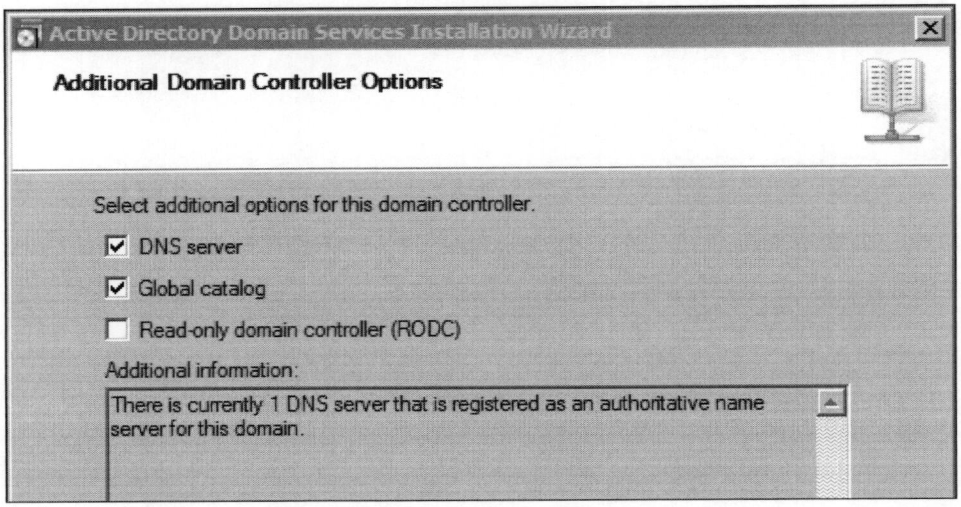

We will examine some of our DNS configuration, and in the following screenshot, we can change the path for the `SysVol` and log files, if we want. As we will use the default values, we just click on **Next**, and then we are presented with a screen to set the recovery mode administrator's account password:

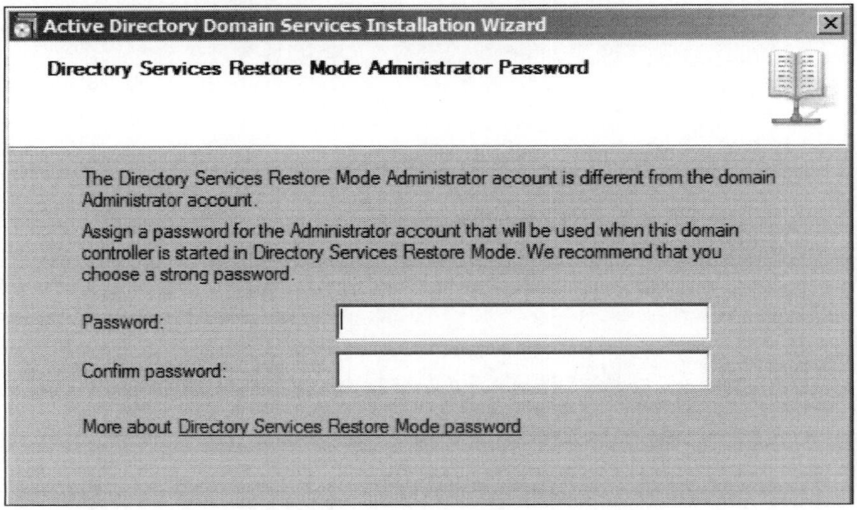

We need to choose a strong password as advertized and click on **Next**, review all our answers, and then click on **Next** for the last time. We will see the progress screen that shows us the process to be added to our new server as an additional Domain Controller to our Active Directory Domain:

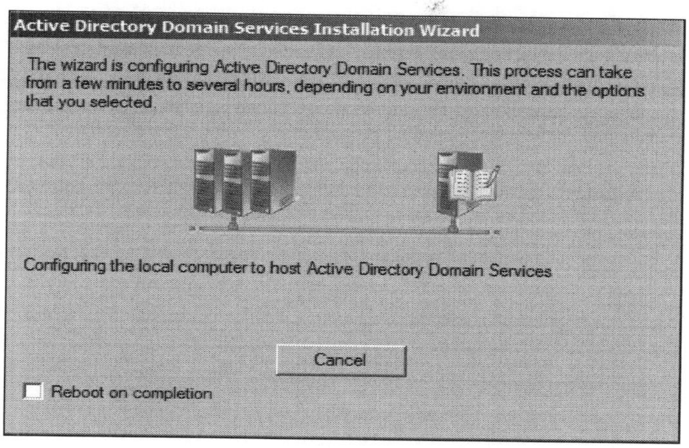

Just click on **Finish** in the last screen, and we'll need to restart the computer, as shown in the following screenshot:

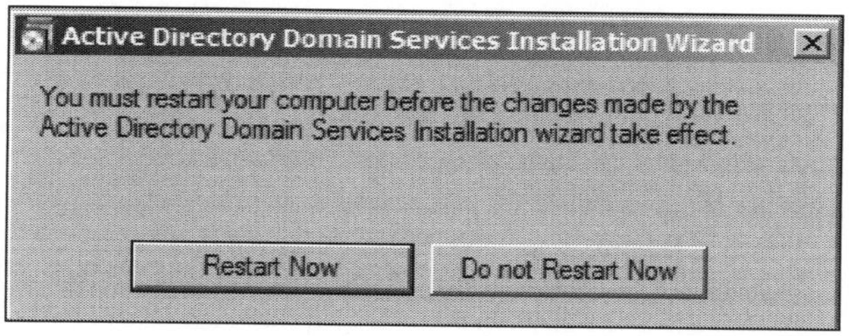

After the restart, open the **Active Directory Users and Computers** (`dsa.msc`) snap-in, and click on **Domain Controllers**. We should see both servers listed, as shown in the following screenshot:

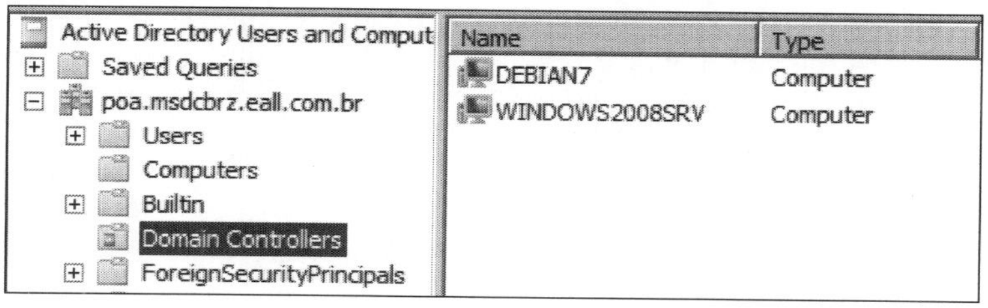

Now let's open our Server Manager and navigate to our DNS Services and check whether our DNS configuration was replicated and whether everything is fine, as DNS is very important to our Active Directory Services. Take a look at the following screenshot:

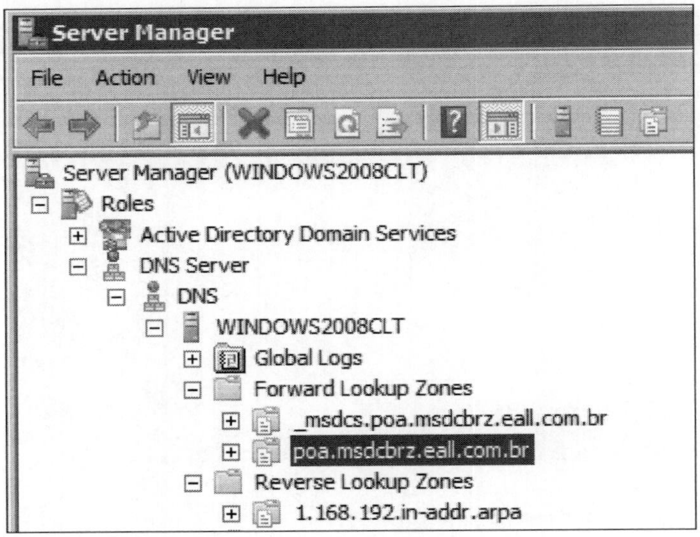

As we can see in the preceding screenshot, our **Forward Lookup Zones** and **Reverse Lookup Zones** folders are present, and if we right-click on our domain—which is `poa.msdcbrz.eall.com.br`—and click on **Properties**, we can check the **Name Servers** tab and check whether we have our two DNS Servers registered (PDC and WINDOWS2008CLT):

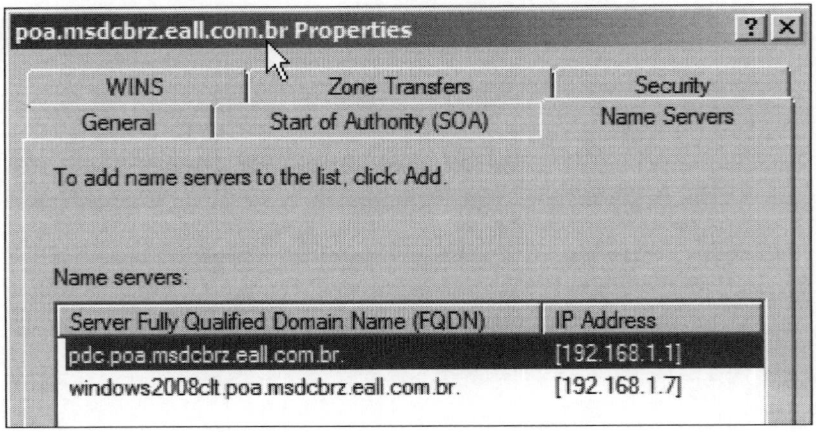

In the preceding screenshot, we can see that our new Active Directory Server was added perfectly to our domain, so we can use the `repadmin` command to verify that everything is up to date and the synchronization process between the two Domain Controllers is fine as shown in the following screenshot:

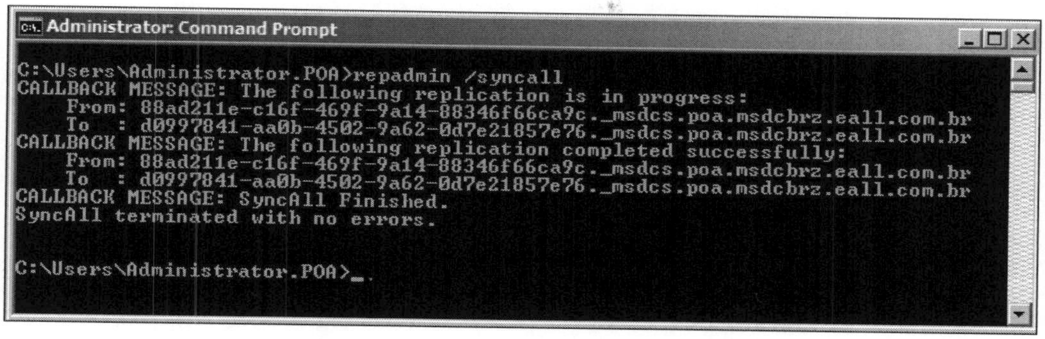
Administrator: Command Prompt
C:\Users\Administrator.POA>repadmin /syncall
CALLBACK MESSAGE: The following replication is in progress:
From: 88ad211e-c16f-469f-9a14-88346f66ca9c._msdcs.poa.msdcbrz.eall.com.br
To : d0997841-aa0b-4502-9a62-0d7e21857e76._msdcs.poa.msdcbrz.eall.com.br
CALLBACK MESSAGE: The following replication completed successfully:
From: 88ad211e-c16f-469f-9a14-88346f66ca9c._msdcs.poa.msdcbrz.eall.com.br
To : d0997841-aa0b-4502-9a62-0d7e21857e76._msdcs.poa.msdcbrz.eall.com.br
CALLBACK MESSAGE: SyncAll Finished.
SyncAll terminated with no errors.
C:\Users\Administrator.POA>_

So, with this procedure, we can be sure that everything is updated and our Domain Controllers are in sync.

> In a GNU/Linux system, we can use the `dig` utility to test our brand new DNS server and confirm that it is answering the DNS queries, issuing the following command:
>
> **`dig poa.msdcbrz.eall.com.br mx @windows2008clt`**

Summary

In this chapter, we learned about the different roles that the Samba 4 Server can play on the network. We also learned how to basically manage the server using a Microsoft Windows Server 2008. We have installed the tools needed to manage it, and all the installation process was explained. The reader was introduced to the Group Policy feature and also learned how to implement the centralized change and configuration management for users and machines using this powerful administrative functionality. The reader also learned how to create a custom management console to have all the management tools that we have used until this point in one place.

We have learned how to get the authentication and authorization working on Samba 4 for GNU/Linux Systems using the Debian distribution as an example. We have seen how to configure two important subsystems from the GNU/Linux systems authentication and name resolution: **Pluggable Authentication Modules (PAM)** and the **Name Service Switch (NSS)**. Also covered in this chapter were the status and current limitations of some replication code and the trust-relationship characteristics of the Samba 4 Server as an Active Directory Domain Controller. We also explained how to add a Microsoft Windows Server 2008 as an additional Domain Controller that shows you the directory/DNS replication feature.

In the next chapter, we will learn how to replace a Microsoft Windows Active Directory Server with a Samba 4 Server as well as the key points of consideration to have in mind before performing such a task.

4

Replacing a Microsoft Windows Active Directory Server

This chapter is intended to show how to replace a Microsoft Windows Server AD (such as Microsoft Windows Server 2008 R2 or Windows Server 2012) with a Samba 4 Active Directory Server, and thus, we will cover the following points:

- The key consideration points we need to keep in mind when planning such a task, and the common concerns one may have before replacing an **Active Directory Domain Controller** (**AD DC**).
- Our example environment will comprise a standalone AD DC, but if you apply the techniques shown in this chapter in an environment with more than one AD DC, you should be able to adapt the procedure with just a few changes.
- After we have covered all the key points, and some backup/recovery and rollback techniques have been considered, we will go to the planning phase with examples and tests to actually validate our final replacement procedure. We need to have all these validations beforehand, as it is crucial to be able to guarantee that after the replacement operation, our final environment will be sane and provide all the resources to our clients as our prior server setup did.
- Then, we will show the step-by-step procedure to execute the replacement of our Microsoft Windows Server 2008 R2 with a Samba 4 Server as the AD DC in our example network. Based on our consideration points and test procedures, we will show you where to look and apply the validations to make sure that the process was successful and the environment is fully available from the clients' perspective.

Key points to consider before replacing an AD DC

Backup, as simple as that. When planning a replacement for a production server or changing the configuration on a system that provides essential services for many users, the first line in our procedure plan needs to guarantee up-to-date backup. This is not a rollback procedure because a rollback may have a restore procedure as a step, but normally we are referring to two different tasks. We have many scenarios where we can execute a rollback procedure that does not restore data from the backup.

Do not delete any data; the ability to quickly and consistently recover the system to the last operational state, where users are not prevented from using the services they need, is an established best practice that we need to pursue while planning and implementing the replacement of the AD DC or any other critical network service.

When we have a clear, up-to-date, and reliable backup of our AD DC, we need to think about the **Mean Time to Recover/Repair** (**MTTR**) that our business or organization will *accept* in case anything goes wrong. Normally, the restore procedure during backup is the task that will take longer; but, in the case of complex issues arising during a maintenance execution, it is the bullet-proof fallback. The rollback can incorporate a last-resort operation that contemplates the complete restoration of the state of data and services from the backup operation; but, it is advised that you work on a rollback procedure in which small issues can be fixed without the (normally) time-consuming restore procedures. This is because small fixes are faster most times.

For the following procedures, it's assumed that the reader has a working backup system [6], and in our specific case, we expect that this procedure/software is aware of the Active Directory and provides restore capabilities or the direct rollback features of the AD DS content. It's assumed that the tasks presented in this chapter will be executed in a lab environment where there is the option to simulate the "real" environment and any issues faced can be identified and fixed in a later execution on the production network. It's invaluable to test big changes in a controlled and simulated lab environment as it provides the possibility to validate the final result (for example, the state of the services after the change), and in the case of blocking issues, it verifies whether or not the rollback is effective and as quick as predicted.

So, we will go through a quick overview of some tools and techniques available for us to identify possible issues, how to save the Active Directory state, and then implement tests and validations to confirm whether or not the replacement was successful. If the replacement was not successful, we will learn how to fix some specific issues.

> Don't execute this procedure when it is in production as we will delete and recreate some objects as part of the learning exercise!

Planning the replacement – tests and validations

One important feature that is present on Microsoft Windows Server 2008 R2 is the Active Directory snapshot capability. For our task, this is a powerful feature as it gives us the option to capture the state present in our AD DC at a specific point in time. So, we can view or utilize that information in the future to fix or replace specific objects in case we face any issues; thus, we will utilize it for our replacement plan. The Active Directory snapshot uses the **Volume Shadow Copy Service (VSS)**, a rich interface that permits coordination between applications and backup software, which allows you to have live, consistent backups [7].

Let's see how that works and how we can make use of this feature in our replacement plan. The following is a screenshot of our standalone Microsoft Windows Server 2008 R2 Active Directory DC, showing some standard users and organizational units:

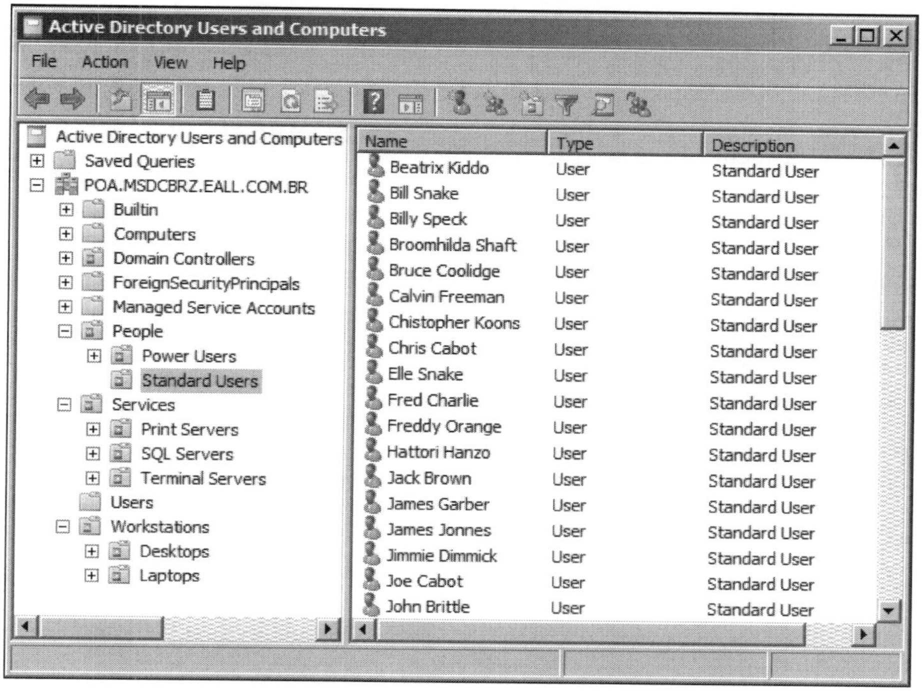

Now, we will go through the procedure to create an Active Directory snapshot [5] and use it to recover some objects. The utilities we will use are `ntdsutil` [8], `dsamain`, `fc`, `sort`, and `csvde`. The `ntdsutil` utility is a very powerful tool that needs to be used with caution as it has the ability to perform advanced database changes of the **Active Directory Domain Service** (**AD DS**). In our example, we have Microsoft Windows Server 2008 R2, which has this tool built in as we have the server acting as the AD DC for our network. If you do not have it installed, it is included in the **Remote Server Administration Tools** (**RSAT**) bundle.

Basically, the steps we need to perform in order to use the snapshot feature are: create, mount, connect (do some work on the snapshot), disconnect, and if we do not intend to maintain the snapshot, destroy it. For our use case, we will not preserve the snapshot as it exists just for support in our replacement procedure. So, after executing, validating, and using it, we will delete the snapshot. In a real-world scenario, it is very common to maintain the snapshot for a while until the administrators are convinced that the new environment is sane.

> It's important to remember that in case we want to preserve the snapshot, further security measures are needed as it contains sensitive information.

The `ntdsutil` utility is an interactive tool, but can be invoked with all the necessary arguments in one line. We will execute it by passing all the arguments in the same line as that can help us learn how to create automated routines and embed these commands later in administration scripts. The `dsamain` [9] tool will be used to access the AD snapshot's data, and all the steps of the procedure will be executed using the domain administrator's account. At the command prompt (navigate to **Start** | **Command Prompt**), execute the following commands:

```
C:\Users\Administrator>ntdsutil "activate instance ntds" snapshot
  create "list all" q q
ntdsutil: activate instance ntds
Active instance set to "ntds".
ntdsutil: snapshot
snapshot: create
Creating snapshot...
Snapshot set {32934713-4bc1-440f-90ff-9ceb0c683452} generated
successfully.
```

```
snapshot: list all
 1: 2013/07/03:23:49 {32934713-4\bc1-440f-90ff-9ceb0c683452}
 2:    C: {35fa1577-e1e1-4a50-b748-28c51fd0ce63}
snapshot: q
ntdsutil: q
C:\Users\Administrator>
```

In the preceding command execution, we can see all the outputs received from `ntdsutil`. We have created the snapshot and listed it (using the `list all` command) in the same command line. We have two lines numbered in the snapshots list, but in fact, `ntdsutil` shows two lines for each snapshot created (the first one has the date of creation and the second contains the snapshot's index and GUID). To mount the snapshot, we can use either the index or the GUID; as we have just one snapshot and it's much easier than referencing the whole GUID, we'll mount it using the index, as follows:

```
C:\Users\Administrator>ntdsutil "activate instance ntds" snapshot
  "list all" "mount 2" q q
ntdsutil: activate instance ntds
Active instance set to "ntds".
ntdsutil: snapshot
snapshot: list all
 1: 2013/07/03:23:49 {32934713-4bc1-440f-90ff-9ceb0c683452}
 2:    C: {35fa1577-e1e1-4a50-b748-28c51fd0ce63}
snapshot: mount 2
Snapshot {35fa1577-e1e1-4a50-b748-28c51fd0ce63} mounted as
C:\$SNAP_201307032349_VOLUMEC$\
snapshot: q
ntdsutil: q
C:\Users\Administrator>
```

As we can see in the preceding output, the snapshot was mounted and the volume path was defined. So, we can go directly to that volume in Explorer by entering the path (`C:\$SNAP_201307032349_VOLUMEC$`) at the **Start | Search program and files** box. After the Explorer window shows the snapshot volume content, navigate to the **Windows | NTDS** folder.

We will need the full path for the `ntds.dit` file to pass it as an argument for the `dsamain` utility. So, we need to right-click on it while holding down the *Shift* key and choose **Copy as path**. After that, in a command prompt window, execute the following commands (paste the `ntds.dit` path that we just saved in the clipboard after the `-dbpath` option):

```
C:\Users\Administrator>dsamain -dbpath \
"C:\$SNAP_201307032349_VOLUMEC$\Windows\NTDS\ntds.dit" \
-ldapport 20389


EVENTLOG (Informational): NTDS General / Service Control : 1000
Microsoft Active Directory Domain Services startup complete, version
  6.1.7600.16385
```

Notice that we have used an alternative port (`20389`) to start the `dsamain` utility as the standard port (`389`) is already used by the standard AD DS service.

Observe that the preceding command is just one line, and the character \ after the `-dbpath` option and the `ntds.dit` file is just stating that the line continues. After a few seconds, we should see that the next line starts with the word `EVENTLOG`, which will inform us that the services have started. We need to leave that command shell open while we work on the snapshot, so we can minimize it to save some space in our desktop. Now, let's open the **Active Directory Users and Computers** MMC and change the Domain Controller to which we are connected. To do so, just right-click on the **Active Directory Users and Computers** option and choose the **Change Domain Controller...** option as shown in the following screenshot:

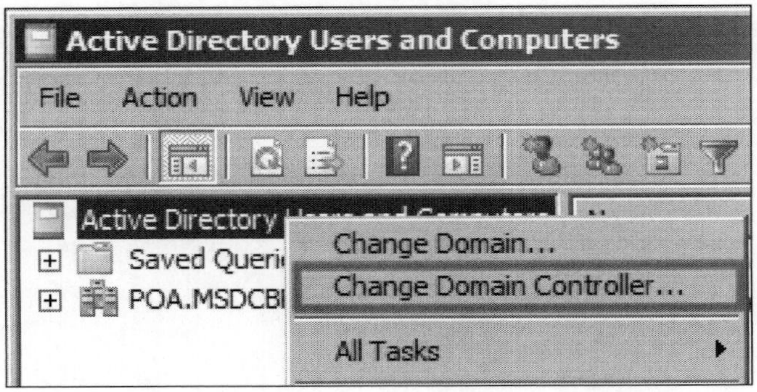

The next step is to add the hostname of our AD DS with the custom port we used in the `dsamain` invocation (for example, `20389`) as we intend to access our snapshot's database:

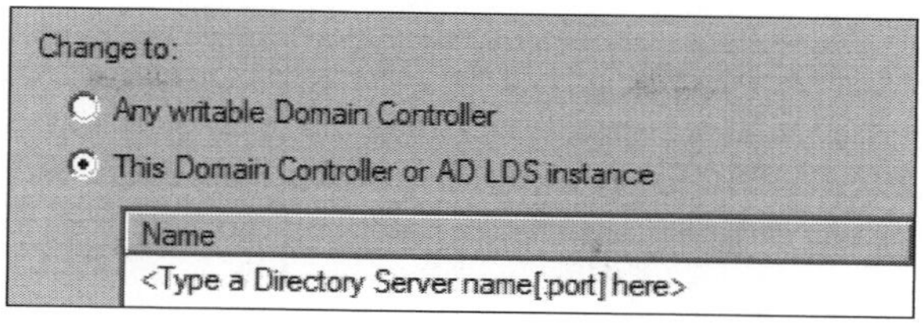

We just need to click on the **<Type a Directory Server name[:port] here>** field as shown in the preceding screenshot, and enter our information (in our example, we will enter: `WINDOWS2008SRV:20389` and click on **OK**).

> We can connect to our snapshot directly by issuing the following command at the **Start** | **Run** menu:
>
> **`dsa.msc /server=windows2008srv:20389`**

Now, we should have two **Active Directory Users and Computers** windows opened: one connected to our live Active Directory Services and the other connected to our snapshot's database (for example, `ntds.dit`). To verify which one we are working with, just hover the mouse over **Active Directory Users and Computers** (top level), and we'll see a pop-up showing the server we are connected to (for example, the snapshot connection has the port `20389` at the end). After we navigate through our **Organizational Units** (**OU**) and have verified that we have a consistent and up-to-date snapshot, we can close this window.

In the remaining window that is connected to the live AD DS, navigate to the **People** | **Standard Users** OU, choose one user object (for example, `hahanzo`), and delete it: just right-click on the user and choose **Delete**; we will be prompted to confirm the deletion and if we agree, we can just choose **Yes**. The deletion of a user is similar to that shown in the following screenshot:

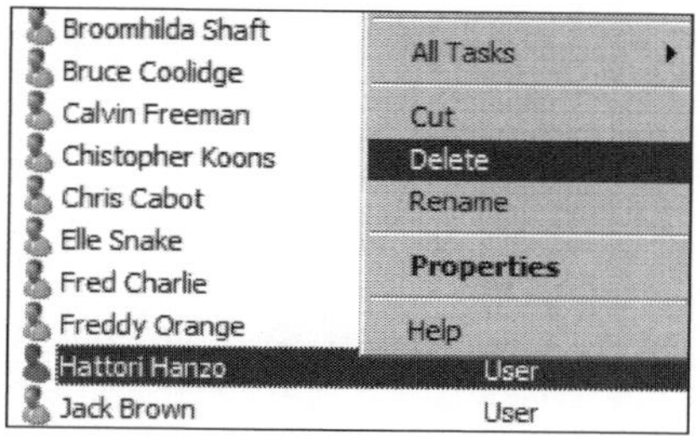

So, from 50 users in our example environment, we have a missing object on the AD (in this case, a user object) at the **Standard Users** OU. Now, we will show you how to recover from such a situation if this happens in our replacement procedure.

> Remember that this is a general planning example procedure that can be used to fix many sorts of problems we may face in our AD DS environment, even on occasions where we are not specifically replacing a Domain Controller.

Exporting directory entries

Let's open another command-prompt window (do not use the same window in which the `dsamain` utility is running) and execute the following commands:

```
C:\Users\Administrator>csvde -s windows2008srv -T 20389 -d\
"ou=Standard Users,ou=People,dc=poa,dc=msdcbrz,dc=eall,dc=com,dc=br"\
 -r "(objectClass=user)" -c \
"ou=Standard Users,ou=People,dc=poa,dc=msdcbrz,dc=eall,dc=com,dc=br"\
 "" -l sAMAccountName -f standardusers-snap.csv
Connecting to "windows2008srv"
Logging in as current user using SSPI
Exporting directory to file standardusers-snap.csv
Searching for entries...
Writing out entries
...............................................
Export Completed. Post-processing in progress...
49 entries exported
The command has completed successfully
C:\Users\Administrator>
```

Cool! It seems like we have 49 entries exported (that is, 49 users) on the snapshot (the fiftieth user is `djfox` on the **Power Users** OU). The `-c` option that we have used is to replace the full DN with another (in our case, an empty string: ""), just to make the resulting `.csv` file easier to read.

> We are just listing objects from the `user` class (the `-r` option/filter), and we just want the usernames (for example, the `sAMAccountName` attribute).

If we look at the content of the `standardusers.csv` file, we will see that it is a standard comma-separated value file as follows:

```
DN,sAMAccountName
"CN=Chris Cabot,",chcabot
"CN=Joe Cabot,",jocabot
"CN=Freddy Orange,",frorange
"CN=Marvin Nash,",manash
"CN=Beatrix Kiddo,",bekiddo
...
```

In the preceding excerpt, we can see the first line (header) and some standard users of the OU. Now we need to execute a similar command on our live AD to compare the contents. We can use the same command-prompt window in which we generated the first `.csv` file to execute the second export command. The following command is very similar to the first one; here, we will just remove the option `-T`, the port `20389`, and change the name of the `.csv` file:

```
C:\Users\Administrator>csvde -s windows2008srv -d\
"ou=Standard Users,ou=People,dc=poa,dc=msdcbrz,dc=eall,dc=com,dc=br"\
 -r "(objectClass=user)" -c \
"ou=Standard Users,ou=People,dc=poa,dc=msdcbrz,dc=eall,dc=com,dc=br"\
 "" -l sAMAccountName -f standardusers.csv
Connecting to "windows2008srv"
Logging in as current user using SSPI
Exporting directory to file standardusers.csv
Searching for entries...
Writing out entries
...............................................
Export Completed. Post-processing in progress...
48 entries exported
The command has completed successfully
C:\Users\Administrator>
```

With the preceding output, we can quickly identify that we have one less entry on the live AD (the one we deleted) as we had 49 entries exported from the snapshot database and here we have just 48! Let's sort the files and compare them using the following commands:

```
C:\Users\Administrator> sort standardusers.csv /o standardusers-sorted.
csv
C:\Users\Administrator> sort standardusers-snap.csv /o standardusers-
snap-sorted.csv
```

> In the preceding procedure, we are using just one specific Organizational Unit as our validation example, and in our specific case, we have more objects (that is, users). But in a real-world scenario, it is advised that you actually list and compare all the Active Directory objects and validate all the content of our Directory Services. We can compare all the structures and content of the Directory Services in one file or use a script to create specific files from portions of our AD tree to facilitate the debugging. What is important is that you save the resultant file(s) in a safe place where we can use them after the replacement to perform the comparison and find any inconsistencies.

Comparing backup data against live data

So, now that we have both files generated and sorted, we can compare them with the following commands (just pass the two filenames as arguments for the `fc` utility):

```
C:\Users\Administrator>fc standardusers-sorted.csv standardusers-snap-
sorted.csv
Comparing files standardusers-sorted.csv and STANDARDUSERS-SNAP-SORTED.
CSV
***** standardusers-sorted.csv
"CN=Freddy Orange,",frorange
"CN=Jack Brown,",jabrown
***** STANDARDUSERS-SNAP-SORTED.CSV
"CN=Freddy Orange,",frorange
"CN=Hattori Hanzo,",hahanzo
"CN=Jack Brown,",jabrown
*****
C:\Users\Administrator>
```

We can see that we have a context in the `fc` utility's output, as the text portions around the differences between the files are shown. So, we can easily identify that the missing user is `Hattori Hanzo` (`hahanzo`) as it is the user in the `standardusers-snap-sorted.csv` file between `Freddy Orange` (`frorange`) and `Jack Brown` (`jabrown`). But, there is no line for `hahanzo` in the `standardusers-sorted.csv` file in that context.

In a case like this, we have a lot of options to choose from to fix the issue, and this is an excellent example where a full restore from the backup is not needed. Our company policies will, for sure, dictate our choice; but in the example case, we have a very satisfactory way to restore this object using just the `dsadd` utility and fill it with up-to-date information that we can get from a newly exported `.csv` file in the snapshot. This can be done using the following command:

```
C:\Users\Administrator>csvde -s windows2008srv -T 20389 -d\ "cn=Hattori Hanzo,ou=Standard Users,ou=People,dc=poa,\
dc=msdcbrz,dc=eall,dc=com,dc=br" -f hattorihanzo.csv
Connecting to "windows2008srv"
Logging in as current user using SSPI
Exporting directory to file hattorihanzo.csv
Searching for entries...
Writing out entries
..............................................
Export Completed. Post-processing in progress...
48 entries exported
The command has completed successfully
C:\Users\Administrator>
```

If we look at the header of the resulting `.csv` file, we will see that the attributes we have on it are for the user `Hattori Hanzo`. We can take a look at the attribute headers in the following example:

```
DN,objectClass,cn,sn,description,givenName,distinguishedName,instanceType
,whenCreated,whenChanged,uSNCreated,uSNChanged,company,name,objectGUID,us
erAccountControl,badPwdCount,codePage,countryCode,badPasswordTime,lastLog
off,lastLogon,pwdLastSet,primaryGroupID,objectSid,accountExpires,logonCou
nt,sAMAccountName,sAMAccountType,objectCategory,dSCorePropagationData,las
tLogonTimestamp,mail
```

We just pick the attributes we need, and it is simple to create the new object, as follows:

```
C:\Users\Administrator>


dsadd succeeded:CN=Hattori Hanzo,OU=Standard Users,OU=People,DC=POA,\
DC=MSDCBRZ,DC=EALL,DC=COM,DC=BR
C:\Users\Administrator>
```

After the preceding command, we can check in the **Active Directory Users and Computers** tool and verify whether or not the user `Hattori Hanzo` (username: `hahanzo`) will be present in the **Standard Users** OU again. We will just need to inform the user to change the password at their first login, because we had recreated the object with a standard password.

Again, this is satisfactory in our example environment; but if we want to preserve some operating system attributes and not break any application that can identify the user as a new user, we can import the `hahanzo` user object to the live AD using the `.csv` exported file directly from the snapshot. The only point you need to pay attention to is in the export procedure using the `csvde` utility, as in order for the import to be successful, there are lists of attributes that are prohibited by the AD from being imported using a connection that is not encrypted (such as `csvde`).

We can use the `-r` option, as we did previously, for the `csvde` utility (to create a filter) and export just the attributes that are allowed; or, we could export all attributes, edit the `.csv` file, and exclude the attributes that are prohibited, such as [10]: `badPasswordTime`, `adPwdCount`, `lastLogoff`, `lastLogon`, `logonCount`, `memberOf`, `objectGUID`, `objectSid`, `primaryGroupID`, `pwdLastSet`, and `sAMAccountType`.

> A third alternative would be to use the `ldifde` [11] tool, but it has the same drawback (that is, the password import limitation) as the `csvde` tool.

As a general rule, in cases where we have a problem executing the maintenance operation in the Active Directory, the important points to be noted are as follows:

- Identify the issue
- Execute the rollback
- Fix the procedure for later execution

The most important part is understanding the many points discussed here and making a decision based on the technical aspects as well as company rules and policies (for example, security policies). However, for the majority of object types, either `csvde` or `ldifde` utilities can be used to export the data from the snapshot and import it seamlessly in the affected AD, and thus can be used as powerful support tools to create rollback procedure and quickly fix procedures to any general Active Directory maintenance. Save them in your virtual utility belt!

We can find some commercial and free tools on the Internet that provide frontends for these procedures/tools, and the export and import procedures from the snapshots to the live AD are made very simple. A very popular example of a free option is the **Directory Service Comparison Tool** [12] by Fredrik Lindstrom. The author of this book does not take any responsibility for the reliability of third-party tools, though.

Replacing the Active Directory Domain Controller

With the backup and rollback plan in place, we can proceed to the replacement procedure, but first, a word about DNS services. We know that Active Directory Services are a collection of services integrated for administrators to use and manage essential network services. But, it's important to handle the replacement procedure by focusing on the DNS part of those services that are separate from the whole AD DC. That's because we have covered the objects recovering with the snapshot feature, but if our DNS records are not consistent and our DNS is not working properly, Active Directory will not work.

Microsoft Windows Server 2008 R2 has a handy configuration file with all the records needed for the proper operation of the AD DS, which is located in `C:\Windows\System32\config\netlogon.dns` and is compatible with Microsoft Windows operating systems prior to Server 2008 or for DNS servers that are not from Microsoft. The latter is just our case, so we will save its content in a TXT file in our Debian 7 brand's new Samba 4 Server. We will use it later on in our procedure.

After the proper installation of the Samba 4 Server and all the dependencies on the machine, we will use it as our new AD DC; we need to be sure that our Kerberos system is working OK. For that, we just need the following configuration in `/etc/krb5.conf`:

```
[libdefaults]
  default_realm = POA.MSDCBRZ.EALL.COM.BR
  dns_lookup_realm = false
  dns_lookup_kdc = true
```

With the preceding configuration in place, we are able to test our Kerberos setup; now just type the following commands (as root):

```
root@debian7:/home/leal# kinit administrator
Password for administrator@POA.MSDCBRZ.EALL.COM.BR:
root@debian7:/home/leal# klist
Ticket cache: FILE:/tmp/krb5cc_0
Default principal: administrator@POA.MSDCBRZ.EALL.COM.BR

Valid starting     Expires            Service principal
08/07/2013 14:10  09/07/2013 00:10  krbtgt/POA.MSDCBRZ\
.EALL.COM.BR@POA.MSDCBRZ.EALL.COM.BR
  renew until 09/07/2013 14:10
```

As is confirmed in the preceding output, we know that we are able to get a valid token, and we can go ahead and start the game by adding our Samba 4 Server as an additional AD DC for our network [15]:

```
root@debian7:/home/leal# /usr/local/samba/bin/samba-tool domain join poa.
msdcbrz.eall.com.br DC -Uadministrator
Finding a writeable DC for domain 'poa.msdcbrz.eall.com.br'
Found DC WINDOWS2008SRV.poa.msdcbrz.eall.com.br
Password for [POA\administrator]:
```

> If your Samba 4 Server has more than one network interface, you may prefer to execute the preceding command with just the main interface enabled. After that, a `smb.conf` file will be created, and you'll be able to add an interface line by specifying the network and binding interface you want.

After this command, we should be prompted for the administrator's password and after providing that, we will see messages in the console about the process of joining the Active Directory Services as a Domain Controller. The following are the last lines of the output:

```
...
Sending DsReplicateUpdateRefs for all the replicated partitions
Setting isSynchronized and dsServiceName
Setting up secrets database
Joined domain POA (SID S-1-5-21-3395795540-2439876420-4291680193) as
  a DC
```

If we do not get a message like the preceding one at the end of the last procedure, we need to check our Samba 4 installation and make sure that all the steps described in *Chapter 1, Installing the Samba 4 Server*, have been followed and executed correctly. We should have many other informational messages too, and if any `ERROR` message is presented, we should return and check our installation and network connectivity.

Now, the first part of our replacement procedure will focus on DNS and make sure that everything is configured properly, and that we have the needed records synchronized and transferred for our new Samba 4 AD DS. We will demote Microsoft Windows Server 2008 R2 just after we complete all the DNS configurations.

Let's execute the following command to update/create necessary DNS entries:

```
root@debian7:~# /usr/local/samba/sbin/samba_dnsupdate --all-names –
  verbose
```

The preceding command should produce a lot of debug messages, and many important DNS entries should be created automatically. Among these messages, we should see the following entries:

```
...
poa.msdcbrz.eall.com.br.        900 IN A 192.168.1.1
debian7.poa.msdcbrz.eall.com.br.     900 IN A 192.168.1.1
gc._msdcs.poa.msdcbrz.eall.com.br.     900 IN A 192.168.1.1
dd1fb0a6-056f-4a5c-a718-2bca393f88a1._msdcs.poa.msdcbrz.eall.com.br. 900
IN CNAME debian7.poa.msdcbrz.eall.com.br.
...
```

Now, we can start querying our DNS server (our Windows Server 2008 R2 AD) to verify whether or not the `samba_dnsupdate` command worked as expected. From our Samba 4 Server, we will execute the following commands:

```
host -t srv _ldap._tcp.Default-First-Site-Name._sites.dc._msdcs.POA.\
MSDCBRZ.EALL.COM.BR windows2008srv
Using domain server:
Name: windows2008srv
Address: 192.168.1.2#53
Aliases:
_ldap._tcp.Default-First-Site-Name._sites.dc._msdcs.POA.MSDCBRZ.\
EALL.COM.BR has SRV record 0 100 389 debian7.poa.msdcbrz.eall.com.br.
_ldap._tcp.Default-First-Site-Name._sites.dc._msdcs.POA.MSDCBRZ.\
EALL.COM.BR has SRV record 0 100 389 windows2008srv.POA.MSDCBRZ.\
eall.com.br.
```

We can query for the specific `CNAME` value for the new DC object GUID using the following commands:

```
root@debian7:/home/leal# host -t CNAME dd1fb0a6-056f-4a5c-a718-2bca3\
93f88a1._msdcs.poa.msdcbrz.eall.com.br.


dd1fb0a6-056f-4a5c-a718-2bca393f88a1._msdcs.poa.msdcbrz.eall.com.br \
 is an alias for debian7.poa.msdcbrz.eall.com.br.
```

> We can find out the new DC GUID by issuing the following command [16]:
>
> ```
> ldbsearch -H /usr/local/samba/private/sam.ldb
>   '(invocationid=*)' --cross-ncs objectguid
> ```

We can ask for the `A` record for the `debian7` new Domain Controller using the following command:

```
root@debian7:/home/leal# host -t A debian7.poa.msdcbrz.eall.com.br
debian7.poa.msdcbrz.eall.com.br has address 192.168.1.1
```

DNS reverse resolution is very important, and Microsoft AD seems not to create a reverse zone for the AD Domain by default. Let's test it using the following commands:

```
leal@debian7:~$ host 192.168.1.2
;; connection timed out; no servers could be reached
leal@debian7:~$
```

Our Microsoft Server does not have a reverse resolution configured, and therefore, let's take a look at our new server:

```
leal@debian7:~$ host 192.168.1.1
;; connection timed out; no servers could be reached
leal@debian7:~$
```

So, the best option is to configure reverse resolution to have fully working DNS. We can open the DNS administration pane by navigating to **Start** | **Administrative Tools** | **DNS**. On the main screen, just expand the main server (for example, **WINDOWS2008SRV**) and choose **Reverse Lookup Zones**, as shown in the following screenshot:

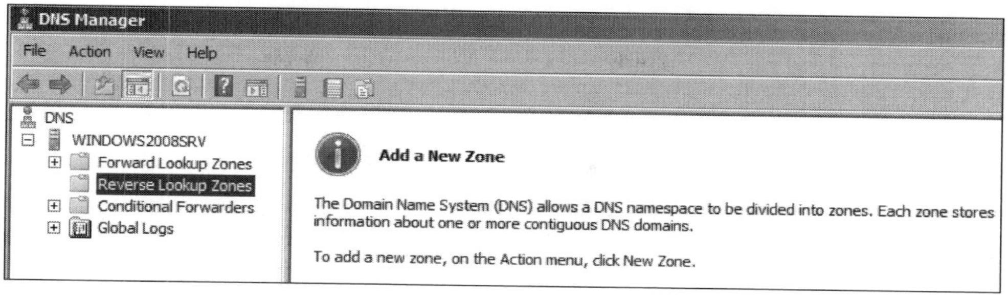

To add a new zone, just click on the **Action** menu and choose **New Zone** as shown in the following screenshot:

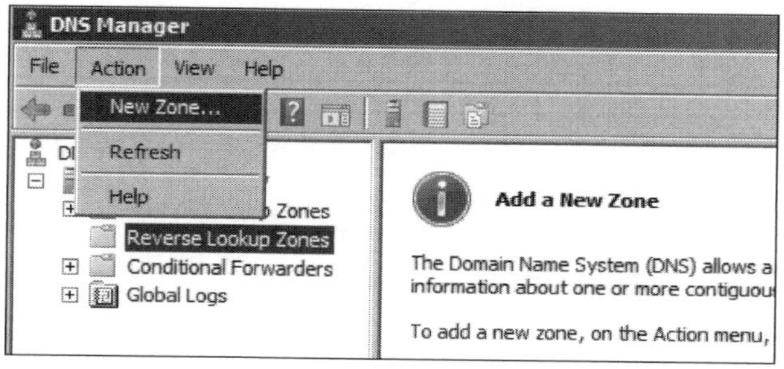

The next step is a straightforward process as we just need to follow **New Zone Wizard**. After the initial **Welcome** screen, we see a screen on which we are able to choose **Store the zone in Active Directory...**, and we should leave that box checked together with the **Primary zone** option. On the third screen, we will choose the replication to **all DNS servers running on domain controllers in this domain....** We'll create an IPv4 reverse lookup zone, and the following screenshot shows the configuration for the **Network ID** value:

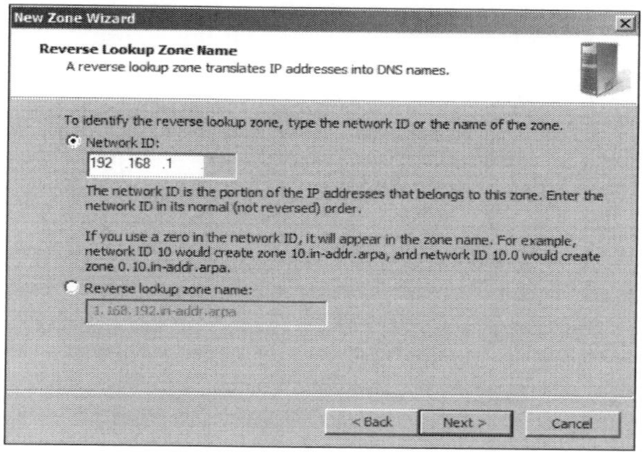

For the DNS updates, we will choose the option to just allow secure dynamic updates, and we can finish the wizard. Now that our **1.168.192-in-addr.arpa** zone is created and up and running, let's create some records and test the resolution again. To do so, we will need to select our brand new reverse DNS zone: right-click on it and choose **New Pointer (PTR)...**, as shown in the following screenshot:

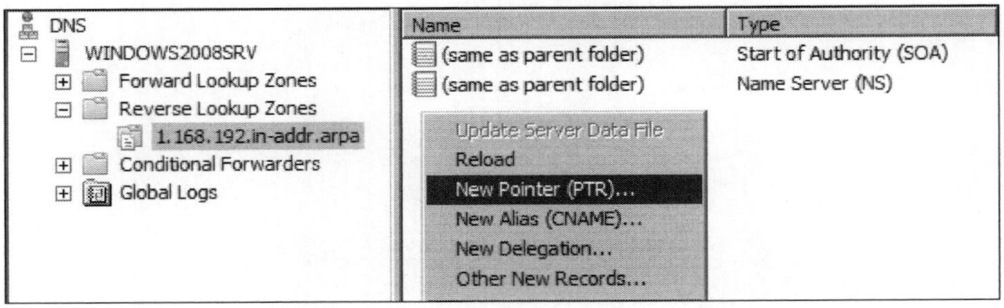

The **New Resource Record** screen will show the **Host IP Address** field almost completely filled; we just need to add the host details. There is a checkbox on this screen about the update for the records, and we need to choose in accordance with your company's policies. The **New Resource Record** screen looks as shown in the following screenshot:

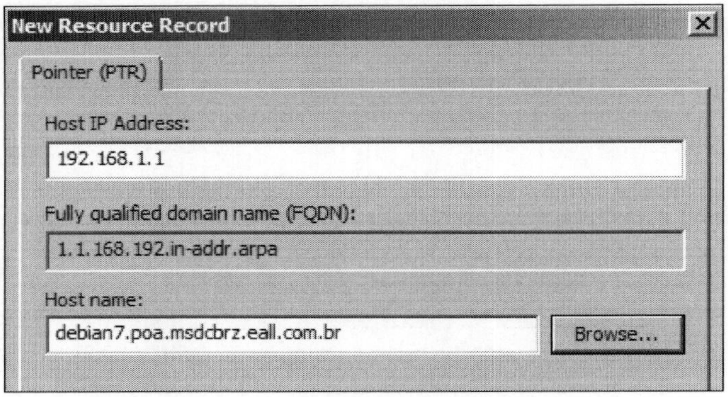

After we have created the entries that we need for our network, we can test our reverse resolution right away using the following commands:

```
leal@debian7:~$ host 192.168.1.2
2.1.168.192.in-addr.arpa domain name pointerwindows2008srv.poa.msdcb\
rz.eall.com.br.
leal@debian7:~$
```

Now, we can run the `samba_dnsupdate` command once more and start Samba using the following commands:

```
root@debian7:/home/leal#/usr/local/samba/sbin/samba_dnsupdate --all-names
--verbose
...
root@debian7:/home/leal# /usr/local/samba/sbin/samba
root@debian7:/home/leal#
```

Now, before moving on to the operations on the AD itself, we will change all the main DNS records of our network to point to our new Samba 4 AD Server. It's important to execute this procedure while the current Microsoft Windows Server 2008 R2 is still online as some records can be very difficult to reconfigure if we do not do this at the right time. Take a look at the following command execution on the Samba 4 Server:

```
leal@debian7:~$ dig -t any poa.msdcbrz.eall.com.br
; <<>> DiG 9.8.4-rpz2+rl005.12-P1 <<>> -t any poa.msdcbrz.eall.com.br
;; global options: +cmd
;; Got answer:
;; ->>HEADER<<- opcode: QUERY, status: NOERROR, id: 31663
;;flags: qr aa rd ra; QUERY: 1, ANSWER: 4, AUTHORITY: 0,ADDITIONAL: 1

;; QUESTION SECTION:
;poa.msdcbrz.eall.com.br.   IN   ANY
;; ANSWER SECTION:
poa.msdcbrz.eall.com.br. 900   IN   A   192.168.1.1
poa.msdcbrz.eall.com.br. 600   IN   A   192.168.1.2
poa.msdcbrz.eall.com.br. 3600   IN
  NSwindows2008srv.poa.msdcbrz.eall.com.br.
poa.msdcbrz.eall.com.br. 3600   IN   SOA
  windows2008srv.poa.msdcbrz.eall.com.br. hostmaster.poa.msdcbrz.eall.
com.br. 32 900 600 86400 3600
;; ADDITIONAL SECTION:
windows2008srv.poa.msdcbrz.eall.com.br.   3600 IN   A 192.168.1.2
;; Query time: 5 msec
;; SERVER: 192.168.1.2#53(192.168.1.2)
;; WHEN: Wed Jul 10 00:01:33 2013
;; MSG SIZE  rcvd: 165
```

The preceding information is very important as we need these records (for example, NS records) to point to our new AD Server. A better way to look at the different entries we have in our DNS configuration is by executing the following commands:

```
root@debian7:~# /usr/local/samba/bin/samba-tool dns query localhost
  poa.msdcbrz.eall.com.br @ ALL
Password for [administrator@POA.MSDCBRZ.EALL.COM.BR]:
  Name=, Records=4, Children=0
    A: 192.168.1.2 (flags=600000f0, serial=22, ttl=600)
    A: 192.168.1.1 (flags=600000f0, serial=22, ttl=900)
    NS: windows2008srv.poa.msdcbrz.eall.com.br. (flags=600000f0,
      serial=22, ttl=3600)
    SOA: serial=21, refresh=900, retry=600, expire=86400,
      ns=windows2008srv.poa.msdcbrz.eall.com.br.,
        email=hostmaster.poa.msdcbrz.eall.com.br. (flags=600000f0,
          serial=22, ttl=3600)
  Name=_msdcs, Records=0, Children=0
  Name=_sites, Records=0, Children=1
  Name=_tcp, Records=0, Children=4
  Name=_udp, Records=0, Children=2
  Name=debian7, Records=1, Children=0
    A: 192.168.1.1 (flags=f0, serial=23, ttl=900)
  Name=DomainDnsZones, Records=0, Children=2
  Name=ForestDnsZones, Records=0, Children=2
...
```

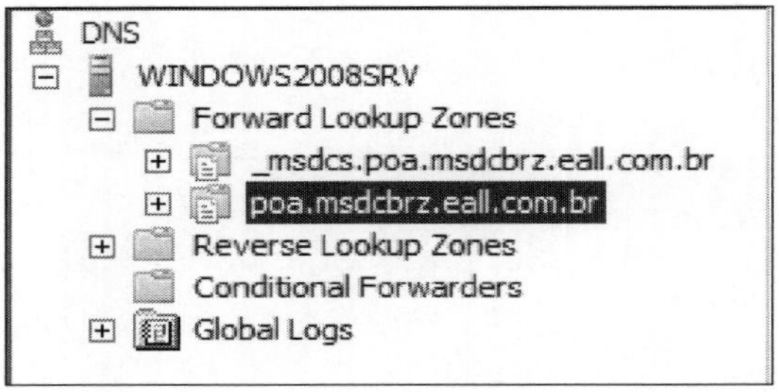

At this time, `samba-tool` is not able to update the SOA records, so we will update the records directly on the Microsoft Windows Server's administrative tool.
We open the DNS tool, select our domain, and right-click on our domain to choose the properties:

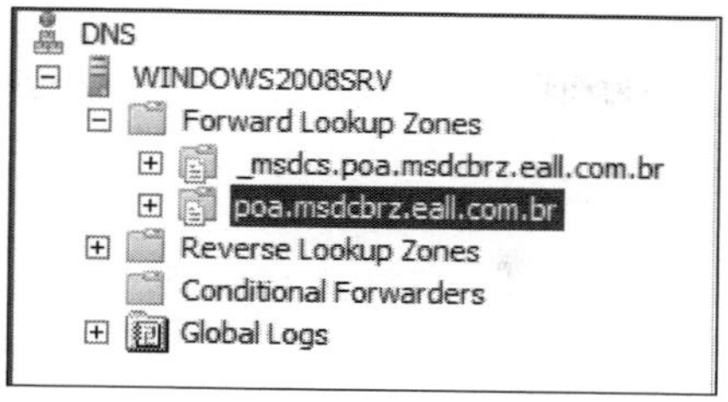

In the **Properties** window, we need to click on the **Start of the Authority (SOA)** tab and change the **Primary server** value from **windows2008srv.poa.msdcbrz.eall.com.br** to **debian7.poa.msdcbrz.eall.com.br** (don't forget to increase the serial number in that window), as shown in the following screenshot:

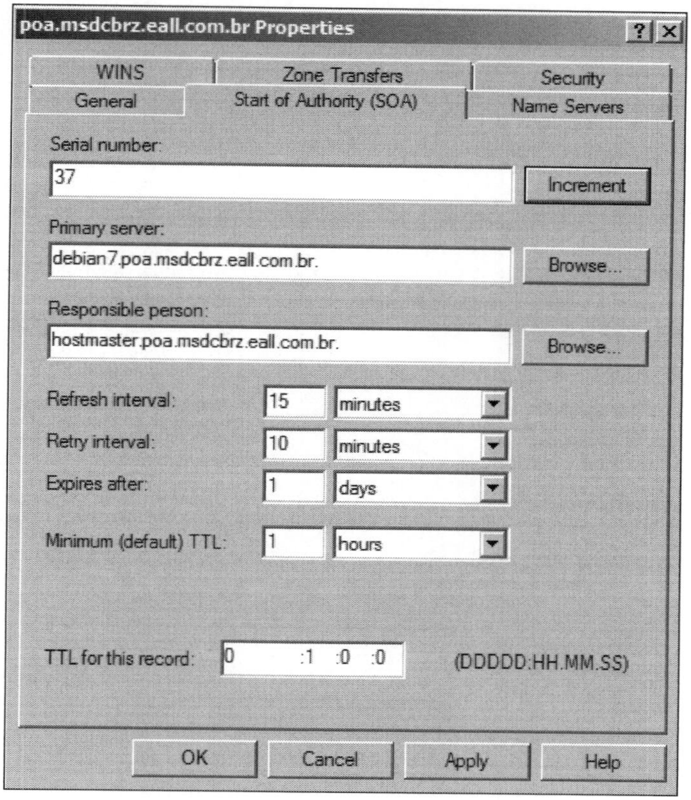

However, before we apply the changes to the SOA record, which is still in the properties of our Domain, we will select the **Name servers** tab and click on **Add...**, as we will add our `debian7` Samba 4 Active Directory Server to the **Name Servers** list. After adding the name of our server, we can click on the **Resolve** button next to the input box, and the IP address for our server will be filled correctly as shown in the following screenshot:

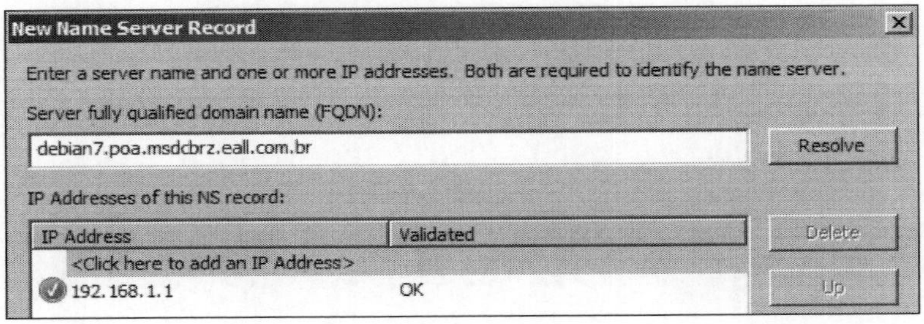

Now we can click on **OK**, and when we get back to the **Name Servers** tab on the **Properties** window, we can click on **Apply** and **OK** again. Let's go back to our Debian 7 Samba 4 server and test and see what our SOA and NS records look like. We will use the following commands to test our SOA and NS records:

```
root@debian7:~# /usr/local/samba/bin/samba-tool dns query localhost poa.
msdcbrz.eall.com.br @ ALL --password 'w1ndow$$'
  Name=, Records=5, Children=0
    A: 192.168.1.2 (flags=600000f0, serial=35, ttl=600)
    A: 192.168.1.1 (flags=600000f0, serial=35, ttl=900)
    NS: windows2008srv.poa.msdcbrz.eall.com.br. (flags=600000f0,
      serial=35, ttl=3600)
    NS: debian7.poa.msdcbrz.eall.com.br. (flags=600000f0, serial=35,\
      ttl=3600)
    SOA: serial=33, refresh=900, retry=600, expire=86400,
      ns=debian7.poa.msdcbrz.eall.com.br.,
        email=hostmaster.poa.msdcbrz.\
eall.com.br. (flags=600000f0, serial=35, ttl=3600)
  Name=_msdcs, Records=0, Children=0
  Name=_sites, Records=0, Children=1
  Name=_tcp, Records=0, Children=4
  Name=_udp, Records=0, Children=2
  Name=debian7, Records=1, Children=0
    A: 192.168.1.1 (flags=f0, serial=36, ttl=900)
```

```
Name=DomainDnsZones, Records=0, Children=2
Name=ForestDnsZones, Records=0, Children=2
Name=WINDOWS2003CLT, Records=1, Children=0
  A: 192.168.1.10 (flags=f0, serial=20, ttl=1200)
Name=WINDOWS2008CLT, Records=1, Children=0
  A: 192.168.1.11 (flags=f0, serial=21, ttl=1200)
Name=windows2008srv, Records=1, Children=0
  A: 192.168.1.2 (flags=f0, serial=3, ttl=3600)
```

We can see the serial number that we have increased when we updated the SOA record in the preceding output, and we can also see that our `debian7` server is configured as the primary server (notice that now we have both servers as name servers of our domain). So, now we can remove **windows2008srv**; going back to our Microsoft Windows Server 2008 R2 DNS administration tool, we go back to the **Properties** | **Name Servers** tab and remove **windows2008srv.poa.msdcbrz.eall.com.br** from the **Name Servers** list. Our zone will look similar to that shown in the following screenshot:

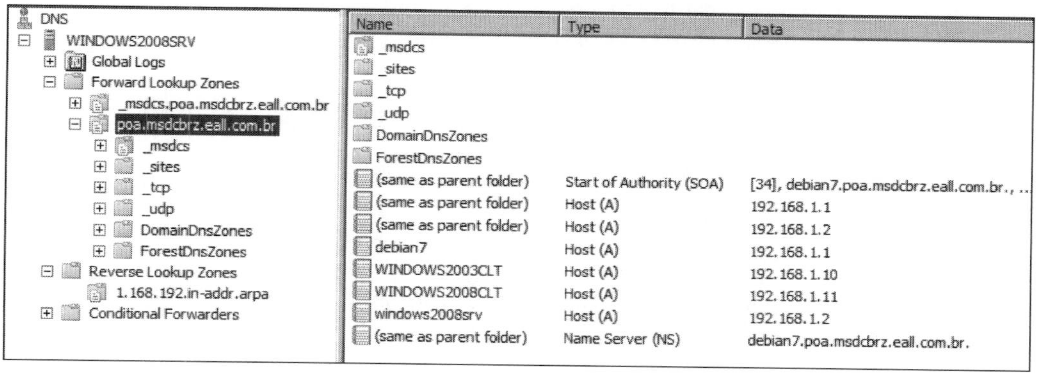

Now, we need to right-click on the `_msdcs` folder (which is inside `poa.msdcbrz.eall.com.br`), as shown in the preceding screenshot, and select **Properties**. So, we can add the `debian7` Samba Server to the list of name servers too, as shown in the following screenshot:

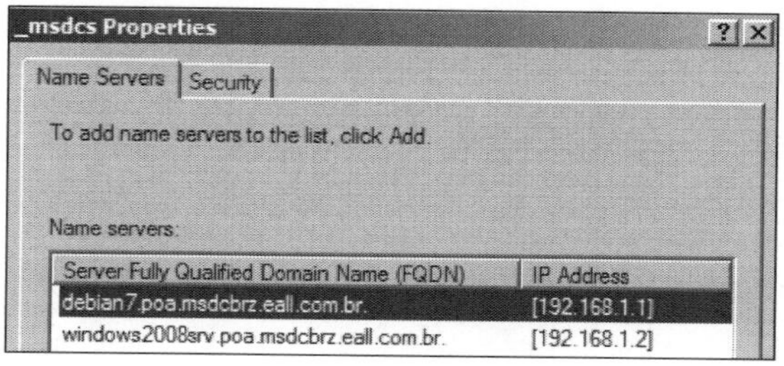

We need to execute the same procedure for **_msdcs.poa.msdcbrz.eall.com.br** as we did for **poa.msdcbrz.eall.com.br**. Right-click on it, choose **Properties**, and in the **Start of Authority (SOA)** tab, change the preferred server name and add `debian7` as the server name in the **Name Servers** tab.

Before going to our Microsoft Windows Server 2008 R2, we need to make sure we run the knowledge Consistency Checker [`14`] using the following commands:

```
root@debian7:/home/leal# /usr/local/samba/bin/samba-tool drs kcc -
  Uadministrator windows2008srv.poa.msdcbrz.eall.com.br
Password for [POA\administrator]:
Consistency check on windows2008srv.poa.msdcbrz.eall.com.br
  successful.
root@debian7:/home/leal#
```

With the preceding message indicating that the consistency check on our Microsoft Windows 2008 Server R2 was successful, we can go ahead and test the replication between the two Domain Controllers. We can go to our Windows Server to look at how the interaction/replication between the two Domain Controllers is occurring. So, we just need to open a command prompt (by navigating to **Start | Command Prompt**), and execute the following commands:

```
C:\Users\Administrator>repadmin /replsummary
Replication Summary Start Time: 2013-07-08 16:46:54

Beginning data collection for replication summary, this may take awhile:
  .....
Source DSA          largest delta    fails/total %%   error
 DEBIAN7                  19m:47s     0 /   3    0
 WINDOWS2008SRV               :23s     0 /   5    0
Destination DSA     largest delta    fails/total %%   error
 DEBIAN7                      :24s     0 /   5    0
 WINDOWS2008SRV           19m:48s     0 /   3    0

C:\Users\Administrator>
```

Now, let's execute the following commands for a full synchronization from `windows2008srv` to `debian7` to ensure that every **naming context** (**NC**) is up to date:

```
C:\Users\Administrator>repadmin /syncall /A debian7
Syncing all NC's held on debian7.
Syncing partition: DC=POA,DC=MSDCBRZ,DC=EALL,DC=COM,DC=BR
```

```
...
CALLBACK MESSAGE: SyncAll Finished.
SyncAll terminated with no errors.
...
Syncing partition: CN=Schema,CN=Configuration,DC=POA,DC=MSDCBRZ,DC=EALL,D
C=COM,DC=BR
...
Syncing partition: CN=Configuration,DC=POA,DC=MSDCBRZ,DC=EALL,DC=COM,DC=
BR
...
Syncing partition: DC=DomainDnsZones,DC=POA,DC=MSDCBRZ,DC=EALL,DC=COM,DC
=BR
CALLBACK MESSAGE: The following replication is in progress:
...
Syncing partition: DC=ForestDnsZones,DC=POA,DC=MSDCBRZ,DC=EALL,DC=COM,DC
=BR
CALLBACK MESSAGE: SyncAll Finished.
SyncAll terminated with no errors.
C:\Users\Administrator>
```

What we can see is that all the known partitions were replicated without errors. We need to look carefully at the replication of these partitions as this is a crucial process for the Active Directory Services. So, now we can work on the **Flexible Single Master Operation** (**FSMO**) roles: Schema Master, Infrastructure Master, Naming Master, RID Master, and PDC.

As we have just one AD DC on our network, all the roles are on the Microsoft Windows Server 2008 R2, and because we are replacing this server, we need to transfer all of them to our brand new AD DC. To do that, we will use the `ntdsutil` utility. For each of the roles mentioned earlier, we need to execute the following command (for example, just changing the role):

```
C:\Users\Administrator>ntdsutil roles connections "connect to server
  debian7" q "transfer schema master" q q
ntdsutil: roles
fsmo maintenance: connections
server connections: connect to server debian7
Binding to debian7 ...
Connected to debian7 using credentials of locally logged on user.
server connections: q
```

```
fsmo maintenance: transfer schema master
Server "debian7" knows about 5 roles
Schema - CN=NTDS Settings,CN=DEBIAN7,CN=Servers,CN=Default-First-\
Site-Name,CN=Sites,CN=Configuration,DC=POA,DC=MSDCBRZ,DC=EALL,DC=COM\
,DC=BR
Naming Master - CN=NTDS Settings,CN=WINDOWS2008SRV,CN=Servers,CN=Def\
ault-First-Site-Name,CN=Sites,CN=Configuration,DC=POA,DC=MSDCBRZ,DC=\
EALL,DC=COM,DC=BR
PDC -CN=NTDS Settings,CN=WINDOWS2008SRV,CN=Servers,CN=Default-First-\
Site-N\ame,CN=Sites,CN=Configuration,DC=POA,DC=MSDCBRZ,DC=EALL,DC=CO\
M,DC=BR
RID - CN=NTDS Settings,CN=WINDOWS2008SRV,CN=Servers,CN=Default-First\
-Site-Name,CN=Sites,CN=Configuration,DC=POA,DC=MSDCBRZ,DC=EALL,DC=CO\
M,DC=BR
Infrastructure - CN=NTDS Settings,CN=DEBIAN7,CN=Servers,CN=Default-F\
irst-Site-Name,CN=Sites,CN=Configuration,DC=POA,DC=MSDCBRZ,DC=EALL,D\
C=COM,DC=BR
fsmo maintenance: q
ntdsutil: q
```

Observe that the schema role was transferred to the new `debian7` AD DC, and after to repeat the preceding commands for the remaining four roles, we can remove the global catalog from Microsoft Windows Server 2008 R2. Navigate to **Start** | **Run...** and execute the command as exemplified in the following screenshot:

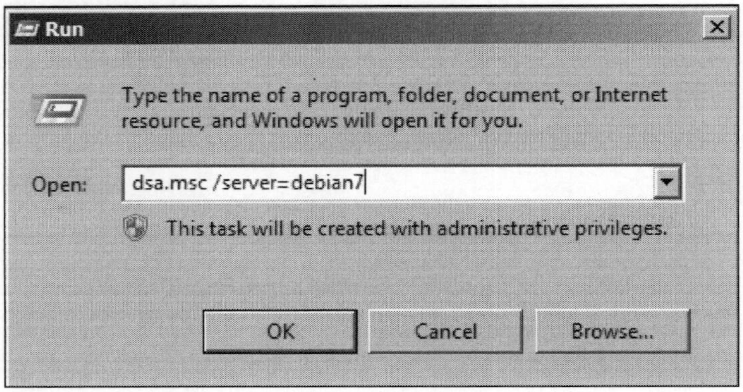

Now, we will expand our domain (for example, **POA.MSDCBRZ.EALL.COM.BR**), click on **Domain Controllers**, and right-click on the server we are replacing (for example, `windows2008srv`), select properties, and click on **NTDS Settings...** as shown in the following screenshot:

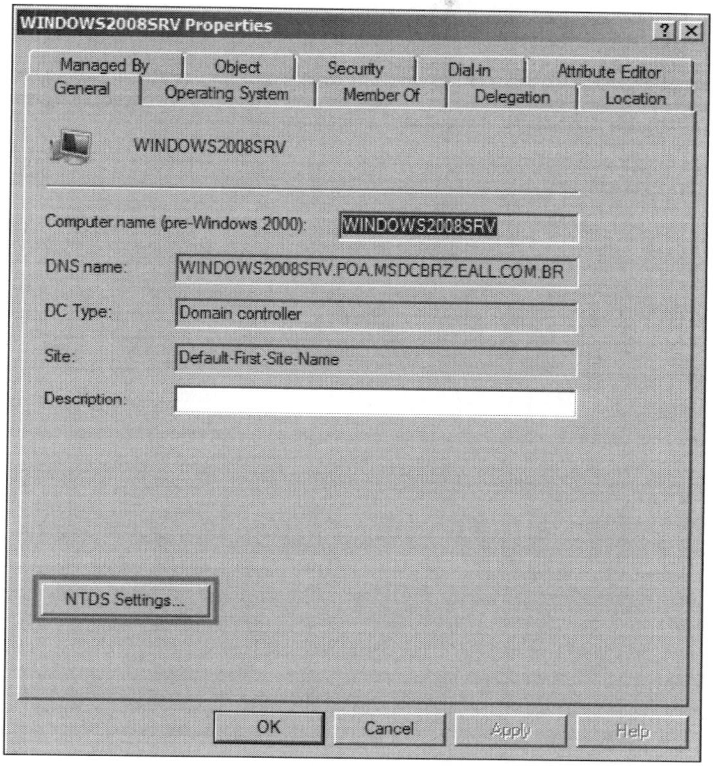

In the following window, we will remove `windows2008srv` server as the global catalog for our domain. For that, we just need to uncheck the **Global Catalog** box (shown in the following screenshot), click on **Apply**, and then click on **OK**:

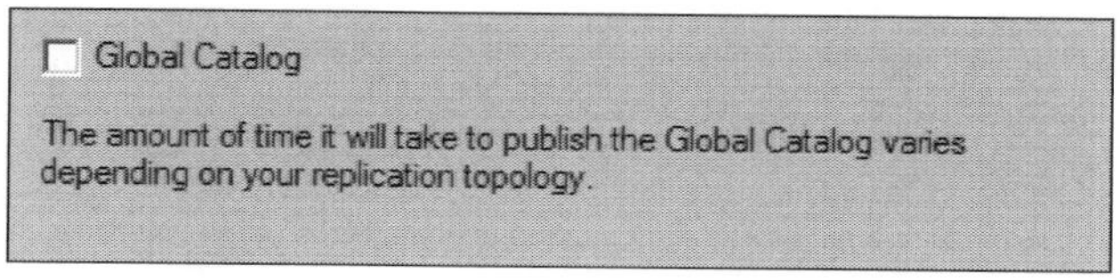

Before demoting our Microsoft Windows Server 2008 R2, let's configure our DHCP server on the new `debian7` Active Directory. We have some configurations pointing to the IP `192.168.1.2`, which is the IP for `windows2008srv`, as we can see in the following lines of our DHCP's configuration file:

```
...
  option domain-name-servers 192.168.1.2;
  option netbios-name-servers 192.168.1.2;
  option ntp-servers 192.168.1.2;
...
```

We need to change those configurations to make them the IP of our new AD (for example, `debian7`): `192.168.1.1`. Just issue the following script at a root shell on the `debian7` server:

```
root@debian7:/home/leal# cp -pRf /etc/dhcp/dhcpd.conf /etc/dhcp/dhcpd.
conf-bkp && sed -e 's/192.168.1.2/192.168.1.1/g' /etc/dhcp/dhcpd.conf >
/etc/dhcp/dhcpd.conf-dnspatch && mv /etc/dhcp/dhcpd.conf-dnspatch /etc/
dhcp/dhcpd.conf && echo OK
OK
root@debian7:/home/leal#
```

Now we can start the DHCP server using the following command:

```
root@debian7:/home/leal# /etc/init.d/isc-dhcp-server start
[ ok ] Starting ISC DHCP server: dhcpd.
root@debian7:~#
```

The last step is to demote Microsoft Windows Server 2008 R2. The utility to execute this procedure is `dcpromo`, and we can execute it by navigating to **Start** | **Run...**, as shown in the following screenshot:

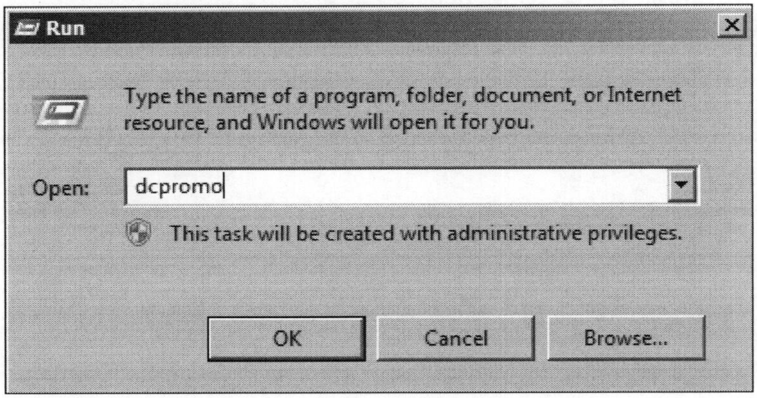

Now, we just follow **Active Directory Domain Services Installation Wizard** to uninstall the Active Directory from the `windows2008srv` server. One important point to keep in mind is to leave the checkbox unchecked when we are asked to delete the domain. If we are presented with a screen informing us that this is the only DNS server on the network, just click on **OK** as shown in the following screenshot:

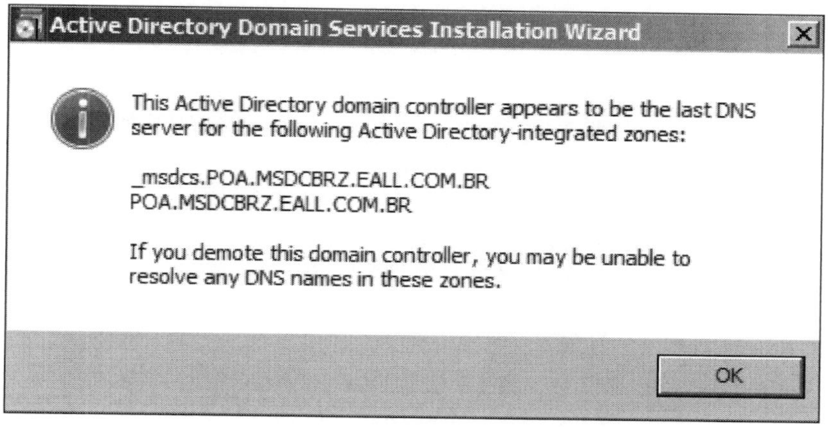

After we get a message informing us that this server, by the end of the process, will be a member server, we'll have a progress indication window like that shown in the following screenshot:

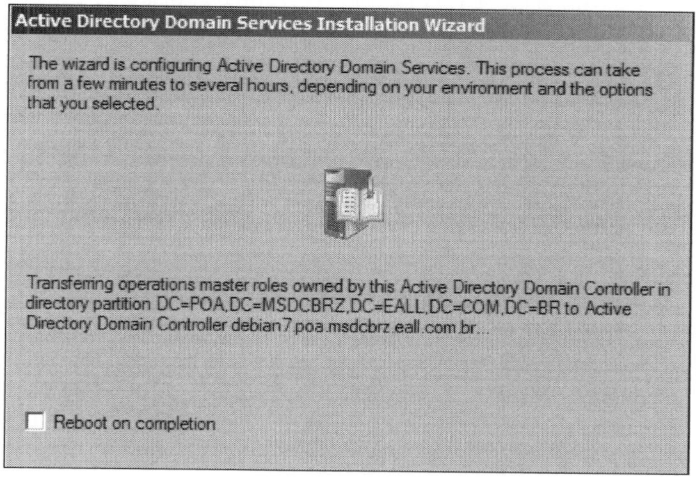

Sometimes, we get some errors when demoting a Microsoft Windows Server from the Active Directory role, but we can continue with the process as we will fix any error and clean up the metadata and old DNS entries in the following steps. When the process has ended, we just restart the Microsoft Windows Server 2008 R2 machine as shown in the following screenshot:

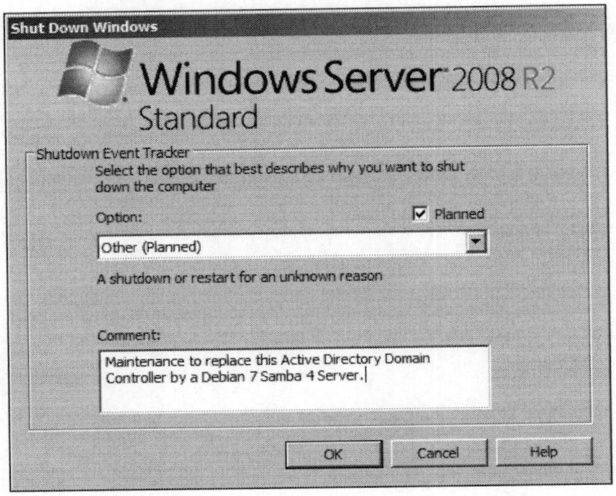

When Microsoft Windows Server 2008 R2 restarts, we will execute a metadata cleanup to guarantee that no deprecated data from the replaced Active Directory Server remains in our environment. Execute the command shown in the following screenshot as an administrator:

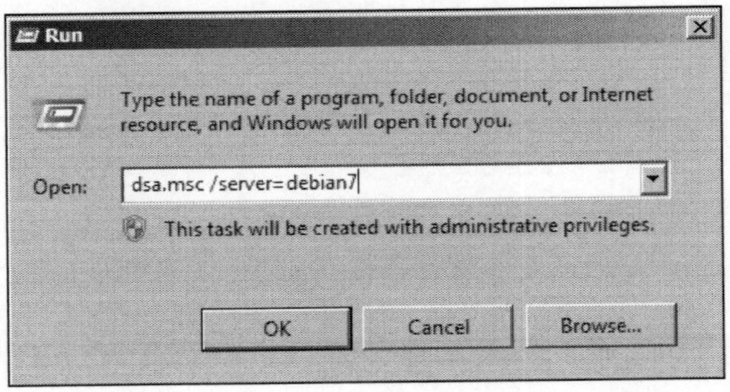

Expand the domain (for example, `POA.MSDCBRZ.EALL.COM.BR`) and select **Domain Controllers**, right-click on Microsoft Windows Server 2008 R2 (for example, **WINDOWS2008SRV**), and select **Delete** as shown in the following screenshot. If we agree with the message in the confirmation screen that appears next (for example, is it the right server we want to delete?), we choose **Yes**.

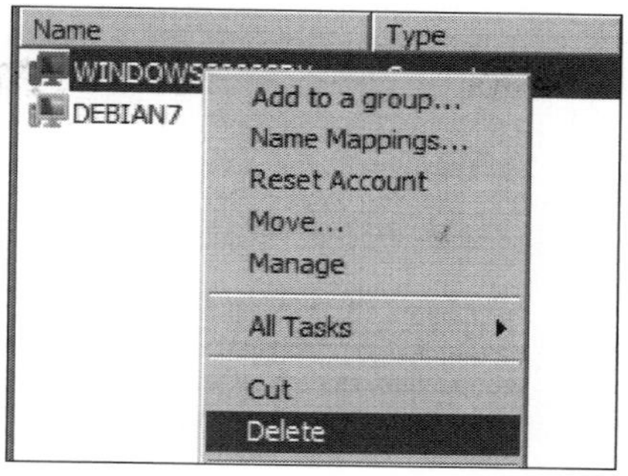

We will receive another screen in which we need to check the **This Domain Controller is permanently offline and can no longer be demoted using the Active Directory Domain Services Installation Wizard (DCPROMO)** box as shown in the following screenshot:

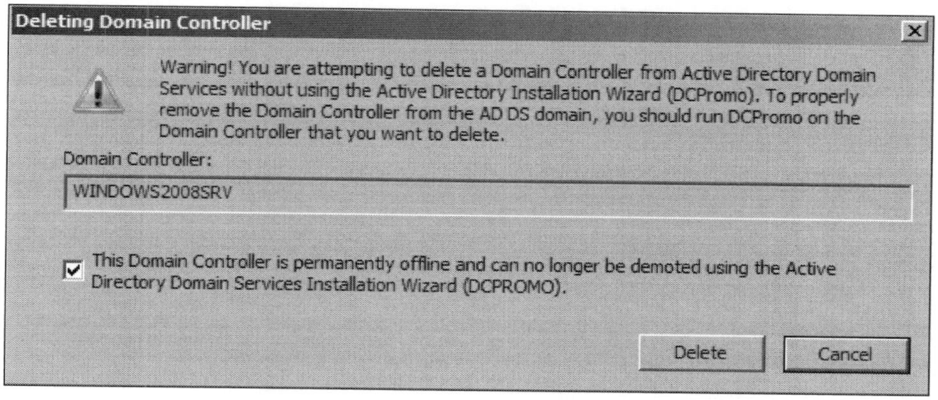

After a few seconds, we should have just one server (for example, `debian7`) in the **Domain Controllers** container, and we can shut down our Microsoft Windows Server 2008 R2.

Now, we will clean up any DNS entries that were left behind during the `dcpromo` demotion. We will use the `netlogon.dns` file on the new GNU/Linux Samba 4 Server AD DC (named `dns.txt`) and have one more handy automation script from the *Implementing Samba 4* book.

First, execute the following command on the Debian 7 Samba 4 Server:

```
root@debian7:~# /usr/local/samba/bin/samba-tool dns delete 192.168.1\
.1 poa.msdcbrz.eall.com.br @ NS windows2008srv.poa.msdcbrz.eall.com.\
br --password 'w1ndow$$'
```

```
Record deleted successfully
root@debian7:~#
```

Now execute the `_msdcs` command:

```
root@debian7:~# /usr/local/samba/bin/samba-tool dns delete 192.168.1\
.1 _msdcs.poa.msdcbrz.eall.com.br @ NS windows2008srv.poa.msdcbrz.ea\
ll.com.br --password 'w1ndow$$'
Record deleted successfully
root@debian7:~#
```

Let's exclude `CNAME` from the GUID of `windows2008srv` using the following command:

```
root@debian7:~#`grep -i cname dns.txt | awk -F. '{print "/usr/local/\
samba/bin/samba-tool dns delete 192.168.1.1 _msdcs.POA.MSDCBRZ.EALL.\
COM.BR", $1, "CNAME WINDOWS2008SRV.POA.MSDCBRZ.EALL.COM.BR"}'`
Password for [administrator@POA.MSDCBRZ.EALL.COM.BR]:
Record deleted successfully
root@debian7:~#
```

Now we use the `fixdns.sh` script to perform all the remaining cleanups for us. Execute the following command (the `dns.txt` file must be in the current directory):

```
root@debian7:/home/leal# ./fixdns.sh -f 192.168.1.1
```

> We can use the option `-h` to get help from the script or just execute a consistency check (using the `-c` option), without changing anything in our Active Directory Server. It's advised that you first execute the script with the option `-c` and after reviewing the changes, execute the script using the `-f` option.

The preceding script will read all the entries from the `dns.txt` file (that has all the default/standard AD DNS entries) and fix any inconsistencies that the demotion could have in our AD database (such as by removing the entries for that demoted AD Server). The output should be something like the following commands:

```
Record Type [   A   ]: POA.MSDCBRZ.EALL.COM.BR. Number of entries: 1
[OK], registered: [OK].
Record Type [   A   ]: gc._msdcs.POA.MSDCBRZ.EALL.COM.BR. Number of
entries: 1 [OK], registered: [OK].
Record Type [   A   ]: DomainDnsZones.POA.MSDCBRZ.EALL.COM.BR. Number of
entries: 1 [OK], registered: [OK].
```

```
Record Type [    A    ]: ForestDnsZones.POA.MSDCBRZ.EALL.COM.BR. Number of
entries: 1 [OK], registered: [OK].
Record Type [   SRV   ]: _ldap._tcp.POA.MSDCBRZ.EALL.COM.BR. Number of
entries: 1 [OK], registered: [OK].
Record Type [   SRV   ]: _ldap._tcp.Default-First-Site-Name._sites.\
POA.MSDCBRZ.EALL.COM.BR. Number of entries: 1 [OK], registered: [OK].
...
```

At this point, the Debian 7 Samba 4 Server is our only AD DC, and we can go to the last and very important step of our procedure.

Replacement tests and validations

Let's start with the DNS validations; first, we'll validate the SOA and NS records for our `poa.msdcbrz.eall.com.br` domain as follows:

```
leal@debian7:~$ dig -t any poa.msdcbrz.eall.com.br
...
;; ANSWER SECTION:
poa.msdcbrz.eall.com.br. 900   IN  A  192.168.1.1
poa.msdcbrz.eall.com.br. 3600   IN  NS
  debian7.poa.msdcbrz.eall.com.br.
poa.msdcbrz.eall.com.br. 3600   IN  SOA
  debian7.poa.msdcbrz.eall.com.br. hostmaster.poa.msdcbrz.eall.com.br. 52
900 600 86400 3600
...
```

Now let's see how the entries are for `_msdcs.poa.msdcbrz.eall.com.br`:

```
...
dig -t any _msdcs.poa.msdcbrz.eall.com.br
;; ANSWER SECTION:
_msdcs.poa.msdcbrz.eall.com.br.  3600 IN  NS
  debian7.poa.msdcbrz.eall.com.br.
_msdcs.poa.msdcbrz.eall.com.br.  3600 IN  SOA
  debian7.poa.msdcbrz.eall.com.br. hostmaster.poa.msdcbrz.eall.com.br. 30
900 600 86400 3600
...
```

> When executing commands that need a password, it is a good practice not to provide the password at the command line as it is saved in the history of the server. We are presenting different ways to call the system's utilities to make sure that the reader knows about the many options available.

We can use the following `samba-tool` utility to query all our DNS records as we did earlier in the chapter:

```
root@debian7:~# /usr/local/samba/bin/samba-tool dns query localhost poa.
msdcbrz.eall.com.br @ ALL --password 'w1ndow$$'
  Name=, Records=3, Children=0
    A: 192.168.1.1 (flags=600000f0, serial=43, ttl=900)
    NS: debian7.poa.msdcbrz.eall.com.br. (flags=600000f0, serial=43,
ttl=3600)
    SOA: serial=52, refresh=900, retry=600, expire=86400, ns=debian7.
poa.msdcbrz.eall.com.br., email=hostmaster.poa.msdcbrz.eall.com.br.
(flags=600000f0, serial=52, ttl=3600)
  Name=_msdcs, Records=0, Children=0
  Name=_sites, Records=0, Children=1
  Name=_tcp, Records=0, Children=4
  Name=_udp, Records=0, Children=2
  Name=debian7, Records=1, Children=0
    A: 192.168.1.1 (flags=f0, serial=48, ttl=900)
  Name=DomainDnsZones, Records=0, Children=2
  Name=ForestDnsZones, Records=0, Children=2
  Name=WINDOWS2003CLT, Records=1, Children=0
    A: 192.168.1.10 (flags=f0, serial=20, ttl=1200)
  Name=WINDOWS2008CLT, Records=1, Children=0
...
```

A good method to test our DNS and its interaction with our AD DS is by adding another machine to the domain. We have a Microsoft Windows 2012 Server that we will use to test our new AD DC. In the following screenshot, we can see the dialog box asking for the administrator's credentials to add the server to the domain:

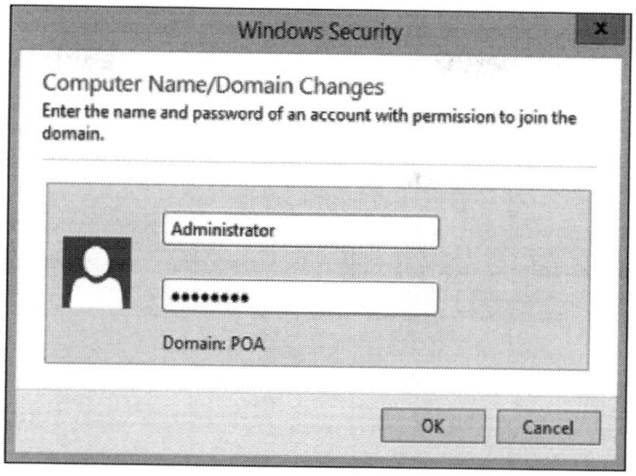

The following screenshot shows the traditional Welcome message after a successful domain join:

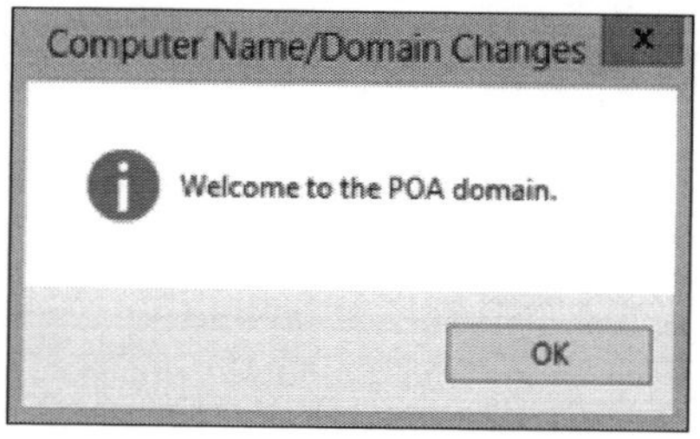

From our Debian 7 Samba 4 shell, we can observe whether or not the DNS entries were created properly for our new server using the following command:

```
root@debian7:~# host -t A windows2012srv
windows2012srv.poa.msdcbrz.eall.com.br has address 192.168.1.13
root@debian7:~#
```

We can verify the registry in the output of the `samba-tool` utility as follows:

```
root@debian7:~# /usr/local/samba/bin/samba-tool dns query localhost
  poa.msdcbrz.eall.com.br windows2012srv A --password 'w1ndow$$'
  Name=, Records=1, Children=0
    A: 192.168.1.13 (flags=f0, serial=110, ttl=1200)
root@debian7:~#
```

Now, we can start to look at our directory: we can test the login of a user to our brand new Microsoft Windows 2012 Server and test the login in some machines that were part of the domain before we performed our replacement procedure. Using one of the Member Servers, we can look at our Active Directory structure and start to look at our OUs, users, and computers. However, as we have our `csv` file saved with the information acquired from our last snapshot, we will extract the list of users from our live AD and compare it with our snapshot's list.

We have our `snapshot-snap-sorted.csv` file saved in our `home` directory on the Debian 7 Samba Server (for example, `/home/leal`), and now we'll extract a live list. Just execute the following command in the command prompt in a member server with RSAT installed (right-click on **Command Prompt** and select **Run as Administrator**):

```
C:\Users\Administrator> csvde -s debian7 -d\
"ou=Standard Users,ou=People,dc=poa,dc=msdcbrz,dc=eall,dc=com,dc=br"\
 -r "(objectClass=user)" -c \
"ou=Standard Users,ou=People,dc=poa,dc=msdcbrz,dc=eall,dc=com,dc=br"\
 "" -l sAMAccountName -f standardusers.csv
Connecting to "debian7"
Logging in as current user using SSPI
Exporting directory to file standardusers.csv
Searching for entries...
Writing out entries
...............................................
Export Completed. Post-processing in progress...
49 entries exported
The command has completed successfully
C:\Users\Administrator>
```

We can see that we have 49 entries exported, but let's execute the following command to compare between the files to make sure that we don't have any inconsistencies in our `Directory` database:

```
C:\Users\Administrator> sort standardusers.csv /o standardusers-
  sorted.csv
```

Now, we can use the Notepad to edit the file and copy the whole content to a file in the Debian 7 Samba 4 Server. Just choose the best option to place the files side-by-side and let's compare their contents as follows:

```
leal@debian7:~$ diff standardusers-snap-sorted.csv standardusers-
  sorted.csv
leal@debian7:~$
```

The files are exactly the same, which means we have all the users present in our new Active Directory Server. I would like, once more, to encourage the creation of many files and the exposure of many attributes for all the crucial objects from the Active Directory prior to performing the replacement procedure. The only point to pay attention to is that some attributes are highly volatile and can make the comparison of the files difficult as they tend to produce "garbage" in the comparisons (such as date, time, and so on). However, the quality of the tests and the validation we perform after our maintenance operations are the ultimate measure of the success or failure of any task in IT.

Summary

In this chapter, we went through the whole process of understanding the key points to be taken into consideration while planning for an Active Directory Domain Controller replacement, learned the different aspects of backup and rollback procedures that we need to have in place beforehand as well as how to create and execute a plan for the replacement of a Microsoft Windows Server 2008 R2 AD DC with a Samba 4 Server.

Also, we learned about many applications and utilities already available on the Microsoft Windows Server 2008 R2 that can be used together to create powerful tests and validations for the replacement procedure as well as how to use some of them to apply effective and quick fixes for some issues that we may encounter during general maintenance procedures on the directory.

We have pointed to external resources and utilities to help readers elaborate even more and execute the procedures as simply and efficiently as possible using examples of scripts and command lines to automate many complex tasks, making the whole replacement process a lot easier to understand. In the next chapter, we will learn about some of the biggest differences between the Samba software Versions 3 and 4, the key points of consideration before planning an upgrade, and how to effectively upgrade from Samba Server Version 3 to the new Version 4.

5

Upgrading from Samba Server Version 3

In this chapter, the reader will learn some of the biggest differences between the Samba software Versions 3 and 4, and based on that, will understand the impact and the relevant considerations before planning a successful upgrade. The main aspects of such differences will be focused on the different working models and the new features and benefits that the upgrade can leverage. We will go over the plan, tests, and validations that the reader needs to pay attention in order to be able to execute and help evaluate the success of such an upgrade procedure.

Scripts and command-line examples will be used to help the readers identify where to look, what information might be important to gather, and how to compare the final result to the prior environment from a functional standpoint.

We will learn about a step-by-step procedure to execute the upgrade and all the commands and scripts needed to go from Samba 3 to Samba 4's fully functional Domain Controller network services.

We will describe a guideline that can be well suited and requires just a few changes for small and medium installations, but bigger and more complex environments will need adjustments and customizations. The variety of configurations in production of the Samba Server Version 3 use cases are huge, and we will not be able to handle all the variations that our readers have implemented in their respective environments, but all the procedures and use case examples presented here should work as a rich base.

Distinguishing between Samba Versions 3 and 4

From the Samba Version 4 release notes made by the Samba project [16], we got information on the addition of the DNS server and NTP protocols that are integrated in the new Samba 4 code, LDAP server and **Kerberos Key Distribution Center (KDC)**—both accounted within the Active Directory Services, support for SMB Version 2.1 with preliminary support for Version 3.0, and the Python scripting interface—all of which we will highlight as great and bold, new capabilities.

These new features can make the Samba Server Version 4 look appealing from an upgrade perspective for the Samba Server Version 3 users. It can also stimulate new installations, as it can be a strong choice to provide full network services as open source and as a free alternative in comparison to Microsoft Windows Servers.

The classic model (NT4 Domains) is still supported and present in the Samba Server Version 4, but the new version's real gain for users and system administrators is the ability to use all the new features introduced by Microsoft with the development of the Active Directory Domain Controller services. All these are associated with the concepts of delegations, group policies, new security model, and so on.

The fact is that the Samba Server Version 3 is a rock-solid software. The file and print's server code is very stable and has been working for many, many years. Besides this, the Samba Server Version 4 has implemented a new approach and daemons for these services; the new project's software version still has support for the old and bulletproof file/print server daemons and those are the ones that are recommended for production purposes at the time of this writing.

Many users are really happy with the file and print services from Samba Server Version 3. As a great portion of the use cases and base installations of the Samba Server is for the purpose of these services, many users remain with the Version 3 in production, where the scary problem is to support the new Microsoft Windows Operating System versions.

So, for the users who are looking at and exploring the upgrade process, the real difference and the main feature that encourages them to take the upgrade path most of the time, which are the Active Directory services present on Samba 4. The new code has integrated the DNS and LDAP server and KDC. So, many users from the previous versions that could be intimidated by the need to deal with external and complex software combinations (for example, DNS/Bind or OpenLDAP) for small and medium installations can now have a really robust and complete solution for the Samba project's new release.

Key points for consideration before the upgrade

It's never too much to remember that the only guarantee we can have when dealing with technology services and maintenance procedures on production systems is the backup—straight and simple.

The upgrade process from the Samba Server Version 3 to Version 4 will have a phase where the software's rollback can be a very difficult task or maybe not even possible. So, a backup not just of the Samba Servers involved, but of the domain's other important machines is really crucial too. This is to make sure that the environment can be brought back online to a consistent and operational state at any time.

Another important point in the planning phase is to take into consideration the size and complexity of the network services' environment. We need to consider how many clients, servers (directly or indirectly involved), and how much time is needed (and available) for the upgrade procedure. Different environments may require different approaches, and a big network and/or a short maintenance windows may require a staged upgrade.

We will focus, as is the sole objective of this book, on the Samba 4 Server as a complete system to provide all services for which it is intended. In a real scenario, we need take a look at the auxiliary services that we use, instead of Samba or other services that are not involved in the upgrade process directly but can or might get impacted. This is a case-by-case analysis, and the reader needs to pay serious attention to these services, and having a checklist and enumeration of all these services and applications is a mandatory step.

Prepare the upgrade procedure taking into account the time that will be available to execute the whole upgrade process, and remember that the time to validate and test it is a part of the process. Take notes on the number of users, groups, machines, and all configured resources that are relevant for the upgrade process. This information is the key for the validation of the whole procedure. Create a checklist of service names (for example, endpoints) and applications that can be impacted, and schedule the upgrade accordingly. We will use some scripts and command-line examples to extract the information from the system, but it is a good idea to have some kind of checklist with quick access to the global aspects of the environment to facilitate and help spot on any issues.

As the Samba Server Version 3 has no built-in DNS server, we'll cover a Bind9 implementation in the upgrade procedure as an example of the DNS side of the upgrade process and its integration with the ISC-DHCP server it's a very common implementation among users of Samba 3. The reader has a choice to maintain Bind as the DNS server after the upgrade or move the resolution services for the Samba Server Version 4 (in this book, we will implement the latter option). Last but not least, the Samba Server Version 4 software needs to be installed and tested prior to the upgrade process with all needed dependencies in all Samba 3 systems that we will upgrade.

Establishing an upgrade plan

The upgrade plan needs to be created focusing on the environment that it will be applied, but we will have some general rules that can be a base for many environments, a generic procedure for the gathering of information, tests, validations, and a practical upgrade example that can be used as a base for a final plan.

In our example case, we will deal with a Microsoft Windows NT4-like domain for one of the EALL Company sites, based in Porto Alegre/RS - Brazil. This site is controlled by one Samba Server Version 3 as the **Primary Domain Controller** (**PDC**) for that region (for example, POA), and two Samba Servers Version 3 acting as Domain Member Servers for each Division/Department of the EALL site in Porto Alegre.

The company is very inclined towards Microsoft products, and the three GNU/Linux systems were installed for the POA's network services as a global decision to lower the IT costs. EALL is successful with Samba's adoption, and as the company has other offices in many places around the world, it has resulted in big savings year over year, as dozens of Debian GNU/Linux PDCs and print/file servers do not need license fees.

Another big advantage the company has while implementing Samba 3 to provide the network services is that it has more flexibility to scale as the file servers present performance problems from time to time, so other filers can be easily deployed without incurring additional license costs. This provided us with a big gain in the quality of the services for the users, better architecture (services are decoupled), reducing complexity, and lowering overall downtime in hardware and software maintenance.

Now, the company sees a huge opportunity to evolve its Microsoft Network with the new Samba 4 release and use it as a free and open source pilot for the **Active Directory Services** (**ADS**). At some of its other sites, the company is already using ADS on newer versions of the Microsoft Windows operating system.

Our Samba 3 upgrade will be focused on three basic sets of services:

- **Authentication services**: These include machines, users, and groups (Samba3)
- **File/print services**: These include files and printer shares (Samba3)
- **DNS services**: These include the name resolution (Bind9)

Every Samba 3 installation needs to have a combination of the core services listed earlier: at least one name resolution system and one (usually both) set of Samba 3 services (in one or more servers).

The Samba services can be provided completely in just one server or distributed in different servers for performance, architecture decision, company policies, and so on. As we go through this procedure, we will see that it is much easier to manage and deal with a medium to big network complexity, with the services that are decoupled. Also, we can handle the whole upgrade procedure in small and separate steps.

In any case, if your specific environment has just one server providing all the services we have mentioned here, there is no problem, as in the end, the process that will be executed will be focused on the services, and thus will be executed on the server where that service resides. Therefore, if we have a site where we have decentralization of services in different servers or in just one server, then all the services are provided by a standalone server. We should notice that the downtime needed to execute all the upgrade procedures in one server alone, which provides all services, can be bigger and much more complex, though. This is why this upgrade can be a very good opportunity to review the architecture of the Samba services and adjust it as needed.

Another important aspect of handling the process at these three different sets of services is that we have specific procedures for each step. So, the upgrade step for the file and print servers, for example, can be replicated as we have more than two Domain Member Servers that are the exact same way. Then, we can establish priorities, and for bigger and more complex environments, we can execute a staged upgrade.

In our example case, we have the file and print services in specific Domain Member Servers that are dedicated to the departments of our company. So, we can handle them with the different priorities and department's maintenance windows, accordingly.

Here is some general information we need at hand for our network, and soon, we will see how to gather them all:

General system and environment information	
Server #1	
The Samba Server version	3.6.6
Role	Primary Domain Controller (Network Logon Services and User's profiles)
Hostname	PDC
IPs	192.168.1.1 (eth1), 10.10.10.1 (eth0)
Other services	DHCP Server (ISC), DNS Server (Bind9), NTP, and CUPS
Shares	Profiles (`/home/POA/`)
Backend	Tdbsam
Server #2	
The Samba Server version:	3.6.6
Role	Domain Member Server (file and print services)
Hostname	`ACCSRV01`
IPs	192.168.1.5 (eth0)
Other services	CUPS
Shares	ACC Division (`/shares/*`)
Server #3	
The Samba Server version	3.6.6
Role	Domain Member Server (file and print services)
Hostname	`DEVSRV01`
IPs	192.168.1.6 (eth0)
Other Services	CUPS
Shares	Devel department (`/shares/*`)
General Samba network information	
Domain	POA.MSDCBRZ.EALL.COM.BR
Network	192.168.1.0
Netmask	255.255.255.0
Default router	192.168.1.1
DHCP Server	192.168.1.1
DNS zone files	`/var/lib/bind/db.poa.msdcbrz.eall.com.br{rev}`
Number of users	51
Number of groups	9

General Samba network information	
Workstations/desktops	Microsoft Windows 2003 and XP
Application servers	Microsoft Windows Server 2003
Maintenance time	2 hours

The preceding information is presented here as a basic example, and we will look at how we actually gathered it in the next section. We will save much of the information in the text files to facilitate the validations after we have concluded the upgrade, but this information is very important to provide quick access to very crucial information; it also works as a formal document that can be attached to the maintenance plan.

After all tests and validations, our upgrade procedure will be executed in a single place for all the Samba Servers. Feel free to add any other information that you think is necessary to the preceding document or attention points to check before and/or after the upgrade. One good example is some consideration about external storage devices, if any (for example, `volumes/luns`), backing shares. In our example, the EALL Company uses local disks (for example, Direct Attached) to all Samba shares, so there was no need to mention it in the preceding document.

> If you followed our Samba 4 installation instruction, the binaries should be compiled with all features needed for the upgrade as we have installed the main dependencies, and the Samba's configuration script should automatically detect and enable them. Don't proceed to the upgrade phase without making sure that all the features that are needed are present on the Samba 4 installation (for example, CUPS and ADS).

Creating tests and validations before the upgrade

Our tests' and environment's validations will start on a clone of the currently installed software—a subset that is representative of our production environment. So, the first task is to establish a small group of machines to clone in a virtual or physical environment to be used to create our tests and validations, and also to exercise our upgrade procedure. After the upgrade, we will execute the same tests described here, and we will know exactly what the expected results are.

The best way to do this is to create a lab in a virtual environment, we will not test any hardware upgrade, and all the device drivers and components needed for the proper execution of the production software are assumed to be in place and in a working condition. So a virtual environment is a perfect fit, and we will execute some checks on it to guarantee that the environment is working as expected and no misconfigurations exist.

> In case you use a virtual environment for your tests, create snapshots of all machines in this environment after you have it all set up to be able to go back and forth on the procedure and restart the whole process when necessary.

In software upgrade procedures, it's very common to face problems after the upgrade that actually were present before the upgrade process. This can mislead the result or unhide a latent issue at the wrong time. Thus, we will use this phase and test environment to validate the current system configuration, and if any issues are discovered, they can be fixed prior to the maintenance. On top of that, we can use this procedure until we have a bulletproof process.

So, we will present some commands and scripts that can be used to make sure that Samba 3 is working as expected this is very important for the upgrade process to work.

> Do not execute any script directly in the production stage; or, make sure you know what you are doing, because we are not responsible for any disruption or data loss that you may incur while executing scripts and commands in a production network without prior testing.

Let's start with the PDC Server and basic tests, such as listing users and groups. Using a command prompt at the Primary Domain Controller, execute the following command:

```
root@pdc:/root# wbinfo -u
...
miwallace
bekiddo
jocabot
jabrown
...
root@pdc:/root#
```

The preceding command is `wbinfo`, a tool to query information from the `winbind` daemon, and we used the `-u` option to list all the users in the domain. Now, let's see how many users we have:

```
root@pdc:/root# wbinfo -u | wc -l
51
root@pdc:/root#
```

As we can see in our plan, we have 51 users in the domain, which is exactly what we've got as an output from the preceding script (one user is the root account, which is mapped to the administrator on the EALL Samba 3 installation). It's important to note that Debian GNU/Linux has some other personal administrative accounts that are not included on that list as the domain users are totally separated from the host operating system's accounts. EALL's architecture choice is not to authenticate the Debian GNU/Linux host on the Samba 3 PDC itself. Still using the `wbinfo` utility, execute the following command:

```
root@pdc:/root# wbinfo -g
eall group
eall domain users
eall domain admins
...
root@pdc:/root# wbinfo -g | wc -l
9
root@pdc:/root#
```

In the preceding output, we have two other important points of information about the system that we will upgrade: the list of groups and the total number of groups in the domain. As we did in the users listing, we have omitted the whole list of names in each group for brevity. However, it's a good idea to save both the full listings for future validation:

```
root@pdc:/root# wbinfo -u | sort > samba3users.txt && echo OK
OK
root@pdc:/root# wbinfo -g | sort > samba3groups.txt && echo OK
OK
root@pdc:/root#
```

The preceding two commands have been created in the `/root` directory, two text files (sorted) with the lists of users, and groups in the domain. Feel free to organize it in a specific directory or send the files to an external server (this is recommended because it's good to have this listing but not on the server on which we will actually execute the upgrade procedure).

> Another command that will provide some of the preceding information is `net rpc info`.

Another good test is to use the `smbclient` utility, and authenticate it against our Samba 3 Server (PDC) and get a good view of the network resources and other important insights about our main Samba 3 Server. Using a test account for the domain (or any other specific account that you know the password), execute the following command:

```
root@pdc:/root# smbclient -L pdc -U 'frorange%w1ndow$$'
Enter frorange's password:
Domain=[POA] OS=[Unix] Server=[Samba 3.6.6]

        Sharename       Type      Comment
        ---------       ----      -------
        Profiles        Disk      EALL Roaming Profiles Share
        IPC$            IPC       IPC Service (EALL Network Services)
Domain=[POA] OS=[Unix] Server=[Samba 3.6.6]

        Server               Comment
        ---------            -------
        ACCSRV01             ACCDivision Office Server
        DEVSRV01             DEV Office Server
        PDC                  EALL Network Services

        Workgroup            Master
        ---------            -------
        POA                  PDC
root@pdc:/root#
```

This is one of the most important commands because it gives us a good view of how our services are decoupled. The preceding output tells us some of the following interesting things:

- We have the main IPC Service for our Samba 3 Server PDC
- One share (Profiles) for the roaming profiles of our domain
- Our workgroup name, POA, and the Samba Server Version 3.6.6

- The PDC server is the master of our domain (Primary Domain Controller)
- We have two other servers: `ACCSRV01` and `DEVSRV01`

> You can use the following syntax to execute the `smbclient` command that provides the password directly on the command line:
>
> **user%password.**
>
> **See the following example:**
>
> **smbclient -L pdc -U ' 'kischultz%w1ndow$$'**

So, this server has two important roles on the EALL network: it is the PDC (controls authentication and authorization) and the Profiles' share. To enhance the decoupling of services on this network, a good option would be to create a specific file server to hold the users' profiles (for example, an HA Filer) and to leave the PDC with just one role in this network. This would facilitate the backup and recovery of this server as it is the only PDC, and if we have the backup of the DB and `smb.conf` files, we can quickly recover from a failure on the main PDC (our most important network service). On top of that, we could focus on an HA solution for the filer that is responsible for the users' Profiles to have a better resilience (for example, a Storage backed Profile share).

The preceding test helped us indirectly validate another important function of our Samba 3 Server—authentication. However, we can use the `ntlm_auth` command to specifically test it, as exemplified in the following command execution:

```
root@pdc:~# ntlm_auth --username=jobrittle --domain=POA
password:
NT_STATUS_LOGON_FAILURE: Logon failure (0xc000006d)
root@pdc:~# ntlm_auth --username=jobrittle --domain=POA
password:
NT_STATUS_OK: Success (0x0)
```

Remember that it is important to test with the wrong password (as we did earlier). Sometimes, we fail to identify problems in our environment because we just test using the same pattern. It's important to test with *wrong pathnames, wrong passwords, usernames that in fact do not exist,* and so on. Many misconfigurations have been a result of a configuration that permits access for any user or any password. Now that's a really bad misconfiguration!

It's recommended that you have your infrastructure automated with recipes and tests. A long time ago, I implemented a system to programmatically provision, test, and validate the infrastructure resources, **Battery of Tests and Validations (BTVA)** of the environment, and it was a really powerful tool to identify and even fix issues on the operating system configuration. Since then, I have used that model when managing any kind of system.

The system was based on **Makefiles** and many scripts to test and validate every corner of the environment that was needed to run a specific application. The essential point about this approach is that you just add tests, and over time, the whole environment just gets better coverage. After a test is written, the same error does not happen twice, and after some time, we have a really strong system to validate our environment.

Now, with devOps [17] and new approaches to handle and implement these kind of automations, it is highly recommended that you have the tests described here incorporated in your tools and provisioning systems.

Here is an example of how we can quickly create a script to execute a good validation of our user's database (we can save the listing for future reference):

```
root@pdc:~# for x in `wbinfo -u`; do wbinfo --name-to-sid $x; done
...
S-1-5-21-1214754503-652539266-1573105461-1023 SID_USER (1)
S-1-5-21-1214754503-652539266-1573105461-1028 SID_USER (1)
S-1-5-21-1214754503-652539266-1573105461-1044 SID_USER (1)
S-1-5-21-1214754503-652539266-1573105461-1008 SID_USER (1)
...
root@pdc:~#
```

If we have any user who is not properly mapped in the Samba database, or if we fail to actually translate a SID to a user/group, we'll have problems ahead. So, I just want to make sure that the reader understands that the more tests and automations we do, the better it will be to validate our upgrade. The examples that have been shown here can be enhanced, and if one test is made for one user as an example, it can be simply modified to make the same test for all users as we just did on the example script earlier.

Now it's time to test our two file/print servers: `ACCSRV01` and `DEVSRV01`. We will use the `smbclient` utility to execute the same test that we performed for PDC as it will show us very detailed information about our two Domain Member Servers. From the command prompt on our PDC Server, execute the following command:

```
root@pdc:~# smbclient -L accsrv01 -U 'legecko'
Enter legecko's password:
Domain=[POA] OS=[Unix] Server=[Samba 3.6.6]

    Sharename        Type      Comment
    ---------        ----      -------
    ---------        ----      -------
IPC$             IPC       IPC Service (ACCDivision Office Server)
    ACCPRTMM01       Printer   1F Printer MM
    ACCPRTLS01       Printer   2F Printer
    PRINT$           Disk      Drivers for Dep. Printers
    ACCPUBLIC        Disk      Public Share
    ACCDIVDOCS       Disk      Accdivision Prospects
    ACCDIVRPTS       Disk      Accdivision Reports
Domain=[POA] OS=[Unix] Server=[Samba 3.6.6]

    Server               Comment
    ---------            -------
    ---------            -------
ACCSRV01             ACCDivision Office Server
    PDC                  EALL Network Services

    Workgroup            Master
    ---------            -------
    ---------            -------
POA                  PDC
root@pdc:~#
```

Again, we could test name resolution and authentication, but on one of our Domain Member Servers this time as this is really important, or users will not be able to access the services from that server. Here is the information we that we got from the preceding test:

- We have the main IPC Service for our Samba 3 Domain Member Server
- We have four file shares: `ACCDIVRPTS`, `ACCDIVDOCS`, `PRINT$`, and `ACCPUBLIC`
- We have two printers: `ACCPRTMM01` and `ACCPRTLS01`
- Our workgroup name, POA and Samba Server Version 3.6.6
- The Primary Domain Controller Server for our Domain: PDC

So, let's take a look at the execution output of this same command, but this time, for our second Domain Member Server:

```
root@pdc:~#  smbclient -L devsrv01 -U ' 'zojarratt'
Enter zojarratt's password:
Domain=[POA] OS=[Unix] Server=[Samba 3.6.6]

   Sharename       Type      Comment
   ---------       ----      -------
  ---------       ----      -------
 DEVPRT01          Printer   General DEV Printer
   DEVCODDS        Disk      DEV COD CODDS
   DEVSRCAP        Disk      DEV SRC AP
   IPC$            IPC       IPC Service (DEV Office Server)
Domain=[POA] OS=[Unix] Server=[Samba 3.6.6]

   Server               Comment
   ---------            -------
   ---------            -------
DEVSRV01             DEV Office Server
   PDC                  EALL Network Services

   Workgroup            Master
   ---------            -------
   ---------            -------
POA                  PDC
root@pdc:~#
```

Here is the interpretation of the preceding output:

- We have the main IPC Service for our Samba 3 Domain Member Server
- We have two shares: `DEVCODDS` and `DEVSRCAP`
- We have one printer: `DEVPRT01`
- Our workgroup name is POA and Samba Server Version 3.6.6
- The Primary Domain Controller Server for our Domain PDC

In Samba, we need to have the domain groups mapped to our Unix groups on the PDC to provide the same authorization to each share that our Domain Member Server provides to our network. So, based on that mapping, it's a good idea to test some of our users and groups to validate that our associations are working as expected.

For an example, take a look at the Unix group, `accdivision`, and its members as this group is mapped to the domain group, `accdivision`:

```
root@pdc:~# grep accdivision /etc/group
accdivision:x:1002:zafalca,cafreeman,qumichael,zisala
root@pdc:~#
```

Executing the following command, we can validate the mapping and save the results:

```
root@pdc:~# net rpc group members "accdivision group" "| tee
>accdivisiongroupmembers.txt
Enter root's password:
POA\zafalca
POA\cafreeman
POA\qumichael
POA\zisala
root@pdc:~#
```

In all the Member Servers, we need to validate the users/group resolutions. So, let's take a look at the NSS configuration for the `DEVSRV01` server as an example:

```
root@devsrv01:~# id djfox
uid=2031(djfox) gid=1513(domain users) grupos=1513(domain
users),2051(eall domain users),2053(devel group)
root@devsrv01:~# getent passwd djfox
djfox:*:2031:1513:djfox:/home/POA/djfox:/bin/false
root@devsrv01:~#
```

Another test that we need to make is to have a Microsoft Windows system test a join into the domain and do some normal activities, such as logon and roaming profiles. We can create one test user and add it to some groups to test the access to the different shares/printers, and after that, we can remove the user. This will test our DHCP Server and its integration with DNS too, helping us guarantee a proper configuration of the whole system. Let's execute some commands to actually test the machine's name resolution on the EALL network:

```
root@pdc:~# host -t A pdc
pdc.poa.msdcbrz.eall.com.br has address 192.168.1.1
root@pdc:~# host 192.168.1.1
1.1.168.192.in-addr.arpa domain name pointer pdc.poa.msdcbrz.eall.com.br.
root@pdc:~# host -t A windowsxp
```

```
windowsxp.poa.msdcbrz.eall.com.br has address 192.168.1.11
root@pdc:~# host -t MX poa.msdcbrz.eall.com.br
poa.msdcbrz.eall.com.br mail is handled by 10 mail.poa.msdcbrz.eall.com.
br.
root@pdc:~# host -t SOA poa.msdcbrz.eall.com.br
poa.msdcbrz.eall.com.br has SOA record pdc.poa.msdcbrz.eall.com.br. root.
poa.msdcbrz.eall.com.br. 2007010408 3600 600 86400 600
root@pdc:~#
```

Tests and validations are executed, and no misconfigurations were found, and that's good. We have saved files with the user and group listings, and we have a plan with all the information about our upgrade maintenance. Now, we are ready to proceed to the upgrade process in our lab environment so that we can validate each step of the upgrade and have an opportunity to fix the process inconsistencies, if any.

Executing the Samba Server upgrade procedure

We will execute our plan following the three service approaches that we mentioned earlier, and we need to start with the PDC Server that provides the Authentication/Authorization Service. The other two will be executed in a sequence, starting with the DNS Services, and the last one will be the file/print services provided by the `ACCSRV01` and `DEVSRV01` servers. The file/print servers can be executed in any order, so we have the flexibility to prioritize one over the other based on factors such as the business impact. In this specific example case, there is no priority or preference, so we have chosen to start with the `ACCSRV01`.

> When executing the procedure in the production, remember that we need to have a backup for our PDC and Domain Member Servers, and for any other servers or clients that we know have crucial data and can't be recreated or easily rebuilt. This is because it can be really difficult to fix/remove a Microsoft Windows Machine after it finds the new Active Directory Server in case we need to rollback our upgrade. So, it's advised that you block the network access for the PDC while you think that it is still not ready to provide the full services.

So, let's turn our attention for the procedure on the main element of our Samba 3 implementation, the **Primary Domain Controller** (**PDC**). The PDC server is the one with this role at the EALL Network, and it has important auxiliary services, such as NTP, DNS, and DHCP servers too. We will work on this server for the two initial phases, and when we have that done, we should have the main functionality of our POA Domain fully working (for example, users, groups, machines, and name resolution).

First, we need to make sure that we don't have groups with the same name as usernames in our Samba 3 Domain, as in the Active Directory, we cannot have usernames and groups sharing the same name, and in case we have, we will need to rename them. If we make use of these groups in the Samba 3 Domain (for example, for file/print services), then we need to replace any references to them on the `smb.conf` files of our file/print servers to reflect the new naming.

So, it's important to take note of all groups that we have renamed, and when we start to work on the file/print servers, we can execute the same change as they reference the groups by names. Here are examples of how we have renamed the two groups:

```
root@pdc:~# export PATH=/usr/local/samba/sbin:\
/usr/local/samba/bin:$PATH
root@pdc:~# net rpc group rename "Domain Users" "EALL Domain Users"
Enter root's password:
root@pdc:~# net rpc group rename "Domain Admins" "EALL Domain Admins"
Enter root's password:
root@pdc:~#
```

> The preceding `export` command is very important as it prefixes the newly installed Samba 4 binaries on our `PATH`, and we will execute all the upgrade procedure commands in this shell. It's a good idea to add this command to our shell startup files (for example, `.bashrc` and/or `.bash_profile`), so we'll always have the new Samba 4 utilities in precedence in our `PATH`. Before we are able to actually remove the old Samba 3 installation, it is very important to reference the right tools.

As we can see in the preceding command execution, we just needed to provide the administrator's password (for example, root) and the group's name gets changed. Another recommendation is to change the name for other standard groups that come with Samba Server 4 if they are present in our Samba 3 installation for any reason; for example, **Domain Guests**, **Domain Computers**, and **Domain Controllers**. All the mapping between the Unix and Domain groups that we may have should still work without issues after the renaming, as the mapping is made by the GID to SID.

To create default group names with the same name as the newly created user is the default behavior of many GNU/Linux distributions, and I have personally never used this group that is created exclusively for a user to implement anything. I prefer actually to get rid of this on the systems I manage. Thus, every new user is created with the default group assigned to the users, and this group is mapped to the EALL Domain Users group. For example, if you want to do the same, but you don't have more than 1000 users, and your GNU/Linux distribution starts to assign users and groups IDs from 1000 onwards (for example, Debian GNU/Linux), the following script will create a new file with the existing users reassigned the primary group of users (GID 100):

```
root@pdc:~#sed 's/[0-9]\{4\}::/100::/g' /etc/passwd > >/etc/passwd-`date
+%Y%m%d-%T` `&& cd && echo OK
OK
root@pdc:~#
```

If the preceding command returned `OK`, a new file will be created with a name like this: `passwd-20130619-13:16:14` (with your execution date and time). Take a closer look at this file and if it is right, you can replace the original `/etc/passwd` with it. Pay attention to the system users to make sure that they were not impacted, but as the system users have very low UIDs and GIDs, they should not be affected by this script. If everything is good, you can edit the `/etc/group` file and delete all the groups that have the same names as the users.

> Normally, default `UMASK` for users is to permit them to read/execute for the primary group (usually, the group specifically created for that same user, as it does not have any other members). If you choose to follow this path, make sure that any security policy or applications will not present any issues. After this change, you will need to fix the directories and files that are pointing to GIDs that actually do not exist anymore. Remember that this is not a necessary configuration for the Samba 3 to 4 upgrade, as the only requisite is to not have groups and users with the same name as the ones in the Samba 3 database.

Stopping and disabling Samba and winbind daemons

Now, we will stop the Samba and `winbind` daemons, and remove the execution bit for the initialization scripts to guarantee that they will not start inadvertently (for example, after a reboot). So, let's execute the following commands at the PDC server:

```
root@pdc:~# /etc/init.d/samba stop && &&/etc/init.d/winbind stop && chmod
-x /etc/init.d/{samba,winbind} }&& echo OK
```

```
[ ok ] Stopping Samba daemons: nmbd smbd.
[ ok ] Stopping the Winbind daemon: winbind.
OK
root@pdc:~#
```

After the execution of the preceding script, if the results are `OK`, we must stop the `smbd/nmbd` and `winbind` daemons, and have both the startup scripts disabled. As our PDC server is the default gateway for our private LAN, we have a public interface configured on this server. The Samba script will use and try to configure all the interfaces configured on the server; thus, we will disable the public interface and enable just the interface that has the connection with the Microsoft Windows network that we are interested:

```
root@pdc:~# ifdown eth0 && echo OK
OK
root@pdc:~#
```

As the preceding command returned `OK`, the interface `eth0` (public) is disabled properly, and we can go to the next step. In this stage, we have the environment ready to execute the `classicupgrade` function of the Samba 4 tool. Just issue the following command as root at a terminal window on the PDC server:

```
root@pdc:~# samba-tool domain classicupgrade --dbdir=/var/lib/samba/
/--use-xattrs=yes --realm=poa.msdcbrz.eall.com.br /etc/samba/smb.conf &&
echo "---====--- Upgrade from Samba 3 to Samba 4 OK 4OK---====---"
...
Fixing provision GUIDs
A Kerberos configuration suitable for Samba 4 has been generated at /usr/
local/samba/private/krb5.conf
---====--- Upgrade from Samba 3 to Samba 4 OK ---====---
root@pdc:~# cp -pf /usr/local/samba/private/krb5.conf /etc && echo OK
OK
root@pdc:~#
```

The preceding command should produce a very verbose output with important information about the upgrade process. This information includes the import of users, groups, machines, the creation of new standard groups, and so on. One such information was highlighted earlier, where the script tells us that a Kerberos configuration file was automatically generated and is ready for the utilization of our domain. We received this message: `Upgrade from Samba 3 to Samba 4 OK`. So, we have copied the Kerberos file to its definitive location.

Editing the Samba 4 configuration file

Now we need to edit the Samba 4 configuration file that was automatically created for us by the `samba-tool` utility, and add the following lines to the global section:

```
(/usr/local/samba/etc/smb.conf):
        interfaces = lo,eth1
        bind interfaces only = Yes
        dns forwarder = 8.8.8.8
```

The first two lines of the previous command specify the interfaces in which we want the Samba 4 Server to listen (in our case, the loopback and `eth1` interfaces; adapt it accordingly to your needs), and in the last line, we added a DNS forwarder configuration to be used for our internal network (Microsoft Windows clients and servers) to resolve names that are not the responsibility of our local DNS Server (for example, not in `poa.msdcbrz.eall.com.br zone`). In a real world, you will need to replace the preceding example's IP address (for example, `8.8.8.8`) with the right IP address of the DNS resolver of your network.

We need to make sure that the NTP Server is configured to signed updates, so basically, we need to have the following lines at the end of our `/etc/ntp.conf` file:

```
ntpsigndsocket /usr/local/samba/var/lib/ntp_signd/
restrict default mssntp
```

Let's restart our NTP Server:

```
root@pdc:~# /etc/init.d/ntp restart
[ ok ] Stopping NTP server: ntpd.
[ ok ] Starting NTP server: ntpd.
root@pdc:~#
```

We need to copy the scripts that we have on the `netlogon` standard share to their new location in our Samba 4 installation:

```
root@pdc:~# cp -pRf /var/lib/samba/netlogon/scripts/* /usr/local/samba/
var/locks/sysvol/poa.msdcbrz.eall.com.br/scripts/ /&& echo OK
OK
root@pdc:~#
```

The preceding result `OK` is the signal that we have finished upgrading Samba 3 from the Primary Domain Controller's perspective, but we have not finished our work on the PDC server just yet as we still have to migrate the DNS Services to the Samba 4 Server. The `samba-tool` utility should have already created all the needed SRV and other DNS basic records for a proper Active Directory installation, but it does not know about some static contents that we may have on our DNS Services for servers and services such as e-mail, pop, and www. So, we can now stop the Bind9, start the Samba 4 services, and execute the following script just by passing the database file for our DNS Server, and it should populate our Samba 4 internal DNS with the missing entries:

```
root@pdc:~# /etc/init.d/bind9 stop
[....] Stopping domain name service...: bind9
waiting for pid 2220 to die
. ok
root@pdc:~# chmod -x /etc/init.d/bind9 && echo OK
OK
root@pdc:~# /usr/local/samba/sbin/samba && echo "Samba 4 Started OK"
Samba 4 Started OK
root@pdc:~# kinit && echo OK
Password for root@POA.MSDCBRZ.EALL.COM.BR:
OK
root@pdc:~# grep -w 'A\|CNAME' /var/lib/bind/db.poa | |\
awk '{print "samba-tool dns add pdc poa.msdcbrz.eall.com.br", \
$1, $2, $NF}' | /bin/sh
Record added successfully
...
root@pdc:~#
```

After the confirmation of the initialization of the Samba 4 Server and each successful entry creation on our Samba 4 DNS Server's database, we should have our static `CNAME` and the records from our BIND9 configuration added to the Samba 4 built-in DNS Server. If some record already exists in the Samba 4 database, it is not an issue as the command will indicate that and will not duplicate it. One last record that needs to be created by hand, if needed, is the MX:

```
root@pdc:~# samba-tool dns add 192.168.1.1 poa.msdcbrz.eall.com.br @ mx
"mail.poa.msdcbrz.eall.com.br 10"
Password for [root@POA.MSDCBRZ.EALL.COM.BR]:
Record added successfully
root@pdc:~#
```

Configuring the reverse zone

With our DNS main zone configured and populated with the static records, we just need to create and add the records for the reverse zone. For that, we just need to execute the following commands at the `pdc` server:

```
root@pdc:~# samba-tool dns zonecreate 192.168.1.1 \
1.168.192.in-addr.arpa -U Administrator%'w1ndow$$!'
Zone 1.168.192.in-addr.arpa created successfully
root@pdc:~#
```

The reverse zone is created, but remember that you will need to replace the network (for example, `1.168.192.in-addr.arpa`) with the real network in your environment. Just as an example, if your network is `10.10.2.0/24`, you would use `2.10.10.in-addr.arpa` instead. Now, to create the PTR records for our hosts, we can use the next script to do the dirty work for us. We are providing the password in the script, so all the records are created without an interaction:

```
root@pdc:~# grep -w 'A' /var/lib/bind/db.poa | |\
awk '{split($3,IP,/\./); print "samba-tool dns add pdc \
1.168.192.in-addr.arpa",IP[4], ],"PTR",$1".poa.msdcbrz.eall.com.br \
-U \x27Administrator%w1ndow$$!\x27"}' | /bin/sh
Record added successfully
Record added successfully
...
root@pdc:~#
```

> Remember the security policies, and as a general rule, it is not a good idea to have passwords in scripts or commands that will be saved on the history file.

Adding the profiles share to the configuration

Now, we can add the `Profiles` share to our Active Directory Domain Controller, which is the only share our PDC is providing to the network. For this, we only need to edit our `/usr/local/samba/etc/smb.conf` file and add the following lines (copied from the Samba 3's `smb.conf` file):

```
[Profiles]
comment = EALL Roaming Profiles Share
path = /home/POA
```

```
read only = No
```

As we have edited our main configuration file, we need to reload it, and so we can bring back online our eth0 interface:

```
root@pdc:~# smbcontrol all reload-config && echo OK
OK
root@pdc:~# ifup eth0 && echo OK
OK
root@pdc:~#
```

Welcome to our brand new Samba 4 Active Directory Domain Controller!

Deciding the upgrade approach for Member Servers

At this time, we can go to the next topic's upgrade tests and validations for the PDC and execute all the checks that have been described until this phase of the procedure. The main services for our Active Directory Network must be fully functional (for example, users, groups, and machines). In case we found any issues that we can fix, rollback before going to the other servers (for example, file/print servers).

After we have confirmed that the right services are working up to this point and as our services are decoupled sufficiently, we have two options for each Domain Member Server at this point:

- Move forward and upgrade them both as and when our maintenance window permits
- Perform just a quick reconfiguration on the Samba 3 Servers (for example, join it to the Active Directory Domain), and continue their upgrade at another opportunity

> For the Domain Member Servers, we should not have any problems if we leave the `smbd/nmbd` daemons running as our PDC should be unconnected from our network. However, it is a good practice to have the Samba 3 services (for example, `smbd/nmbd` and `winbindd`) stopped, and after we finish the upgrade or reconfiguration, we start the services again. However, remember that the Microsoft Windows machines must not contact the new AD before we have everything tested and are sure that a successful upgrade is confirmed.

In both options, all the services will still be working as usual. However, as the reconfiguration of the Samba 3 is quicker than Samba 4, it can be one good option for network environments where many servers need to be upgraded and do not fit in just one maintenance window (the staged upgrade that we mentioned earlier).

Let's use our two Domain Member Servers and exemplify an upgrade to Samba 4 in one and the integration of the Samba 3 to our new Active Directory on the other. We will show you the second option first, and we will use the `ACCSRV01` server for that. Let's edit the Samba 3 Server's configuration file, change the security option, and add the realm for our Domain:

```
[global]
...
Security = ads
realm = POA.MSDCBRZ.EALL.COM.BR
```

Notice that the security option was already present on our `smb.conf` file for our Samba 3 installation, so we just needed to change it to `ads` (earlier, it was domain) and add the realm directive to it. Now let's use the same Kerberos file that the Samba tool has created for us in the PDC upgrade process (`/etc/krb5.conf`):

```
[libdefaults]
        default_realm = POA.MSDCBRZ.EALL.COM.BR
        dns_lookup_realm = false
        dns_lookup_kdc = true
```

Now, on a shell at the `ACCSRV01` server, execute the following command:

```
root@accsrv01:~# net ads join -U administrator -S pdc
Using short domain name -- POA
Joined 'ACCSRV01' to realm 'poa.msdcbrz.eall.com.br'
DNS Update for accsrv01.poa.msdcbrz.eall.com.br failed: ERROR_DNS_UPDATE_
FAILED
DNS update failed!
root@accsrv01:~# /etc/init.d/winbind start
[ ok ] Starting the Winbind daemon: winbind.
root@accsrv01:~# /etc/init.d/samba start
[ ok ] Starting Samba daemons: nmbd smbd.
```

From now on, our old friend, Samba 3, is up and running and ready to continue to provide the file/print services for our Active Directory network, as always. The error about the DNS update is because the `ACCSRV01` server is already registered on our Active Directory Domain Controller's DNS. So, our users can now log in to the Domain (PDC) and access the shares and use the print services from this server, as usual.

At this point, we can go to the next topic, which is *Upgrade tests and validations for Member Servers*, and execute the tests for this phase—listing and using the shares/printers, using some desktop to browse the `ACCSRV01` server, and so on. As we finish the validations (and if everything is fine), we can go back to this topic and continue to the next and final step of upgrading the `DEVSRV01` Domain Member Server to Samba 4.

In *Chapter 3, Managing the Samba Active Directory Server*, we have an example of the configuration of a Domain Member Server where the Debian GNU/Linux are authenticated and integrated on our Active Directory Domain. We can refer to this chapter if we need a similar solution, but here, we will show you a quick configuration to have our `DEVSRV01` file/print server up and running in the same scenario as before, taking into account that in the EALL network, the GNU/Linux host is administrated with the users who are not getting authenticated on the Samba's Domain.

First, we need to create a minimal Samba 4 configuration file for the Domain Member Server function (`/usr/local/samba/etc/smb.conf`):

```
[global]
workgroup = POA
netbios name = DEVSRV01
server string = DEV Office Server
security = ads
realm = POA.MSDCBRZ.EALL.COM.BR
encrypt passwords = true
winbind use default domain = Yes
winbind enum users = yes
winbind enum groups = yes
```

> Remember to match the `idmap` configuration that comes in ranges for your Samba 3 installation. We can add other environments' specific global configuration from Samba 3 that we want to maintain on our Samba 4 installation (for example, log file, bind interfaces, and so on).

We want to add our `idmap` configuration and shares from Samba 3 too:

```
idmap config *:backend  = rid
idmap config *:range = 1000-20000
[DEVCODDS]
comment = DEV COD DS
path = /var/lib/samba/devcodds
read only = No
```

```
valid users = @"POA\Domain Admins"
browseable = Yes

[DEVSRCAP]
comment = DEV SRC AP
path = /var/lib/samba/devsrcap
read only = No
valid users = @"POA\Devel Group"
browseable = Yes

[PRINTERS]
Comment = DEV Dep. Printers
path = /var/spool/samba
Printable = yes
Printing = CUPS

[DEVPRT01]
comment = General DEV Printer
Printer Name = devprt01
path = /var/spool/samba/
printable = yes
browseable = yes
```

Let's copy our Kerberos configuration file to `/etc/krb5.conf`:

```
[libdefaults]
        default_realm = POA.MSDCBRZ.EALL.COM.BR
        dns_lookup_realm = false
        dns_lookup_kdc = true
```

As we have our new Samba 4 and Kerberos configuration files in place, we just need to issue the following commands at the `DEVSRV01` server:

```
root@devsrv01:~# export PATH=/usr/local/samba/sbin:\
/usr/local/samba/bin:$PATH
root@devsrv01:~# net ads join -U administrator
Enter administrator's password:
Using short domain name -- POA
Joined 'DEVSRV01' to dns domain 'poa.msdcbrz.eall.com.br'
```

```
DNS Update for devsrv01.poa.msdcbrz.eall.com.br failed: ERROR_DNS_UPDATE_
FAILED
DNS update failed: NT_STATUS_UNSUCCESSFUL
```

Now, we have our second Domain Member Server upgraded to the Samba 4 software release! The error about the DNS update is the same as our previous one when configuring the `ACCSRV01` server (the DNS entry already exists).As we are working with a 64-bit system, we should use the following commands to configure the Debian NSS libraries to our system:

```
root@devsrv01:~# cd /lib/x86_64-linux-gnu && &&\
mv libnss_winbind.so.2{,-old} && }&&\
ln -s /usr/local/samba/lib/libnss_winbind.so.2 && &&\
ln -s slibnss_winbind.so.2 2libnss_winbind.so && cd && echo OK
OK
root@devsrv01:~#
```

The last step is to start the winbind and Samba daemons (notice that for a Samba 4 member server, we do not start the Samba Server, but we have the specific daemons instead):

```
root@devsrv01:~# winbindd && echo "Winbind Started OK"
Winbind Started OK
root@devsrv01:~# smbd && nmbd && echo "Samba Daemons Started OK"
Samba Daemons Started OK
root@devsrv01:~#
```

The next step is to execute all the tests and validations for the file/print servers in the same way as we did for the `ACCSRV01` server, and if we do not have any failures, our upgrade procedure plan and execution is validated. It's important to keep in mind that the quality of our upgrade process is highly dependent on the quality of our tests and validations, so every test and check that we can add to our validation's kit is welcome!

Upgrading tests and validations for the PDC

As our upgrade procedure started with the PDC (now the Active Directory Domain Controller for our Domain), we need to test and validate it after we have upgraded the PDC server as follows:

```
root@pdc:~# wbinfo -u | wc -l
54
root@pdc:~#
```

From the preceding output, we can see, based on our upgrade plan, that the number of users are diverging (51 before the upgrade and 54 now). So, let's save the user list in one file and use the `diff` command to see what these differences really are:

```
root@pdc:~# wbinfo -u | sort > samba4users.txt && echo OK
OK
root@pdc:~# diff samba3users.txt samba4users.txt
0a1
> Administrator
12a14
> Guest
23a26
> krbtgt
```

No problem at all. The three users are the default users from the new Samba 4 installation: `Administrator`, `Guest`, and `krbtgt`. Let's take a look at our groups:

```
root@pdc:~# wbinfo -g | wc -l
16
root@pdc:~#
```

Again, we have a different number of objects in comparison to the environment before the upgrade, so let's identify what exactly these differences are:

```
root@pdc:~# wbinfo -g | sort > samba4groups.txt && echo OK
OK
root@pdc:~# diff -Naur samba3groups.txt samba4groups.txt
--- samba3groups.txt    2013-08-31 19:52:21.917725440 -0300
+++ samba4groups.txt    2013-08-31 20:15:30.262715229 -0300
@@ -1,5 +1,16 @@
-accdivision group
-devel group
-domain admins
-domain users
-eall group
+Accdivision Group
+Devel Group
+DnsUpdateProxy
+Domain Admins
+Domain Computers
```

```
+Domain Controllers
+Domain Guests
+Domain Users
+EALL Domain Admins
+EALL Domain Users
+EALL Group
+Enterprise Admins
+Enterprise Read-Only Domain Controllers
+Group Policy Creator Owners
+Read-Only Domain Controllers
+Schema Admins
```

> We can use the `comm` utility to perform a comparison between files. Take a look at `man comm` for the options and to learn how to interpret the output.

Again, the only groups that are different on both the files are the new ones created by the new Samba 4 software version. Looking closely, we can see that the two groups that we renamed are present in the list because we have saved the file before we renamed them. Other minor differences are there because of the capital letters changed on Samba 4 (for example, Domain Admins). We can now use the `smbclient` utility to execute a bunch of minor validations on our new Active Directory Domain Controller server:

```
root@pdc:/root# smbclient -L pdc -U 'frorange%w1ndow$$'
Domain=[POA] OS=[Unix] Server=[Samba 4.0.9]

        Sharename       Type      Comment
        ---------       ----      -------
        netlogon        Disk
        sysvol          Disk
        Profiles        Disk      EALL Roaming Profiles Share
        IPC$            IPC       IPC Service (Samba 4.0.9)
Domain=[POA] OS=[Unix] Server=[Samba 4.0.9]

        Server               Comment
        ---------            -------
        Workgroup            Master
        ---------            -------
```

Based on the preceding output, we can see that our server was upgraded from Samba 3.6.6 to Samba 4.0.9, the authentication is working for our test user, and we have the Profiles share available. With a simple script, we can validate our user's database:

```
root@pdc:~# for x in `wbinfo -u`; do wbinfo --name-to-sid $x; done
...
S-1-5-21-1214754503-652539266-1573105461-1047 SID_USER (1)
S-1-5-21-1214754503-652539266-1573105461-1048 SID_USER (1)
S-1-5-21-1214754503-652539266-1573105461-1049 SID_USER (1)
S-1-5-21-1214754503-652539266-1573105461-1055 SID_USER (1)
root@pdc:~#
```

Before we proceed to the final tests of our Active Directory Domain Controller (for example, add a machine to the domain, log in, create users, and so on), let's see if the DNS services are working as they should, and all the records that we need are configured properly:

```
root@pdc:~# host -t SRV _ldap._tcp.poa.msdcbrz.eall.com.br.
_ldap._tcp.poa.msdcbrz.eall.com.br has SRV record 0 100 389 pdc.poa.
msdcbrz.eall.com.br.
root@pdc:~# host -t SRV _kerberos._tcp.poa.msdcbrz.eall.com.br.
_kerberos._tcp.poa.msdcbrz.eall.com.br has SRV record 0 100 88 pdc.poa.
msdcbrz.eall.com.br.
root@pdc:~# host -t CNAME `ldbsearch -H \
/usr/local/samba/private/sam.ldb '(invocationid=*)' \
--cross-ncs objectguid | grep objectGUID | \
 awk '{print $2}'`._msdcs.poa.msdcbrz.eall.com.br.
2319316b-e10b-4568-b3e8-13735c9d6bd9._msdcs.poa.msdcbrz.eall.com.br is an
alias for pdc.poa.msdcbrz.eall.com.br.
root@pdc:~#
```

Now, we can take a look at the specific commands for the `samba-tool` utility to query and verify our Samba's internal DNS server. First, execute the following command:

```
root@pdc:~# samba-tool dns serverinfo pdc \
-U 'Administrator-U'Administrator%w1ndow$$!' | grep psz
pszServerName                : PDC.poa.msdcbrz.eall.com.br
pszDsContainer               : CN=MicrosoftDNS,DC=DomainDnsZones,\
DC=poa,DC=msdcbrz,DC=eall,DC=com,DC=br
pszDomainName                : poa.msdcbrz.eall.com.br
```

```
pszForestName                   : poa.msdcbrz.eall.com.br
pszDomainDirectoryPartition : DC=DomainDnsZones,DC=poa,DC=msdcbrz,\
DC=eall,DC=com,DC=br
pszForestDirectoryPartition : DC=ForestDnsZones,DC=poa,DC=msdcbrz,\
DC=eall,DC=com,DC=br
root@pdc:~#
```

The preceding output is very important and gives us a good overview of the DNS configuration. Using the `samba-tool` utility, we can get another good insight into our Samba DNS configuration and the records that are registered, so we can list the entries for our zone as follows:

```
root@pdc:~# samba-tool dns query pdc pdcpoa.msdcbrz.eall.com.br @ ALL -U
'Administrator%w1ndow$$!'
  Name=, Records=5, Children=0
    SOA: serial=9, refresh=900, retry=600, expire=86400, ns=pdc.
    poa.msdcbrz.eall.com.br., email=hostmaster.poa.msdcbrz.eall.com.br.
    (flags=600000f0, serial=9, ttl=3600)
    NS: pdc.poa.msdcbrz.eall.com.br. (flags=600000f0, serial=1, ttl=900)
    A: 192.168.1.1 (flags=600000f0, serial=1, ttl=900)
    AAAA: 0000:0000:0000:0000:0000:0000:0000:0001 (flags=600000f0,
    serial=110, ttl=900)
    MX: mail.poa.msdcbrz.eall.com.br. (10) (flags=600000f0, serial=9,
    ttl=900)
  Name=_msdcs, Records=0, Children=0
  Name=_sites, Records=0, Children=1…
root@pdc:~#
```

The preceding output can be very long, as it will depend on how many entries we had on our DNS server (hosts, aliases, and so on). We can use the `samba-tool` utility to show general information and list our entries for the DNS reverse zone too:

```
root@pdc:~# samba-tool dns zonelist pdc --reverse \
-U 'Administrator-U'Administrator%w1ndow$$!'
  1 zone(s) found
pszZoneName: 1.168.192.in-addr.arpa
Flags       : DNS_RPC_ZONE_DSINTEGRATED DNS_RPC_ZONE_UPDATE_SECURE
ZoneType    : DNS_ZONE_TYPE_PRIMARY
Version     : 50
dwDpFlags   : DNS_DP_AUTOCREATED DNS_DP_DOMAIN_DEFAULT DNS_DP_ENLISTED
pszDpFqdn   : DomainDnsZones.poa.msdcbrz.eall.com.br
root@pdc:~#
```

Here is how we can use `samba-tool` to list our reverse zone entries:

```
root@pdc:~# samba-tool dns query pdc 1.168.192.in-addr.arpa \
@ ALL -U 'Administrator%w1ndow$$!'
Name=, Records=2, Children=0
  SOA: serial=6, refresh=900, retry=600, expire=86400, ns=pdc.poa.
  msdcbrz.eall.com.br., email=hostmaster.poa.msdcbrz.eall.com.br.
  (flags=600000f0, serial=6, ttl=3600)
  NS: pdc.poa.msdcbrz.eall.com.br. (flags=600000f0, serial=1, ttl=0)
Name=1, Records=1, Children=0
  PTR: pdc.poa.msdcbrz.eall.com.br (flags=f0, serial=4, ttl=0)
Name=10, Records=1, Children=0
  PTR: WINDOWS2K3.poa.msdcbrz.eall.com.br (flags=f0, serial=5, ttl=0)
Name=11, Records=1, Children=0
  PTR: windowsxp.poa.msdcbrz.eall.com.br (flags=f0, serial=6, ttl=0)
Name=5, Records=1, Children=0
...
root@pdc:~#
```

We can use the `net` command to give us other important information about our Active Directory Services:

```
root@pdc:~# net ads info
LDAP server: 192.168.1.1
LDAP server name: pdc.poa.msdcbrz.eall.com.br
Realm: POA.MSDCBRZ.EALL.COM.BR
Bind Path: dc=POA,dc=MSDCBRZ,dc=EALL,dc=COM,dc=BR
LDAP port: 389
Server time: Qui, 29 Ago 2013 16:30:50 BRT
KDC server: 192.168.1.1
Server time offset: 0
root@pdc:~#
```

With all the preceding tests passed, we can pick a Microsoft Windows machine (for example, 2003 or XP) and try to add it to the Active Directory Domain, and as we already have tested the authentication for test users, we can validate the login from the new joined machine. It's important to test a Microsoft Windows machine that was already in the domain too, and see if the machine will work as usual. Everything must work as if we had not executed any upgrade. After this point, we can go back to the upgrade procedure (the previous topic) to continue upgrading the Domain Member Servers.

Upgrading tests and validations for Member Servers

To validate the upgrade process for our Domain Member Servers, we need to test the file/print shares. The same tests that we will execute here for one file/print server must be executed for all the file/print servers that we have in our environment. So, in our example scenario, we have two Domain Member servers on the EALL POA network, so we need to execute the following tests twice.

First, we need to make sure that we are able to list the users:

```
root@pdc:~# wbinfo -u
...
wiwolf
zisala
joliu
...
root@pdc:~#
```

And groups:

```
root@pdc:~# wbinfo -g
allowed rodc password replication group
enterprise read-only domain controllers
denied rodc password replication group
read-only domain controllers
...
root@pdc:~#
```

The preceding output is something that is pretty familiar to us, as we already know that Samba 4 has some default Active Directory groups and users, and we have performed the tests and validations of the users and groups when we were validating the upgrade at the PDC phase. So, we just need to make sure that the Domain Members could list the Domain users and groups. We need to confirm that the users' issues are being resolved and the name service switch is working as it should. Take a look at the following command execution:

```
root@devsrv01:~# id djfox
uid=2031(djfox) gid=1513(domain users) grupos=1513(domain users),\
2051(eall domain users),2053(devel group)
root@devsrv01:~# getent passwd djfox
```

```
djfox:*:2031:1513:djfox:/home/POA/djfox:/bin/false
root@devsrv01:~#
```

Using `smbclient`, we can get all sort of information that we are used to, and we will be able to see the new Samba version and test the authentication when directly accessing the file/print servers:

```
root@accsrv01:~# smbclient -L accsrv01 -U 'cafreeman%w1ndow$$'
Domain=[POA] OS=[Unix] Server=[Samba 3.6.6]

    Sharename       Type      Comment
    ---------       ----      -------
   ---------       ----      -------
ACCPRTMM01      Printer   1F Printer MM
   ACCPRTLS01      Printer   2F Printer
   PRINT$          Disk      Drivers for Dep. Printers
   ACCPUBLIC       Disk      Public Share
   ACCDIVDOCS      Disk      Accdivision Prospects
   ACCDIVRPTS      Disk      Accdivision Reports
   IPC$            IPC       IPC Service (ACCDivision Office Server)
Domain=[POA] OS=[Unix] Server=[Samba 3.6.6]
    Server               Comment
    ---------            -------
    ---------            -------
ACCSRV01             ACCDivision Office Server

    Workgroup            Master
    ---------            -------
    ---------            -------
POA                  ACCSRV01
root@accsrv01:~
```

Notice that the Samba version will still be 3.6.6 for our upgrade procedure of the `ACCSRV01` output that we got previously as we had not upgraded this server. When testing the `DEVSRV01` server, we should see a different Samba version (for example, 4.0.9).

Using one of the Microsoft Windows machines that are already in the domain, let's perform some print and file share tests, creating two files—one in the `ACCSRV01` server and the other on the `DEVSRV01` server. We will use a test user that has access to the shares on both the servers; use one file to print in at least one printer in each server. After we have logged in to our Microsoft Windows 2003 test machine, we navigate to the network's share and see something similar to the following screenshot:

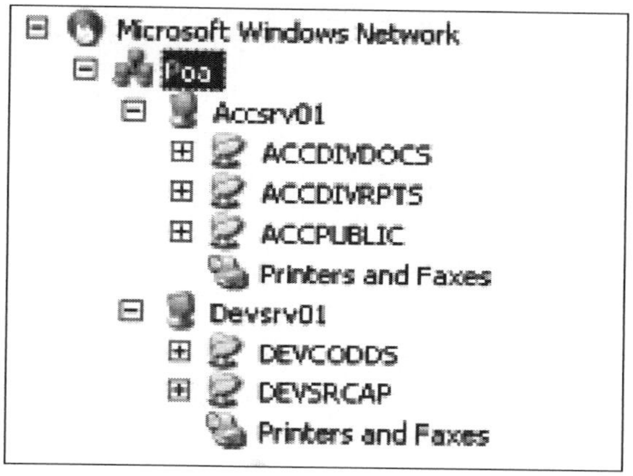

So, we just need to create a file on one folder of each file/print server and send it to at least one printer in each server (for example, `ACCSRV01` and `DEVSRV01`). After this, we can change our desktop background, for example, and log in to another machine to validate that our roaming profiles are working fine, so we can finish our upgrade and welcome our users to the brand new EALL's Active Directory Domain.

> After everything is checked, we can remove the old Samba 3 Server installation: `apt-get` removes Samba `winbind`.

Summary

In this chapter, we learned about the main difference between the Samba Server Version 3 and 4, how to plan and execute an upgrade procedure of the Samba Server, and a step-by-step process to test and validate the upgrade as well. Using the command-line examples and scripts, we showed you how to gather important information from the Samba 3 environment and how to use that information to compare it with the upgraded system and be sure that the transition from Samba 3 to 4 was successful.

A very detailed Samba 3 example scenario was presented with three Samba 3 Servers playing different roles on the network. So, we showed you how to execute a staged upgrade, discussing the benefits of having different servers for different sets of services and providing flexibility to manage the maintenance window, which is very useful for real use cases.

In the next chapter, we will learn about the file and print service capabilities of the Samba 4 Server, and we will discuss some differences between file and print services from Versions 3 and 4 as well as Microsoft Point and Print feature, print drivers versions, and so on.

6
Printing and File Services

This chapter will cover the file and printing services for the Samba 4 Server; we will discuss some differences between the file and printing capabilities of Samba Server Versions 3 and 4.

In this chapter, we will cover the following topics:

- **SMB/CIFS (Common Internet File System)** protocol versions and Samba 4
- Samba 4 file and print server daemons
- Microsoft Windows print driver Versions 3 and 4
- Configuring a printer on the Samba 4 Server host using CUPS
- Sharing the printer on a Microsoft AD network using Samba
- Microsoft Windows Point and Print Samba Server configuration
- File sharing with Samba 4

Introducing SMB/CIFS protocol versions and Samba 4

Starting from the first release of the Samba Server Version 4 (4.0.0), the software now supports the SMB file that serves the protocol Version 2.1 of Microsoft; it also provides preliminary support for the SMB protocol Version 3.0 [18]. The SMBv2.1 has been a great achievement for the Samba project since the introduction of the SMBv2.0 on Samba Version 3.6. Major improvements that Version 2.1 brings, as compared to Version 2.0 (from the Microsoft announcement), are mainly performance enhancements [19], listed as follows:

- Client oplock leasing model
- Large MTU support

- Improved energy efficiency for client computers
- Support for previous versions of SMB

> You can read more about the changes between the protocol Versions 2.0 and 2.1 and more about each individual feature at the official Microsoft reference [19]: `http://technet.microsoft.com/en-us/library/ff625695%28v=ws.10%29.aspx`

The official Samba 4 release announcement has some important information about the continuous development towards the protocol SMB Version 3.0, which is a major version improvement with many new features. From the Microsoft support site, we can get a glimpse of the following features [20]:

- SMB Transparent Failover
- SMB Scale Out
- SMB Multichannel
- SMB Direct
- SMB Encryption
- VSS for SMB file shares
- SMB Directory Leasing
- SMB PowerShell

The reference [20] has great information about each of the preceding features, and the reader will understand why we really need to keep an eye on the development of the Samba 4 software and future 4.x releases.

Introducing the Samba 4 file and print server daemons

Prior to the beta2 release version of the Samba 4 software, the project was mainly investing the new `NTVFS` file server daemon [16]. However, the first stable release of Samba 4 used the old and very stable `smbd` daemon to act as the default file server for the brand new version of Samba 4.0.0.

The release notes, dated December 11, 2012, state that the project will still support and provide continued development on the new `NTVFS` file server to guarantee support to the users who are exploring this new daemon already (for example, the early adopters of the Samba 4 alpha releases).

The new NT-FSA architecture is planned to be the default architecture in the future as it is architected to match the requirements of the new Active Directory Domain Controller model. So, the `smbd` daemon should be replaced as the default Samba's file server in the long term [16] (presently, `smbd` is still the recommended file server).

> Here is a very good thread about **NTVFS vs S3 file server** from December 8, 2011. The following link is a response from Stefan Metzmacher (from `http://www.samba.org/`), which provides us with a great overview about the development process and also tells us how these file servers and daemons were being architected:
>
> `https://lists.samba.org/archive/samba-technical/2011-December/080784.html`

To follow the development process and to keep up to date with the features that are being integrated and tested on the Samba project, it is highly recommended that the reader participate in the mailing lists of the project. These are the best places to discuss the features, get help, learn about different configuration scenarios, and get in touch with the actual developers of the project as they are always present and willing to help.

Some of the mailing lists I would recommend for the reader to participate are as follows (`https://lists.samba.org`):

List	Description
samba	General questions regarding Samba
samba-announce	Low volume list for Samba announcements
cifs-protocol	Discussions on the CIFS and related protocol
samba-technical	Discussions on Samba internals

Just remember to take a look at the archives of the list before posting new threads that might have been answered already, and also remember to post them on the "right" list (for example, basic and general Samba questions should not be directed to the samba-technical mailing list).

Introducing Microsoft Windows print driver Versions 3 and 4

Basically, there are two types of print drivers: **kernel mode** and **user mode** [23]. To understand the different Microsoft Windows print drivers and how these two types of drivers impact the end user, we need to go back to the **Microsoft Operating System (OS)** history and talk a bit about the Microsoft Windows NT 4.0. People who had used the Microsoft OS might remember that printing was a task that could really bring the whole OS down just because of a printer driver failure. That's because NT 4.0 supported just the kernel-mode printer drivers [23], which ran on a privileged operating mode, so due to the failure, these drivers could hang the whole OS (these kinds of drivers are the ones that are there in Version 2).

Starting with Microsoft Windows 2000, a new Version 3 printer driver was introduced, and that printer driver ran on the user mode. The difference is that when running the printer driver on the user mode the error or bug on these drivers will not impact the OS itself, but will be like an ordinary application with very limited impact. Before Vista, this OS version from Microsoft and some others provided support for both types of printer drivers in the compatibility mode [23].

From Microsoft Windows Server 2012 and Microsoft Windows 8 OS onwards, a new printer driver model was designed—Version 4. This new model was architected to improve and fix the known issues with the previous Version 3 driver model [21].

The new Version 4 driver motivations were around a new design consideration for applications present on the Windows store were easier for printer sharing and driver development [21]. Samba 4 does not have support for this new printer driver model yet, but it supports Version 3 as all the other Microsoft Windows OS versions prior to the ones cited earlier, and the ones that are higher than Microsoft Windows 2000, also support this printer driver model.

Configuring a printer on the Samba 4 Server host using CUPS

The first important point to consider here is the fact that we will be configuring Samba to act as a print server for our Active Directory Network. So, we will configure Samba as a print server for the network, but at the backend, we have the **Common UNIX Printing System (CUPS)** software that uses the **Internet Printing Protocol (IPP)** to support printing to local and network printers [22]. Thus, we can look at this as Samba acting as a print server that uses CUPS as the backend spooling and printer management system. Or, we can look at this as a print server that provides CUPS print services to a Microsoft Network through Samba. Either way, this is a rock solid combination!

Another important fact to understand is that there are other printer management software (for example, LPD or LPRng), and Samba can be configured with those systems. As this is a practical book and CUPS is the standard and most prevalent software in many GNU/Linux and in many other OS distributions, we choose to work and show you example configurations with this printing system. We will not cover all the procedures to install and configure a CUPS server as this is out of the scope of this book; but, we will show you how to perform some tasks and, more importantly, how to integrate the CUPS system and configure it with Samba as a print server.

> The official CUPS site has a lot of documents and examples, which can be found at `http://www.cups.org`

The final advice, before we start, is that the compilation of Samba 4 needs to have the CUPS libraries enabled. If you have followed our instructions on the installation of the dependencies and the Samba 4 compilation in this book, Samba should identify the presence of the required header and libraries for the CUPS printing system, and everything should be in place and ready to go.

Our procedure will show you how to make the printer drivers available for our Microsoft Windows network, and thus, each Windows machine that needs to print, will have the option to install the right driver (for the right OS architecture), do all the rendering, and control the format of the print job. When adding a printer to CUPS (actually a "queue"), we need to choose between a raw queue and a filtered one. We can have several queues for the same printer. So, if we need a filtered queue, we can have it. However, we need a raw queue for our Microsoft Windows machines for which we will provide the print services. As we said earlier, the Windows clients will use the specific printer driver and send a rendered job.

There are two options to add a printer queue to a CUPS system using the command line or the Web interface. In the case of a network printer, based on the protocol supported by the printer (for example, AppSocket, IPP, or LPD), we could add a printer queue by issuing the following command on our Samba 4 Server (from CUPS 1.7 documentation):

```
root@debian7:~# lpadmin -p devprt01 -v ipp://10.11.11.1 -L "Devel 001
  PS/Gen 2nd Floor" -E && echo OK
OK
root@debian7:~#
```

> To do the same configuration using the Web interface, we will use the following URL: `http://debian7:631/admin`

The preceding command has used the following four options (`lpadmin`):

- `-p`: This option defines the destination, named printer, or class
- `-E`: This option will enable the printer (queue) to accept jobs
- `-v`: This option sets the device URI for the new printer queue
- `-L`: This option defines the location (note that it is not a description, but it's intended to provide information about the physical location of the printer)

It is very important to note that the `-E` option, when used before the options `-d`, `-p`, or `-x`, forces encryption while connecting to the print/server. So, we need to pay attention to the position of this `lpadmin` option, it is a good practice to use it at the end to enable the queue at the time of the creation.

Now, we can use the following `lpstat` command to list our printers and see if our new printer is listed and our CUPS is aware of it:

```
root@debian7:~# lpstat -p devprt01
printer devprt01 is idle.  enabled since Dom 26 May 2013 16:06:01 BRT
root@debian7:~#
```

Just before starting the configuration of Samba and actually making this new printer available on the network, it is a good idea to test it and see if everything is working, from our CUPS backend to the printer. As we will not test any filter- or driver-related features at this time, we just want to test the connectivity and check that our CUPS server and printer are working fine, and we can use a PS or text file to send to the `devprt01` printer. From a shell on our server, we can use the System V command `lp` or the Berkeley `lpr` utility to send a test page to our printer [25], shown as follows:

```
root@debian7:~# lpr -P devprt01 simpletestpage.txt && echo OK
OK
root@debian7:~#
```

The preceding command has used the `lpr` utility to send the `simpletestpage.txt` file to the `devprt01` printer, so we can be sure that the printer is configured and is working fine with our CUPS server. If the file is printed `OK`, we can go to the next step and work on the configuration of the Samba 4 Server, but in case of any issues, we need to check our CUPS configuration and the network connectivity before proceeding further.

> The `simpletestpage.txt` file is just a very simple text file and can be created as follows:
>
> **echo test > simpletestpage.txt**

Sharing the printer on a Microsoft AD network using Samba

The main directive that we need to have in our Samba 4 configuration file to start configuring it as a print server is the **printers** share. Thus, we need to add a section to our `smb.conf` (for example, `/usr/local/samba/etc/smb.conf`) file as shown in the following code:

```
...
[PRINTERS]
    Comment = DEV Dep. Printers
    path = /var/spool/samba
    Printable = yes
    Printing = CUPS
```

> The `/var/spool/samba` directory should already be created, but if it is not created, we just need to create it and set the right permissions. Remember that you are required to set the sticky bit on the printing spool directory: `chmod 1777 /var/spool/samba`.

The preceding configuration is all we need for the Samba 4 Server to have access to our CUPS server's backend. The comment line is optional, but it is a good source of information for the clients and even system administrators. After adding the general `[PRINTERS]` share, we can add as many printers to our Active Directory network as we plan to share, and we can add them one by one in our `smb.conf` file.

Now, let's add the printer that we have previously configured in our CUPS server to our `smb.conf` file. For this, we just need to create a share with the `Printer Name` value that has the same name as our CUPS queue that we created and indicate the path for our Samba's spool:

```
[DEVPRT01]
    comment = General DEV Printer
    Printer Name = devprt01
    path = /var/spool/samba/
    printable = yes
    browseable = yes
```

After this, we can reload our Samba configuration and make our brand new printer configuration live and available on our network. As a root user, type the following command in a shell on the `debian7` Samba 4 Server:

```
root@debian7:/home/leal# smbcontrol all reload-config && echo OK
OK
```

root@debian7:/home/leal#

From now on, we will have a printer named `devprt01` available on our network, and we can proceed to the configuration of our Point and Print feature, so the clients can automatically download and install the right driver and start using the print services.

Introducing Microsoft Windows Point and Print Samba Server configuration

Microsoft has a **Point and Print** feature [23] in the print subsystem of Microsoft Windows 2000 onwards. This technology enables the users on Microsoft client machines to actually send print jobs to remote printers without the need to manually install each printer driver to every new printer that is available on the network for him or her to use. This itself is a great functionality, but another important feature of the Point and Print technology is that it handles the installation of different drivers for different operating systems and architectures (for example, 32 bits or 64 bits). With the right user credentials, configuration can be made on these without explicit administrator intervention.

To start using this technology and provide this functionality to our Active Directory Domain, we first need to have a specific share on our Samba configuration to hold these drivers. The share name is fixed as the client machines will search for it, and for that reason, we need to configure it with this exact name [24]: `print$`.

> To be able to use the Point and Print feature with different processor architectures, the appropriate driver needs to be installed on the print server [23].

So, to create the `print$` share and be able to start to upload the drivers to the Samba 4 share, we just need to add the following lines of code to our `smb.conf` file:

```
[PRINT$]
    path = /var/lib/samba/pointandprint
    comment = Drivers for Dep. Printers
    writeable = yes
```

> The `/var/lib/samba/pointandprint` directory should be created, which can be accomplished with the following command:
>
> **`mkdir -p /var/lib/samba/pointandprint`**

After we have this share configured on our Samba 4 installation, we can start the process of uploading the needed drivers to our `print$` share. For the configuration of initial print network services, we may need to create a plan to enumerate the printers and the different architectures that we need to access the printer resource. One option is to pick a 64 bit OS version, and install all printer drivers for that Microsoft Windows version using the same machine. This way, both architectures (that is, 32 bit and 64 bit) will be available for installation from one single place.

Now, we will upload the driver (32 bit or 64 bit) for the printer that we have shared on our Samba 4 Server. Based on this example, we should be able to install any other driver that we need to make available to our client machines as we announce more printers on the AD network.

Depending on the Microsoft Windows OS, we have different ways to open the printer driver installation wizard. Have a look at the following procedures:

1. For Microsoft Windows 2003, for example, we can open a connection for our Samba 4 print server as shown in the following screenshot:

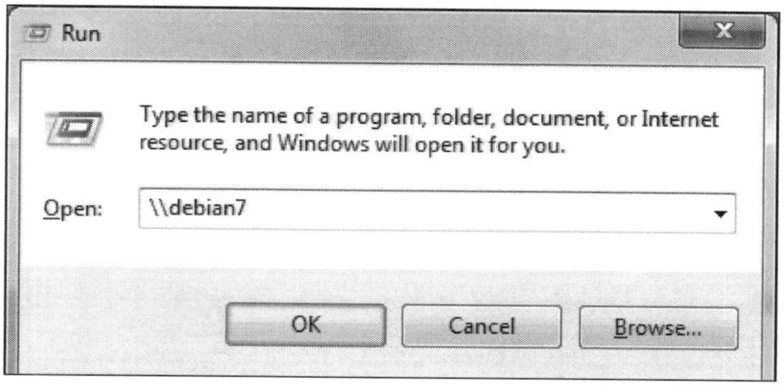

2. After clicking on **OK**, as shown in the preceding screenshot, we should be presented with a file explorer window as follows:

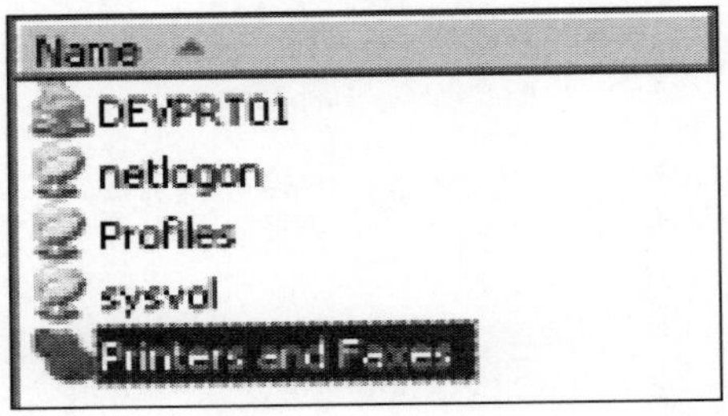

3. Now, we can double-click on **Printers and Faxes** and right-click on the following screen to be able to select the **Server Properties** option:

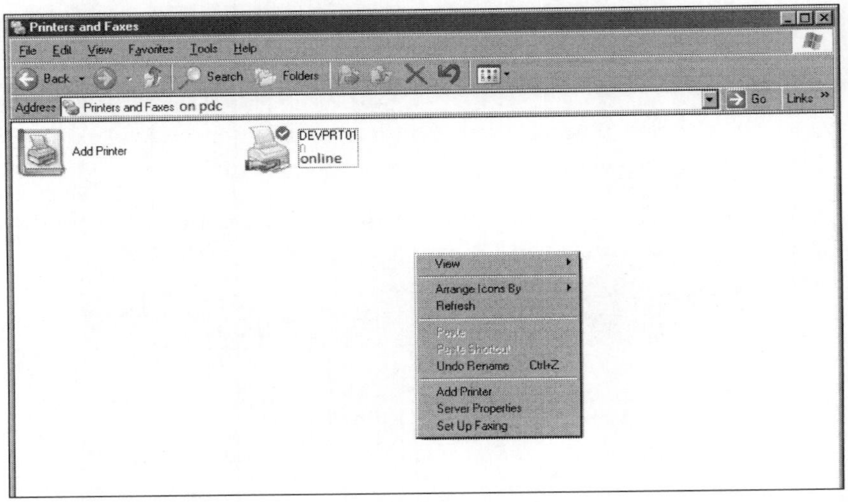

4. From the **Server Properties** window, we need to select the **Drivers** tab as shown in the following screenshot:

5. The next screen will show us an option where we can choose **Add...** to add new drivers, so we can follow the printer driver installation wizard. In the following screenshot, we can see a welcome screen for **Add Printer Driver Wizard** in a Microsoft Windows Server 2008 R2:

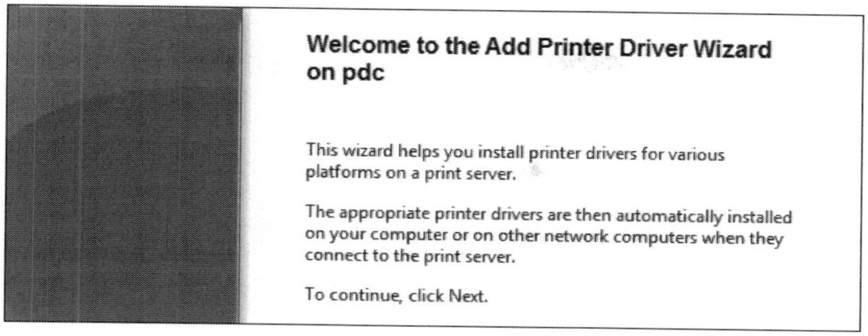

The preceding screenshot is important as it informs us that we can actually install printer drivers for various platforms on a print server. So, we can repeat this procedure to every printer on which we want to install the drivers, we just need to choose the operating system.

6. After we click on **Next**, we have the following screen that will provide us with information on the printer driver type that we will be able to install (**Type 3 - User Mode**). It will also provide us with information on the architecture—**x64** and/or **x86** (64 bits and 32 bits respectively):

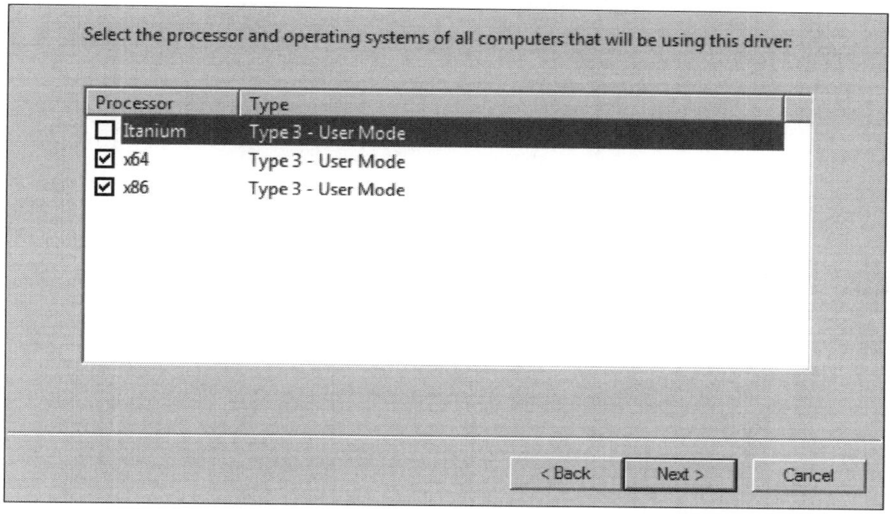

7. We chose both the architectures as we have 32 bit versions of this OS running on our network. After choosing the platform, the next step is to choose the printer driver—the manufacturer and printer models—as shown in the following screenshot:

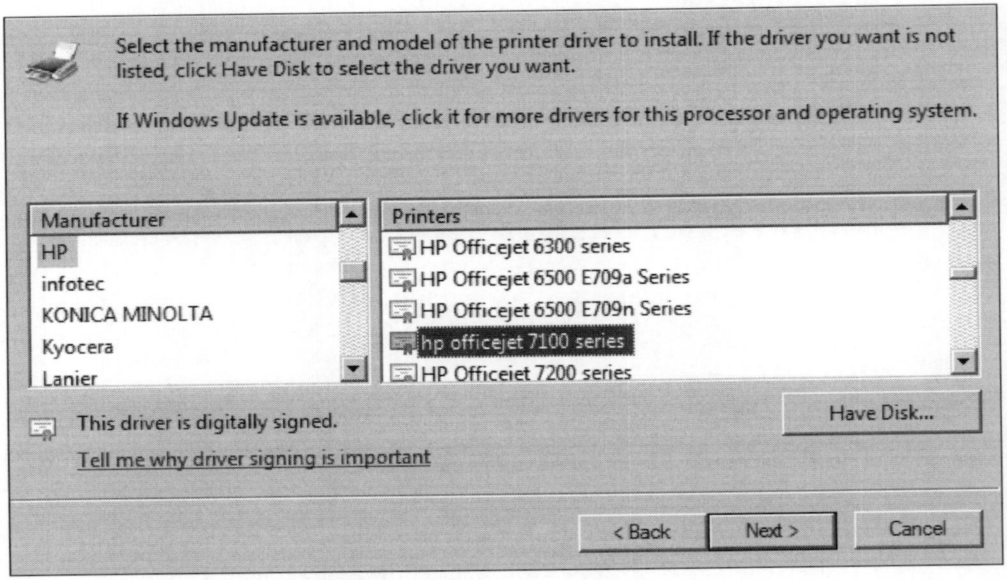

8. In the preceding screenshot, we selected a printer driver, and in the following screenshot, we will get a message about the drivers (and architectures) that will be installed:

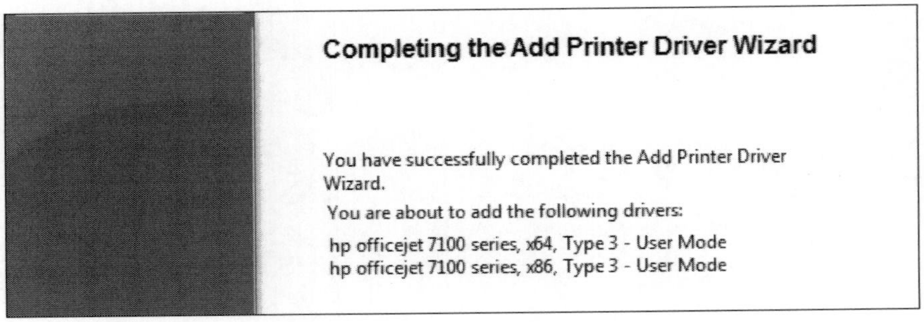

So, we should receive a status window that shows us the progress of the installation (for example, information on the files that are being copied). After this, the **Drivers** tab, which was empty at the beginning of this process, will now have two drivers listed (one printer driver for two platforms).

Another piece of important information in the preceding screenshot is the printer driver's name (**hp officejet 7100 series**); soon, we will use it to associate it with our printer, `devprt01`. So, we can take note of this name now, but we will show you how to list the drivers that we have registered and how to pick their names directly from our Samba 4 Server.

Looking at our Samba 4 Server, we can check our filesystem and list the files that were installed for the x64 version of the driver, as follows:

```
root@debian7:~# ls -1 /var/lib/samba/pointandprint/x64/3/
HPBMIAPI.DLL
HPBMINI.DLL
HPBOID.DLL
HPBOIDPS.DLL
HPBPRO.DLL
HPBPROPS.DLL
HPEACLHN.HPI
HPFIME50.DLL
HPFRES50.DLL
HPO5H83L.GPD
...
```

That's it! Remember that you can be required to provide the Microsoft Windows CD to install the 32 bit version of the printer driver. So, if we select both versions of the printer driver, the installation wizard might require the location to pick the x86 version (for example, when installing from a x64 Microsoft Windows version). It's a good idea to have a copy of the CD or the ISO in a folder or a file server.

The last step is the registration of the printer driver, associating it with our printer. As we said earlier, we have a way to list the drivers of the platforms that we have installed on the server, and for that, we just need to issue the following command:

```
root@debian7:~# rpcclient debian7 -U 'administrator%w1ndow$$!' -c
  'enumdrivers'
...
[Windows x64]
    Printer Driver Info 1:
    Driver Name: [hp officejet 7100 series]
...
root@debian7:~#
```

The preceding command will list all the drivers that we have installed on our Samba 4 Server (for example, `debian7`) for all different platforms. In this example, we have highlighted just the one that we are interested in, and we can see that the name is the same as the one we have in our previous screenshot of the printer driver installation wizard. To associate this driver to our HP printer, we can use the following command [24]:

```
root@debian7:~# rpcclient debian7 -U 'administrator%window$$!' -c
  'setdriver "devprt01" "hp officejet 7100 series"'
Successfully set devprt01 to driver hp officejet 7100 series.
root@debian7:~#
```

In the reference [24], there is an example that shows you how to associate the driver with the printer from a Microsoft Windows machine, but the drawback is that the procedure in Windows changes the printer's name. As described in the link, the administrator can rename it to the old name (but even so, we do not recommend this) after the procedure. In this same link on the Samba wiki, there is a section that describes how to preconfigure the printer and publish it on the Active Directory so that the users can easily find the printer. So, if you want to proceed with these configurations, we highly recommend that you take a look at the reference at the end of this book and actually explore the Samba wiki pages as it has a lot of useful information and how-tos.

Sharing files using Samba 4

One of the most powerful features of the Samba software is its share capabilities for the server-side and the client-side code. We will focus on the server-side features here, and we will also focus on how to make the shares available to our Active Directory environment, but we cannot forget that being able to access these shares from other operating systems (for example, GNU/Linux) is a very important feature too. Samba provides all this as an open source solution since Version 3 is in a very mature state.

Users and system administrators who used Version 3 and earlier versions of the Samba software will see that with the new Version 4, the file share capabilities are much easier to implement and manage. In the earlier versions, we had to basically perform all the configurations on the `smb.conf` file and control what was possible on the filesystem and/or the configuration file (for example, `smb.conf`).

File sharing with Samba 4 is a simple task. Basically, we just need to have a folder where a set of data will reside, and all the configuration around the users and groups who have access to this primary folder and subsequent subdirectories should be managed from a Microsoft Windows machine. The installation procedure used in this book covers the installation of all the features needed for the Samba 4 software to handle **Access Control Lists (ACLs)** and **Extended Attributes (XATTR)**; so, for the next procedures, we will assume that our Samba 4 installation has all the features that are needed. In case you have any issues or lack of capabilities on the Samba binaries installed on your system, please review the Samba 4 installation procedure in the previous chapters.

We've already seen some examples of shares on Samba 4 in our previous topics, such as `PRINTERS`, `PRINT$`, and `HOME` directives, which are basically shares. Standard and special ones, in the end, are the shares configured on the `smb.conf` file and are available to our Microsoft Windows clients on the network. To create a regular share in order to provide cooperative work around files to users and groups in Samba 4 is as simple as performing the following tasks:

- Create the directory to be shared
- Add it to the `smb.conf` file

To create the directory, we can use a command prompt in our Samba 4 Server and execute the following command (assuming that the root of the directory tree exists):

```
root@debian7:~# mkdir /var/lib/samba/devcodds && echo OK
OK
root@debian7:~#
```

Add the directory to the `smb.conf` file:

```
[DEVCODDS]
    comment = DEV COD DS
    path = /var/lib/samba/devcodds
    read only = No
```

We do not need to actually restart the whole server to reload the `smb.conf` file to apply the changes that we have made; we can use the `smbcontrol` command with the `reload` option as exemplified in the following code:

```
root@debian7:~# smbcontrol all reload-config && echo OK
OK
root@debian7:~#
```

At this time, we already have a new share available on our network, and we can access it using a Microsoft Windows machine in our domain (for example, as an administrator) and configure all the permissions we want, and users and groups can directly access the share from there. As Samba 4 is fully compatible with the Active Directory, we don't need to use any old model to restrict the user's access on the `smb.conf` file; we just edit the share permissions from a Microsoft Windows machine and manage its properties.

The following screenshot is an example of the POA's administrator that is editing the share permissions of **DEVCODDS** (Run `\\debian7\devcodds`, right-click on **Properties**, click on the **Security** tab, and click on **Edit**):

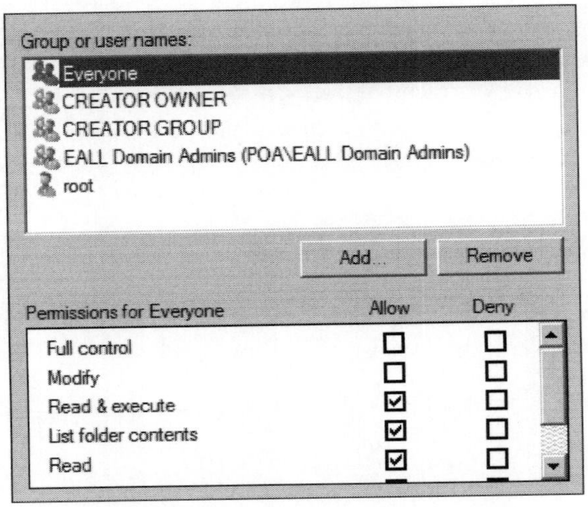

All standard permissions and management controls are available in Samba, and the system administrator can use the granularity he or she requires to control access to the share and subdirectories. This is a huge enhancement for the file shares' administration in Samba and is a feature that will really make the users more comfortable. Many system administrators are used to the integrations and easiness that the Microsoft operating system provides, and Samba being able to accommodate some is a big step forward.

Summary

In this chapter, we looked at the different SMB versions that Samba 4 supports, an overview of the main features of each one, and what to expect from the next Samba 4 releases. We have discussed the file and print daemons, what has changed from the alpha release to the final Samba 4 stable announcement, and learned about the different types of printer drivers in the Microsoft Windows operating systems.

This chapter also covered the installation of a printer/queue on the Samba host using CUPS, how to share that printer using Samba, and the configuration of the Point and Print feature for the Microsoft Windows machines. We explained how to perform the association of the printer driver to the shared printer, and pointed some reference links for further and specific configurations. Also, in this chapter, we explained how to create a file share and configure the permissions in an easy way using the graphical interface of a Microsoft Windows machine, making use of the fully compatible Active Directory capabilities of Samba 4.

In the next chapter, we will learn how to extend the Active Directory schema using Samba 4. We will use scripts and examples to understand the procedures based on a specific example application that makes use of some custom object class and attributes.

7

Extending the Active Directory Schema Using Samba 4

This chapter explains how to extend the default Active Directory schema for some specific applications when using Samba 4 built in as the Active Directory Domain Controller. This chapter covers more advanced topics for which some prior knowledge of LDAP / Active Directory protocol specification and general system administration is preferred.

The process will be explained using examples and scripts to extend the Samba 4 / Active Directory schema, and will use a simple application that uses a specific object class and attribute. This is so you understand how to extend the Samba 4 LDAP schema and accommodate the attribute and class for this application.

The following is the list of topics that will be covered in this chapter:

- Key consideration points when planning an Active Directory schema extension
- Exporting the current Active Directory schema configuration
- A practical example for extending the Active Directory schema
- Applying the Active Directory schema extension
- Tests and validations of the Samba 4 Active Directory schema extension

Planning an Active Directory schema extension

The point we need to have foremost in mind when planning an Active Directory schema extension is the word "schema". As in a **Relational Database Management System (RDBMS)** schema [27], just in case the reader is familiar with database systems, every change we make to the predefined data types or the relationships between tables can lead to unwanted results. So, before going forward, it's important to understand what the changes are and whether or not we really need to make them; as in the case of the Active Directory schema extensions, once created they are not reversible [28].

In the Active Directory world, maybe the schema does not have much of the complexity of an RDBMS schema, but it is a crucial, very important definition all the same, as any error can lead to the unavailability of the service. The Active Directory schema maintains definitions for all objects in the directory; thus, the creation of any new object is validated using the object's definition in the schema before it can be actually written in the directory [29]. Yet, from the Active Directory schema documentation, the object classes and attributes in the default schema configuration are wide and rich, and so intended to meet the needs of most organizations [29].

Another important characteristic of how the Active Directory schema is organized is the fact that the attributes are defined in the schema separated from the classes [30]. This is really important as an attribute, for example, `description`, does not need to be tied to just one object class, as we can have descriptions for jobs, roles, and machines; thus, we do not need to have one specific `description` attribute for each of those objects.

Obviously, the possibility of extending the Active Directory schema is a real and powerful option. Its purpose is legitimate as the default schema does not suit specific use cases; this is because users and companies have different requirements and it's very difficult to have all specifications implemented in a standard configuration (such as, a schema). However, the point is that many use cases can be fulfilled with the standard options, and the general advice is to make sure that the requirements are specific enough where a schema extension is really needed. The Microsoft documentation website has great articles about Active Directory, and is an excellent resource for Active Directory terminology, syntaxes, classes, attributes, and so on [30]. So, the user can look at all the classes and attributes to get familiarized with the structure and data types.

The second point to keep in mind is that after we have realized that a schema extension is really needed by our new application / use case, we need to understand how the directory is organized and how to accommodate our changes in a way that it can coexist with other information we have and will have in the directory. A well-defined procedure is to execute the operation to extend the schema itself, and a proper procedure is to test it and make sure everything is still working and will continue to work as usual.

Some users do utilize some reserved namespaces from the X.500 standard or other options for private use. Here, we will show you how to do it properly, as the next step necessary to extend the Active Directory schema is to register with the **Internet Assigned Numbers Authority** (**IANA**) and asking for a **Private Enterprise Number** (**PEN**) [26]. IANA is the entity responsible for the global coordination of many Internet protocol resources (there are no costs; obtaining a PEN assignment is free of charge).

> An Active Directory forest has just one schema and it is replicated to all the domain controllers on that forest, but only the schema master has control over its structure and content [29].

The Private Enterprise Number is needed as the classes and attributes (`classSchema` and `attributeSchema`) use an object identifier (OID) that is derived from the uniqueness of the PEN we received from IANA. Let's look at the **EALL** example OID `1.3.6.1.4.1.42768.2.1`, so we can understand the whole tree as these objects are referenced in the following figure [37]:

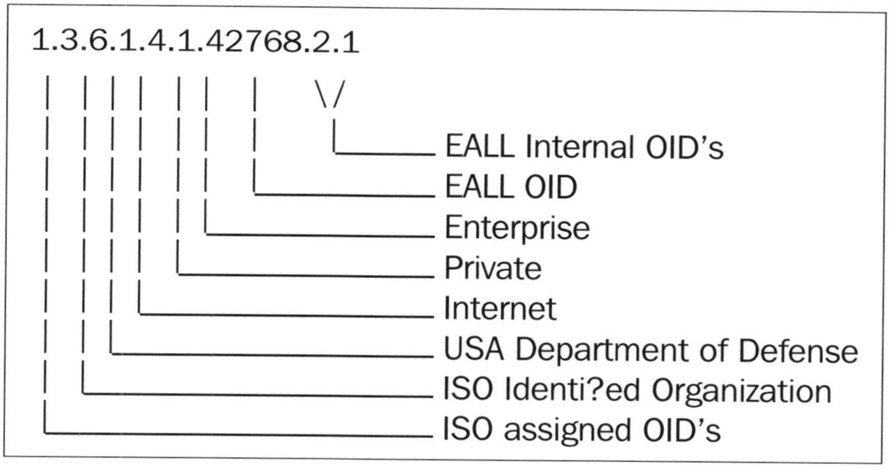

As you can see in the preceding figure, we have a hierarchy that starts with the top authority (which is the root; in this case, ISO), until we get to the EALL (for example, Marcelo Leal) that owns the OID `42768`, and where a more specific and fully controlled division can be executed in the EALL site. In the next steps, we will see how to create a division in our PEN and start to organize our new classes and attributes to include them in our Active Directory services. Now, let's look at the OIDs from the output of the following command executed on a Samba 4 Active Directory Domain Controller:

```
root@addc:~# ldapsearch -x -h localhost -s base | grep supportedCap
supportedCapabilities: 1.2.840.113556.1.4.800
supportedCapabilities: 1.2.840.113556.1.4.1670
supportedCapabilities: 1.2.840.113556.1.4.1791
supportedCapabilities: 1.2.840.113556.1.4.1935
supportedCapabilities: 1.2.840.113556.1.4.2080
root@addc:~#
```

Based on the Microsoft documentation [32], we can get great insights about the capabilities of this Samba 4 AD DS, as we've shown in the following table:

1.2.840.113556.1.4.800 (LDAP_CAP_ACTIVE_DIRECTORY_OID)	The LDAP server is running Active Directory and as Active Directory Domain Services (AD DS).
1.2.840.113556.1.4.1670 (LDAP_CAP_ACTIVE_DIRECTORY_V51_OID)	If the server is running as an AD DS, the presence of this capability means that the LDAP server is running at least the Microsoft Windows Server 2003 version of Active Directory. If the server is running as AD LDS, it means that the LDAP server is running at least the Windows Server 2008 version of AD.
1.2.840.113556.1.4.1791 (LDAP_CAP_ACTIVE_DIRECTORY_LDAP_INTEG_OID)	The LDAP server on the domain controller is capable of signing and sealing on an NTLM authenticated connection.
1.2.840.113556.1.4.1935 (LDAP_CAP_ACTIVE_DIRECTORY_V60_OID)	This OID means the server is running at least the Windows Server 2008 version of AD.

So, based on the preceding table, we can correlate the capabilities present on the Samba 4 version we are using as the Active Directory Domain Controller, and the correspondent Microsoft Windows Server 2008 R2 operating system Active Directory Domain Services [32]. From the capabilities described on the referenced website, we can see that the only feature not present in our Samba 4 Server AD DS for our matching to be 100 percent is `LDAP_CAP_ACTIVE_DIRECTORY_PARTIAL_SECRETS_OID`. However, as you can see in the notes of the web page, that capability is only exposed by the respective server in specific conditions (for example, RODC, which is an additional DC in a domain that hosts read-only partitions of the AD database).

Exporting the current Active Directory schema configuration

As usual, for us, for all procedures that will change the state and configuration of our Active Directory services, we will base our AD DS schema extension with a prior plan in place to test and validate our results. Thus, we can make sure that the environment is functional after the schema extension and everything is stable as before.

Microsoft Windows servers have a great tool that we can use to generate a file (the LDIF file) with all our schema configurations: `ldifde`. To use this tool, we just need to be logged into a Microsoft Windows server (for example, 2008 R2) and execute the following script in a command-line prompt window:

```
C:\Users\Administrator.POA> cd Desktop
C:\Users\Administrator.POA\Desktop>ldifde -f old-adds-schema.ldif \
-d CN=Schema,CN=configuration,DC=poa,DC=msdcbrz,DC=eall,DC=com,DC=br
Connecting to "adds.poa.msdcbrz.eall.com.br"
Logging in as current user using SSPI
Exporting directory to file old-adds-schema.ldif
Searching for entries…
Writing out entries ...........................................
...............................................................
.........................
1550 entries exported
The command has completed successfully
C:\Users\Administrator.POA\Desktop>
```

If the preceding command is executed successfully, we should have a file named `old-adds-schema.ldif` in our current directory; its content should be like that shown in the following excerpt:

```
dn: CN=LDAP-Display-Name,CN=Schema,CN=Configuration,DC=poa,DC=msdcbrz,\
DC=eall,DC=com,DC=br
changetype: add
objectClass: top
objectClass: attributeSchema
cn: LDAP-Display-Name
instanceType: 4
whenCreated: 20121113212243.0Z
```

> It seems that there is an option to use custom OIDs inside Microsoft's private number, but we will not cover that in this book and prefer to point out the procedure so users and companies can have their own address space.

We need to save the `old-adds-schema.ldif` file in a well-known place on our server, as we will use it after executing our AD DS schema extension to conduct an assessment of the changes we have made. Another important tool to be used in conjunction with this file after executing the schema extension is the AD DS / LDS Schema Analyzer. This tool should be installed on Microsoft Windows Server 2008 R2 if this server has Active Directory Lightweight Directory Services installed as we do on the server exemplified in the following screenshot:

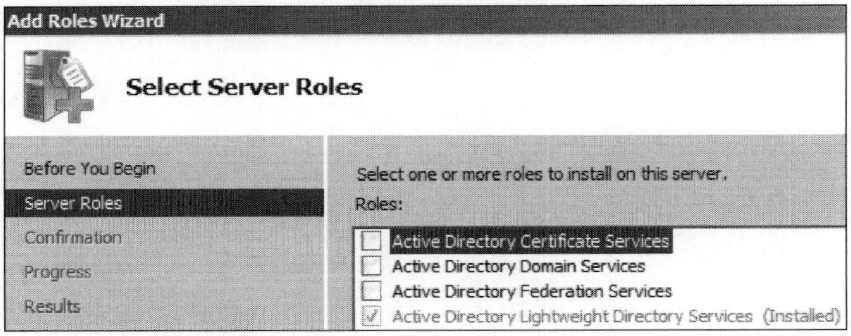

In case if it has not been installed yet, we could install it using the **Add Roles Wizard**, shown in the preceding screenshot, in a quick and simple process.

Extending the Active Directory schema in practice

Here, we will take a look at the requirements of our example application and the attribute it needs in Active Directory in order to work properly. It's important to keep in mind that the attribute presented here is not the most relevant part, except the procedure we will present and the points related to naming convention. Very often, I use an existing attribute to accomplish what this example application requires, but again, the procedure is the most important part here.

> In a real-life scenario, you should not extend the Active Directory schema if you can use an existing attribute.

For security, a system administrator implements an authentication module (for example, the PAM module) to add another layer on the authentication process and enhance access control on the GNU/Linux servers in the environment they manage. As the schema they were using earlier was a custom version on OpenLDAP, which utilizes this module on an Active Directory environment, they need to extend its schema.

The module is named `pam_hostscheck`, and it needs an attribute named `allowedhost` containing the hostname of the host on which some user is trying to authenticate: permit (for example, `allowedhost=myservername`) or decline the authentication process. Note that we can have many `allowedhost` instances for each user object (for example, it's a multivalue attribute), as a user may be allowed to access many machines. The attribute can contain some wildcards that the application knows (for example, `netgroups`) and other tricky options, but that is application-specific, and the content of the attribute is not very important for our AD DS schema extension.

With this task at hand, the first concern we need to address should be that related to the attribute's name. We need to think about the present and the future and choose a name that will not conflict with other applications we may need to use. The system administrator has created this module with a cool feature to help in this matter: we can specify the name of the attribute that the module will use in a configuration file. So, for the EALL company, if the system administrator decides to use `eALLallowedHost` as the attribute's name, there's a very low probability that it will clash with other attribute names we may use in the future.

Extending the Active Directory schema

Before we are able to extend the Active Directory schema in Samba 4, we need to enable the schema extension feature as it is disabled by default [33]. According to the referenced Samba documentation, you can enable this feature by adding a specific option in the Samba configuration file (`/usr/local/samba/etc/smb.conf`), or directly on the command line [33]. We have opted for the latter.

As we need to execute three modifications on the directory for our example case, we will do it in three distinct steps to make it clearer, as I believe this way is better to understand the whole process. So, we will start adding the `eALLallowedHost` attribute to the AD DS, and to do that, we need to create an LDAP Data Interchange Format (LDIF) file with all the information about this new attribute to extend our AD schema. The following is the LDIF file for this (`/root/eALLallowedHost.ldif`):

```
# Samba 4 Active Directory Schema Extension for PAM_HOSTSCHECK
# byLeal
# Attribute: eALLallowedHost
dn: CN=eALLallowedHost,CN=Schema,CN=Configuration,DC=poa,DC=msdcbrz,DC=ea
ll,DC=com,DC=br
objectClass: top
objectClass: attributeSchema
attributeID: 1.3.6.1.4.1.42768.2.1
cn: eALLallowedHost
name: eALLallowedHost
attributeSyntax: 2.5.5.12
lDAPDisplayName: eALLallowedHost
Description: Hostname the user is allowed to authenticate
oMSyntax: 64
-
```

In the LDIF file, the first three lines are just comments (for example, about what the file is, who created it, and the attribute name to be created). We can have as many comment lines as we think are needed to organize and provide information for the people that will handle this piece of configuration.

In an LDIF file, we always have a **Distinguished Name** (**DN**) that is composed of a common name for the object itself (for example, `eALLallowedHost`), and the **Relative Distinguished Names** (**RDN**), which in this case, is `cn=schema,cn=configuration`, plus a constant string for the Domain Component (DC): `DC=poa,DC=msdcbrz,DC=ea ll,DC=com,DC=br`.

The directive `objectClass` will define some characteristics (for example, type) of this object (for example, `top`, `attributeSchema`). We have a display name, a name, and a description; additionally, we have `attributeSyntax (Unicode String)` and `oMSyntax` as they are mandatory for all new attributes we create (the first is an OID and the latter is an integer) [34]. The `attributeID` is based on our registered OID (for example, EALL's registered OID) and the specific number assigned within the company for that new attribute.

> To organize the new classes and attributes, the EALL company has chosen to reserve the number 1 for classes and 2 for attributes. So, 1.1 is the first new class created and 2.1 is the new first attribute.

Now we have the first `LDIF` file ready, and we can actually execute the first Active Directory schema extension. Remember to never (and I will say it again: never) execute an AD DS schema extension in production directly. All the procedures here need to be executed and tested in a lab environment, and just after you are satisfied that the procedure has proven consistent and without negative impact on your simulated environment, you can plan for an implementation in production. That being said, let's look at the following command to extend the AD DS schema:

```
root@addc:~# ldbmodify -H /usr/local/samba/private/sam.ldb \
/root/eALLallowedHost.ldif --option="dsdb:schema update allowed"=true
Modified 1 records successfully
root@addc:~#
```

> Remember to have the `$PATH` bash variable configured with the correct location of the Samba 4 installation before all other paths in your shell, for example, `export PATH="/usr/local/samba/sbin:/usr/local/samba/bin:$PATH"`.

As you can see in the preceding output, the command was executed and one record was modified successfully. This is good news! The next step is to add to the schema a new custom user class (for example, `eALLUser`), so we can associate this class with the standard user class and make our schema extension less intrusive. The following is the `eALLUser.ldif` file:

```
# Samba 4 Active Directory Schema Extension for PAM_HOSTSCHECK
# byLeal
# ------
# Class: eALLUser
```

```
dn: CN=eALLUser,CN=Schema,CN=Configuration,DC=poa,DC=msdcbrz,DC=eall,DC=c
om,DC=br
objectClass: top
objectClass: classSchema
cn: eALLUser
name: eALLUser
governsID: 1.3.6.1.4.1.42768.1.1
mayContain: eALLallowedHost
rDNAttID: cn
lDAPDisplayName: eALLUser
Description: EALL Custom User Class
objectClassCategory: 3
-
```

> I don't remember talking about backup in this chapter. So, here we go… Before changing, maintaining, or even looking at a production server, perform a backup. Then, do it again. That's cool; I just said it and I already feel better!

The most important differences between the LDIF file we just saw and the first one are the `objectClass` type and the `mayContain` clause. Observe that in this specific case, we are creating a class (for example, `classSchema`) and not an attribute as we did earlier in the chapter. The procedure to add a class to our AD DS schema, shown as follows, is pretty much the same as described earlier:

```
root@addc:~# ldbmodify -H /usr/local/samba/private/sam.ldb \
/root/eALLUser.ldif --option="dsdb:schema update allowed"=true
Modified 1 records successfully
root@addc:~#
```

So far, so good! We are almost done; the last step we need to perform is to add our `auxiliaryClass` class to the user class, and for that, we can use our third and last LDIF file (`User.ldif`), as follows:

```
dn: CN=User,CN=Schema,CN=Configuration,DC=poa,DC=msdcbrz,DC=eall,DC=com,D
C=br
changetype: modify
add: auxiliaryClass
auxiliaryClass: eALLUser
-
```

Now we can execute the last command to finish our AD DS schema extension, as follows:

```
root@addc:~# ldbmodify -H /usr/local/samba/private/sam.ldb \
/root/User.ldif --option="dsdb:schema update allowed"=true
Modified 1 records successfully
root@addc:~#
```

All executions went well and by now, we should have the new `eALLUser` class available on our AD DS; as you may remember, this new class may contain our new attribute `eALLallowedHost`. So, now we will use a Microsoft Windows 2008 Server machine that is a member of our domain in order to configure this attribute to two EALL users to make sure that the new attribute is available and really ready to be used. Follow the ensuing steps:

1. After we have logged onto the Microsoft Windows machine, we will execute the **Active Directory Services Interfaces Editor** tool (`adsiedit.msc`) to manage the new attribute for our users, as shown in the following screenshot, as the standard **Active Directory Users and Computers** (**ADUC**) Microsoft Windows tool to manage users does not work with custom attributes by default (for example, in standard mode):

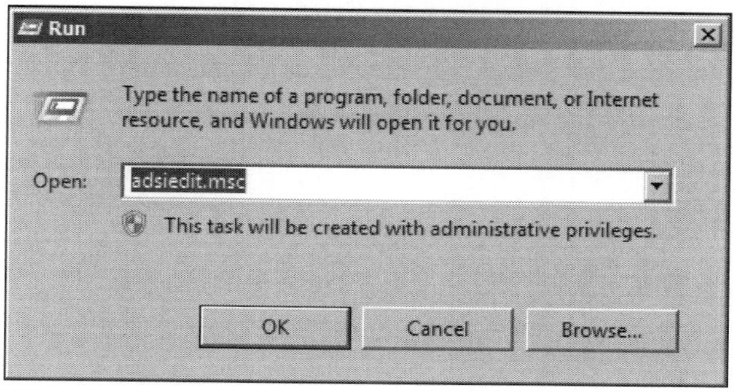

2. There is a PowerShell script in the references [40] to perform a schema conflict analysis on LDIF files against the production schema. After some executions, it seems to be another good resource publicly available at the Technet Microsoft website. Looking at the source code, the drawback seems to be that the OID for Microsoft is hardcoded, and using any other OID will result in errors. The following is an excerpt of the code:

   ```
   $OIDCheck = $values[1].StartsWith("1.2.840.113556.1").
   ```

   Besides, insights provided by the script on the LDIF file can be valuable.

3. After we have been presented the default window for the ADSI Edit tool, we need to click on the top-most menu in the **Action | Connect to...** option, which will give us a **Connection Settings** window, as shown in the following screenshot:

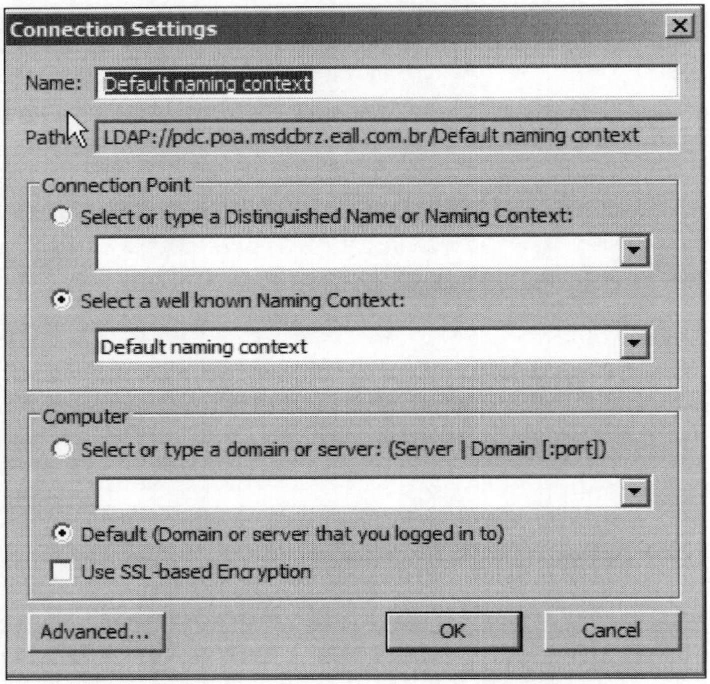

4. Just click on **OK**, as the default naming context should point accurately to our domain. Just double-click on the tree structure and expand the domain component to select `CN=Users`, as shown in the following screenshot:

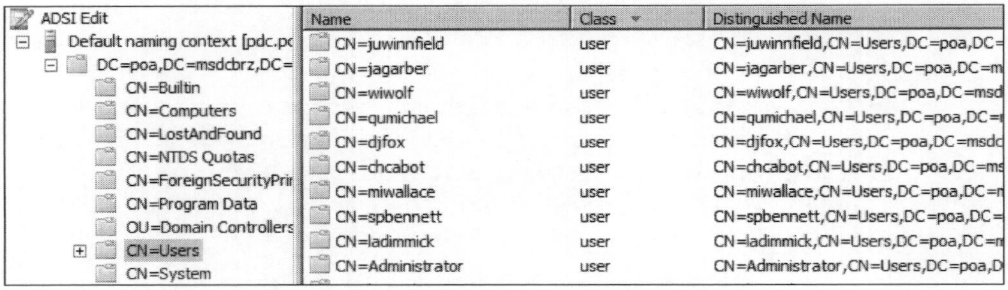

5. We will use two users for our configuration test: `djfox` and `joliu`; so, the procedure we will show for the first user will be the same as that for the second one, and that's why the second execution will be omitted. Just right-click on the `djfox` user and choose **Properties**, as shown in the following screenshot:

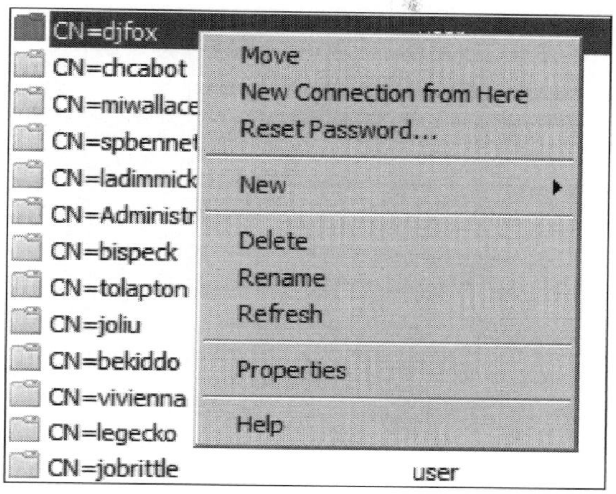

6. An **Attribute Editor** window (**CN=djfox Properties**) will appear, listing all the attributes for that user. If we select the first one and start to edit `eALLallowedHost`, we should be routed directly to this attribute, as shown in the following screenshot:

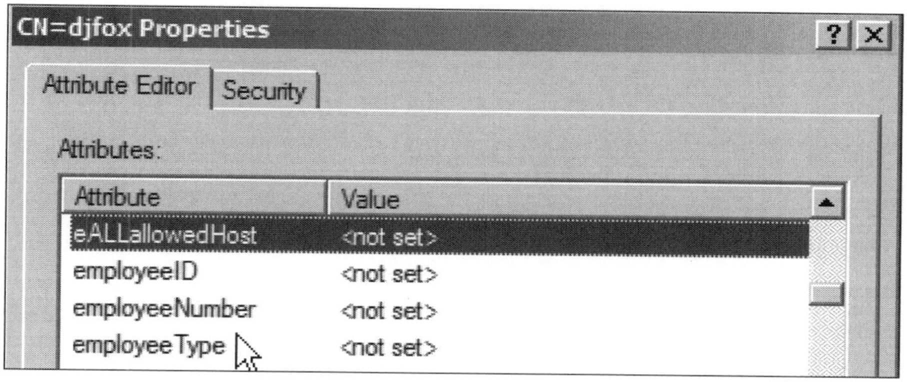

7. Now, we double-click on the `eALLallowedHost` attribute, as shown in the following screenshot, and fill the value-entry field with the name of the GNU/Linux machine's host to which we want this user to be able to log in, and click on **OK**.

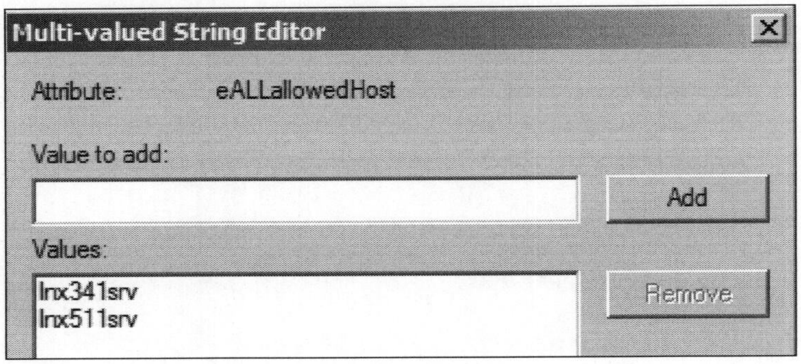

8. So, after we execute the same procedure for our second user (for example, `joliu`), we can close the ADSI Edit tool and go back to our Samba 4 Active Directory command-line prompt. Now, we will execute a simple search on the Active Directory to look for our brand new attribute and confirm that the changes and configurations we made on the schema are all working as expected, as shown in the following commands:

```
root@addc:~# ldbsearch -H /usr/local/samba/private/sam.ldb \
'(eALLallowedHost=*)' username eALLallowedHost
# record 1
dn: CN=djfox,CN=Users,DC=poa,DC=msdcbrz,DC=eall,DC=com,DC=br
eALLallowedHost: lnx341srv
eALLallowedHost: lnx511srv

# record 2
dn: CN=joliu,CN=Users,DC=poa,DC=msdcbrz,DC=eall,DC=com,DC=br
eALLallowedHost: lnx341srv
eALLallowedHost: lnx511srv
...
root@addc:~#
```

So, we ran a quick search using the `ldbsearch` utility from the Samba project, and basically searched for any object on the directory that had the attribute `eALLallowedHost` configured on it; for those objects, we asked to be shown the `username` and `eALLallowedHost` attributes. As expected, the two users that configured the `eALLallowedhost` attribute were returned in the preceding query, and now the system administrator can configure the users with the hostname of the hosts or groups of hosts to which the users need access. Thus, the `pam_hostscheck` module can be configured to use the `eALLallowedHost` attribute to execute a similar search in Active Directory Domain Services, and allow or deny the user authentication process. Using `pam_hostscheck` as a requisite module can be a powerful security barrier, as users that do not have access to that machine will not even be provided a username/password challenge.

> I had written the `pam_hostscheck` module many years ago, and today, we have other new and more efficient means to accomplish what I had implemented in that module. However, it was a very effective tool and a good opportunity to learn about PAM, LDAP, and schema extensions.

As the ADSI Edit tool is powerful and not intended for use in day-to-day procedures to manage users, and as we can have operators or even people who are not from the IT staff managing EALL's company users, we need to have this attribute handled in an easier manner. One option is to enable the advanced features in the Active Directory Users and Computers snap-in (ADUC).

Just take a look at the default properties window from an ADUC snap-in without the advanced features enabled, as shown in the following screenshot:

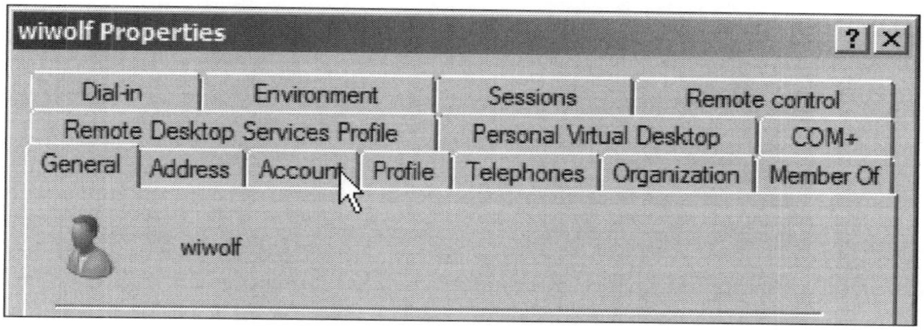

Now, let's go back to the main window of the ADUC snap-in. Just click on the item **View** on the top menu and check **Advanced Features**, as shown in the following screenshot:

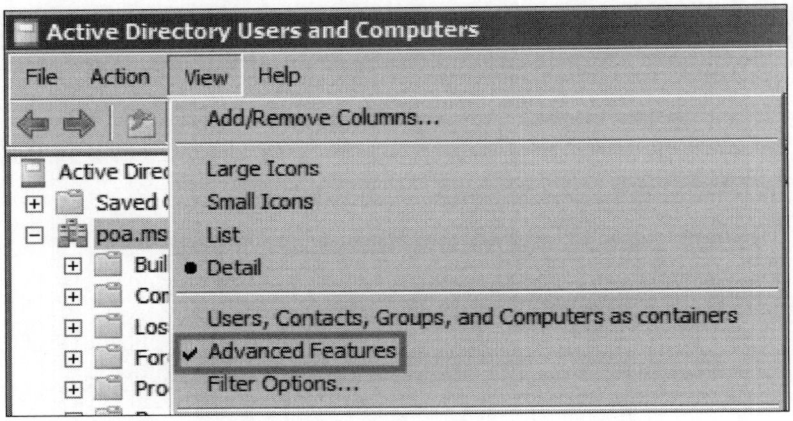

After this procedure, we can just double-click on one of our users and see that the **Properties** screen has changed a bit, as shown in the following screenshot:

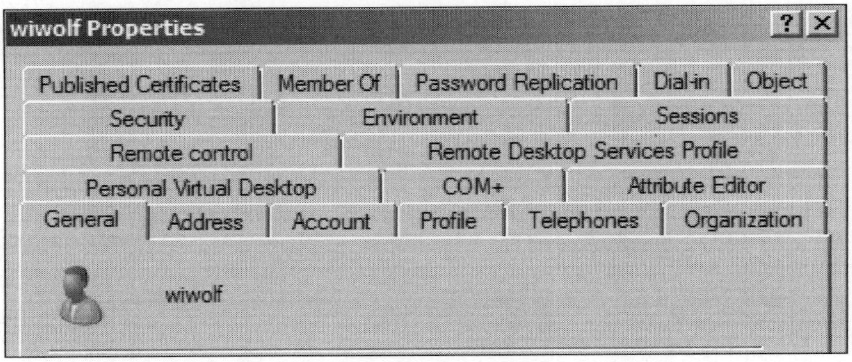

Now if we look closely, we will not only see that we have many more tabs, but also that we have one named **Attribute Editor**. If we select that tab and the first attribute, and start to type the name of our brand new attribute `eALLallowedHost`, we'll find it and be able to edit it in the same way we did using the ADSI Edit tool, as shown in the following screenshot:

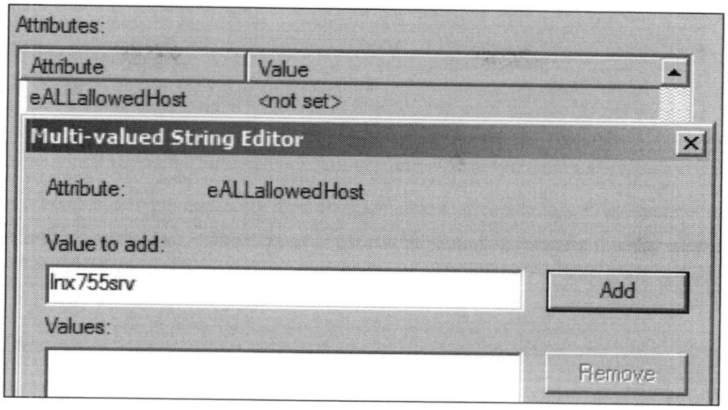

But, wait! We can use the ADSI Edit tool just one more time to add the column **Host Access is Allowed** for our new attribute in the ADUC snap-in! Just execute the `adsiedit.msc` command, but this time, we will connect in a different way.

Because we used ADSI Edit the last time, it will be already connected in the same context as we need it to be in the next execution. So, we need to choose the **Action** item in the top menu and select **Remove** (you can click on **Yes** as it will not remove anything from your AD DS; it will just remove the currently active connection).

Now with a cleaner screen, we can select the **Action** | **Connect to** menu option, but this time, we will choose **Configuration** in the **Select a well known Naming Context** combobox, as shown in the following screenshot:

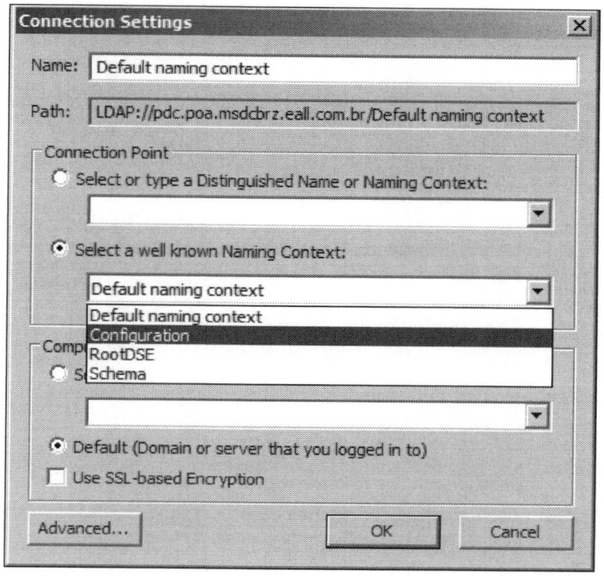

> Active Directory has some extension attributes for use by companies to create custom applications, without them needing to extend the AD DS schema; these are available at `http://msdn.microsoft.com/en-us/library/ms873846%28v=exchg.65%29.aspx`.
>
> The attributes in the specific Exchange Active Directory documentation seem to be for general utilization and are worth looking at before extending the schema if your application can be configured to use generic attribute names.

After the connection is established, expand the `CN=Configuration` and the `CN=DisplaySpecifiers` folders, as shown in the following screenshot:

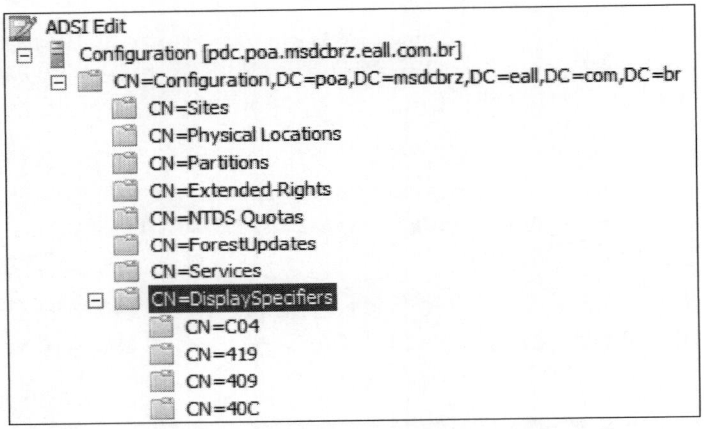

According to the Microsoft documentation [35], the `displaySpecifier` objects are localized user-interface data, and so we should configure them in a locale-specific base. In our case, we will just show an example for the US-English (409) locale container.

Selecting the `CN=409` folder, we can find `CN=default-display` in the right-hand panel (we can click on the **Name** column to order the entries, and so it should be the fourth line). Just double-click on it and select the first attribute in the following window, and then start typing `extraColumns`. You should then see the following screen:

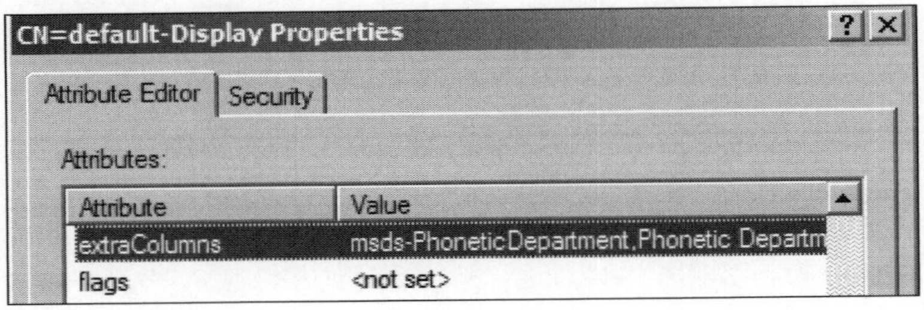

Just double-click on the `extraColumns` attribute, and in the **Value to add:** field, we need to enter the information for our new attribute in the `<ldapdisplayname>,<column header>,<default visibility>,<width>,<unused>` format [36].

The first value `ldapdisplayname` we have specified on our LDIF file as the name of our attribute is `eALLallowedHost`; the column header is the name that will appear in the header of the column and so can be more descriptive; the default visibility is a Boolean value that specifies whether the attribute is by default hidden (`0`) or visible (`1`); the width is the column's width in pixels and can be a positive integer or `-1`, which, in turn, sets the column to the same size as the header; and the last one is unused [36], as shown in the following screenshot:

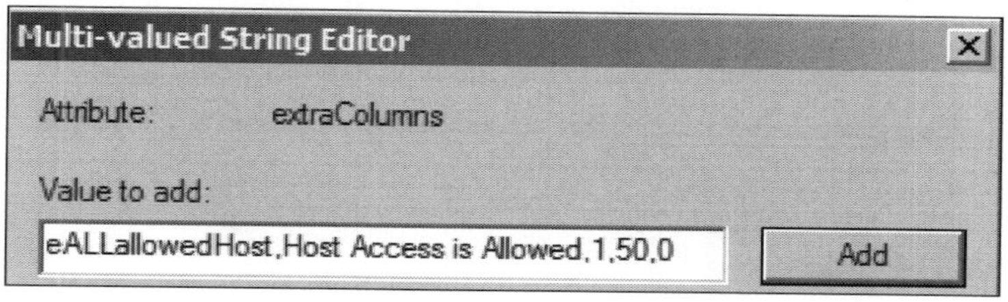

For the default visibility, we have entered `1`, so we will not need to add it later (as the column default will be visible). When you click on **Add**, the string you have entered should be listed with the other values, as shown in the following screenshot:

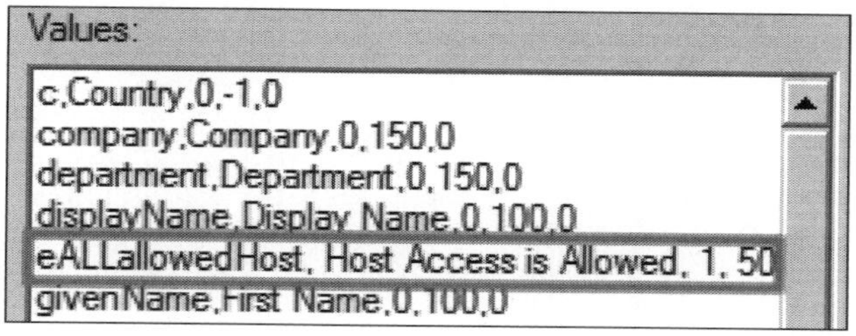

Now, we can click on **OK** twice and close the ADSI Edit tool (we can remove this connection before we close the tool in case we want a clean start the next time). The next step is to open the ADUC snap-in, right-click on **Saved Queries**, and choose **New | Query**. The screen shown in the following screenshot will be presented where we'll name the query **Host Access is Allowed**:

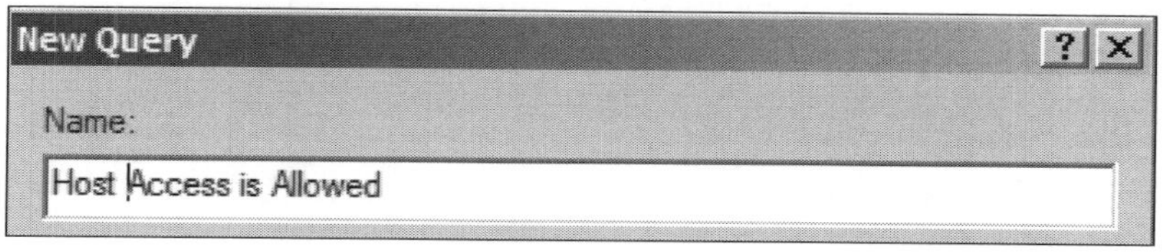

Once you have written the name of the new query, click on the button **Define Query...**, and in the **Find Common Queries** window, select the **Custom Search** option, as shown in the following screenshot:

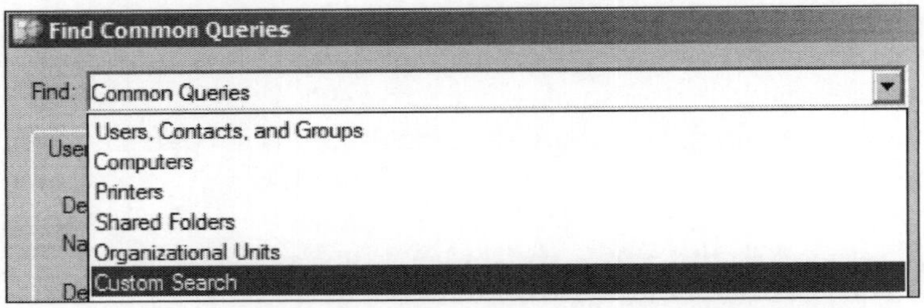

Now, we need to select the **Advanced** tab and run the following simple search to filter all objects (for example, users) that have the `eALLallowedHost` attribute configured, as shown in the following screenshot:

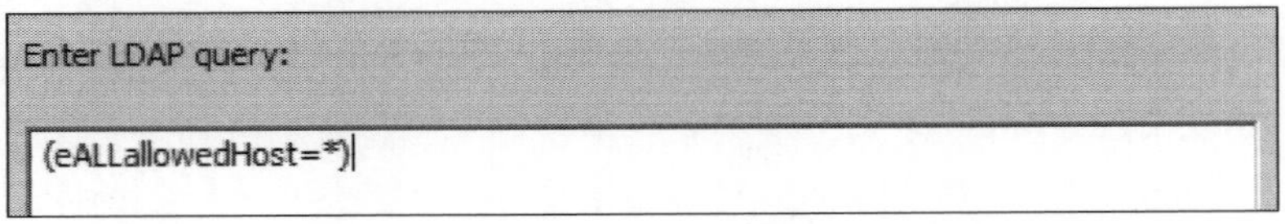

Just click on **OK** twice, and we should see the result of our search on the main screen along with our **Host Access is Allowed** column, as shown in the following screenshot:

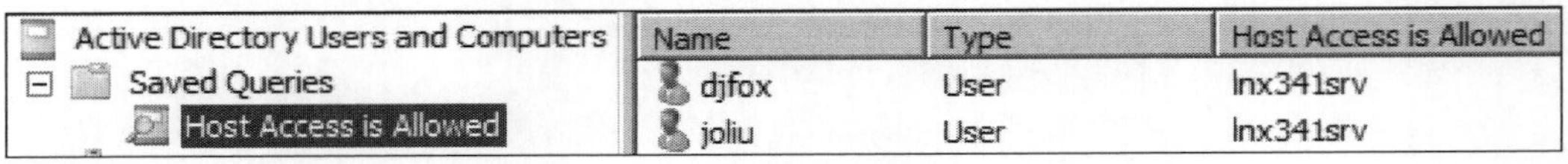

Very handy!

Testing and validating the Samba 4 Active Directory schema extension

When we execute an Active Directory schema extension procedure, my experience in different environments (for example, lab setups for testing) is very similar for Samba 4 and Microsoft Windows servers running Active Directory. In case of failures, they can have different impacts on the services, as follows:

- AD DS doesn't even start
- Some misbehavior while running normal operations (for example, searching or replicating)

For the first case, some start/stop command executions after the AD DS schema extension, followed by server restarts is a good starting point to validate our system and make sure we do not have very bad issues with our Active Directory schema.

For the issues in the second category, we will see some commands that can be used to try to find any inconsistencies as soon as possible, so that they can be fixed and the schema extension can be rolled out onto production. Speaking specifically about the Samba 4 Active Directory implementation, the official page of the project at the time of this writing informed that it sometimes does not generate essential attributes, leading to problems in Samba 4 provisions [33]. There are some issues that can arise after some time when the new schema is running, and that is why extensions need to be extensively tested before being applied in production. All the procedures presented here are intended to be validated in a lab and test environment before the reader analyzes its suitability for production.

We will use the `dcdiag` utility [38] to execute specific tests one-by-one to look at some specific points of the Active Directory services and try to make a good assessment of the environment. We will focus on some specific tests, but feel free to validate as much as you feel is needed for your actual Active Directory deployment. The only attention point I would recommend is to make sure you understand that some limitations do exist when using this tool in a Samba 4 installation (for example, FRS or DFSR), and they are not implemented on this software at the time of this writing [39], so if not supported tests are performed, the results will be misleading.

Using one of the Member Servers of the domain (for example, Microsoft Windows Server 2008 R2), log on as the domain admin and execute the following command and press *Enter*:

```
C:\Users\Administrator.POA> dcdiag /s:addc /test:advertising /v
Now we should get a response like the following:
<OUTPUT SKIPPED some errors about FRS and DFSR <OUTPUT SKIPPED>
Doing initial required tests
   Testing server: Default-First-Site-Name\ADDC
      Starting test: Connectivity
.................. ADDC passed test Connectivity
Doing primary tests
   Testing server: Default-First-Site-Name\ADDC
      Starting test: Advertising
   The DC ADDC is advertising itself as a DC and having a DS.
         The DC ADDC is advertising as an LDAP server
         The DC ADDC is advertising as having a writeable directory
```

```
        The DC ADDC is advertising as a Key Distribution Center
        The DC ADDC is advertising as a time server
        The DC ADDC is advertising as a GC.
.................. ADDC passed test Advertising
<OUTPUT SKIPPED tests omitted by user request OUTPUT SKIPPED>
C:\Users\Administrator.POA> dcdiag
```

We use the `/v` option in our command to see all the tests that have performed. We have used this option so that we know how to look more deeply into each test and find specific issues on the global test commands. For now, we will omit this option and just look at the global test result. The following is the replication test code:

```
C:\Users\Administrator.POA> dcdiag /s:addc /test:replications
<OUTPUT SKIPPED some errors about FRS and DFSR <OUTPUT SKIPPED>
Doing initial required tests
   Testing server: Default-First-Site-Name\ADDC
      Starting test: Connectivity
.................. ADDC passed test Connectivity
Doing primary tests
   Testing server: Default-First-Site-Name\ADDC
Starting test: Replications
.................. ADDC passed test Replications
...
C:\Users\Administrator.POA>
```

> It's important to remember to create a lab environment based on a sane and fully working environment to make sure that every point of our configuration was working just fine before starting our procedure. So, when we perform the tests, we can be sure that if any error occurs after our tests, we can fix or roll back the changes. One tip is to execute all the tests described in this section before and after the AD DS schema extension to have a baseline.

As we discussed earlier, replication can be a problem, but we have seen that we did not have any. But replication can be a broader issue, and even if the result of this command is not OK, we need to look to see if it is a transient failure or actually a problem root on our Active Directory schema extension procedure. Another quick but valuable test is to check if the required logon privileges exist to permit proper replication, as shown in the following commands:

```
C:\Users\Administrator.POA> dcdiag /s:addc /test:netlogons
<OUTPUT SKIPPED some errors about FRS and DFSR <OUTPUT SKIPPED>
Doing initial required tests
   Testing server: Default-First-Site-Name\ADDC
      Starting test: Connectivity
................... ADDC passed test Connectivity
Doing primary tests
   Testing server: Default-First-Site-Name\ADDC
Starting test: NetLogons
................... ADDC passed test NetLogons
...
C:\Users\Administrator.POA>
```

The test of `KnowsOfRoleHolders` is an essential one; sometimes we have a misbehaving AD DS and the problem is as basic as the lack of consistency on the **Flexible Single Master Operations** (**FSMO**) roles:

```
C:\Users\Administrator.POA> dcdiag /s:addc /test:knowsofroleholders
<OUTPUT SKIPPED some errors about FRS and DFSR <OUTPUT SKIPPED>
Doing initial required tests
   Testing server: Default-First-Site-Name\ADDC
      Starting test: Connectivity
................... ADDC passed test Connectivity
Doing primary tests
   Testing server: Default-First-Site-Name\ADDC
Starting test: KnowsOfRoleHolders
................... ADDC passed test KnowsOfRoleHolders

C:\Users\Administrator.POA>
```

We can issue many tests at once, and the following is an example of how to do it:

```
C:\Users\Administrator.POA> dcdiag /s:addc /test:fsmocheck /
test:ridmanager /test:machineaccount /test:kccevent /test:systemlog /
test:topology /test:ncsecdesc
<OUTPUT SKIPPED some errors about FRS and DFSR <OUTPUT SKIPPED>
Doing initial required tests
   Testing server: Default-First-Site-Name\ADDC
      Starting test: Connectivity
```

```
.................... ADDC passed test Connectivity
Doing primary tests
   Testing server: Default-First-Site-Name\ADDC
Starting test: KccEvent
.................... ADDC passed test KccEvent
Starting test: MachineAccount
.................... ADDC passed test MachineAccount
Starting test: NCSecDesc
.................... ADDC passed test NCSecDesc
Starting test: RidManager
.................... ADDC passed test RidManager
Starting test: SystemLog
.................... ADDC passed test SystemLog
Starting test: Topology
.................... ADDC passed test Topology


Running enterprise tests on : poa.msdcbrz.eall.com.br
   Starting test: FsmoCheck
               .................... poa.msdcbrz.eall.com.br passed test
FsmoCheck
C:\Users\Administrator.POA>
```

The tests we executed until now are important general validation routines we need to have in the bag to evaluate the health of any Active Directory deployment. Any errors on these tests are the first indication that something went wrong, and we then need to review our configuration and evaluate our AD DS schema extension.

Before we started our AD DS schema extension, we have created a LDIF file with the content of our current schema configuration, and we have installed the components to use the AD DS/LDS Schema Analyzer tool. Now, we need a new LDIF file with the state of the AD DS with our changes already in place. Let's open a new command-line prompt window and execute the following script inside the directory where we have the other LDIF file:

```
C:\Users\Administrator.POA> cd Desktop
C:\Users\Administrator.POA\Desktop>ldifde -f new-adds-schema.ldif \
-d CN=Schema,CN=Configuration,DC=poa,DC=msdcbrz,DC=eall,DC=com,DC=br
Connecting to "adds.poa.msdcbrz.eall.com.br"
Logging in as current user using SSPI
```

```
Exporting directory to file new-adds-schema.ldif
Searching for entries…
Writing out entries ........................................
............................................................
.........................
1552 entries exported
The command has completed successfully
C:\Users\Administrator.POA\Desktop>
```

If we look closely at the preceding output, we can already see that we have a good starting point for our comparison. If we recall our first execution before the AD DS schema extension, we had 1550 entries, and now we have 1552 (we have added one class and one attribute to the schema).

That seems like a good sign, but as we will see next, it does not actually relate to attributes and classes, as we thought at first. In any case, let's not take anything for granted and not jump to any conclusions yet, as we have a proper tool to help us analyze and give us a better and proper view of the AD DS state.

Now we can execute the following by navigating to **Start** | **Run**:

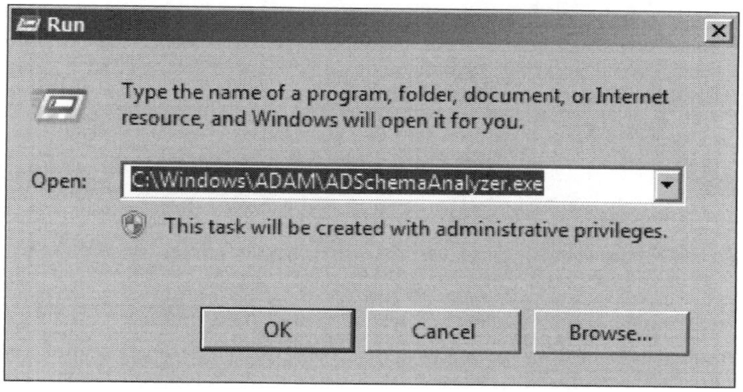

We should get the default **AD DS/LDS Schema Analyzer** tool screen, with three top menu options. Just go to **File** | **Load target schema...** as shown in the following screenshot:

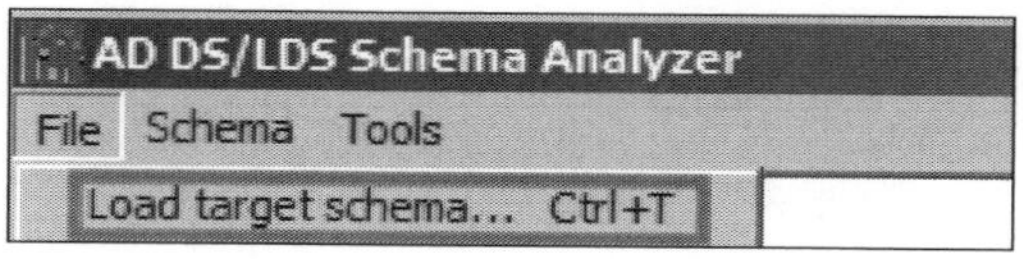

In the screen that will now appear (as shown in the following screenshot), we can click on the **Load LDIF...** button to load the LDIF file from before the AD DS schema extension:

Load LDIF...

Select the `old-adds-schema.ldif` file and press *Enter*. At the bottom of the **AD DS/LDS Schema Analyzer** tool, we will see some progress as the tool loads the entries, and at the end we will see a summary of the loaded schema as shown in the following screenshot:

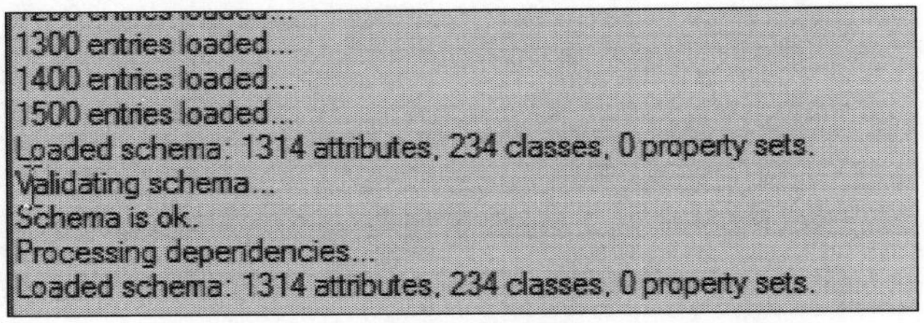
1300 entries loaded...
1400 entries loaded...
1500 entries loaded...
Loaded schema: 1314 attributes, 234 classes, 0 property sets.
Validating schema...
Schema is ok.
Processing dependencies...
Loaded schema: 1314 attributes, 234 classes, 0 property sets.

Ok, now we need to load the base schema so we can use the tool for the comparison. We can do this in the following two ways:

- Connecting directly to the live AD DS
- Using the LDIF file we generated based on the AD DS schema after the extension

We will use the latter. Thus, we just need to click on the top menu and go to **File | Load base schema...**, and in the next screen click on the button **Load LDIF...** as we did for the target schema in the previous step.

Again, a summary of the new loaded schema will appear at the bottom of the tool. Now we can actually see that we have one more class and one more attribute on our Active Directory. After the load, the tool will automatically execute a comparison between the schemas, as we can see in the following screenshot:

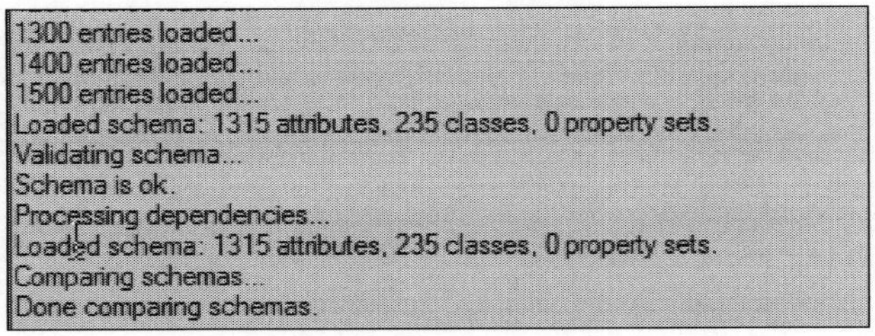
1300 entries loaded...
1400 entries loaded...
1500 entries loaded...
Loaded schema: 1315 attributes, 235 classes, 0 property sets.
Validating schema...
Schema is ok.
Processing dependencies...
Loaded schema: 1315 attributes, 235 classes, 0 property sets.
Comparing schemas...
Done comparing schemas.

Now, to be absolutely certain that all attributes and classes are present on the actual schema, we go to **Schema** | **Hide present elements,** as shown in the following screenshot:

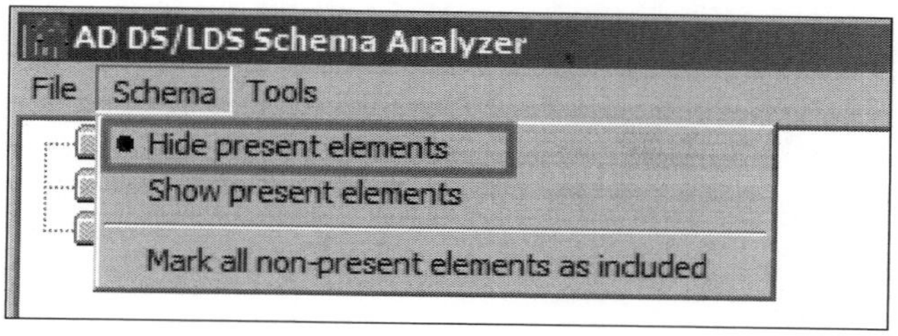

After that, we will see that all the items in the upper panel on the **AD DS/LDS Schema Analyzer** tool are empty. This means that every element is present, as shown in the following screenshot:

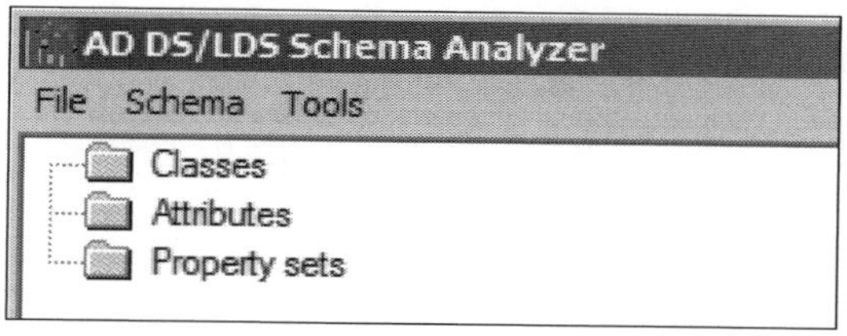

This is one way we can use this handy tool to perform comparisons when we change the AD DS default schema. Now, if we exit the tool and start it again, we can actually perform a similar comparison, but this time loading the target schema as our `new-adds-schema.ldif` file and the base schema as the `old-adds-schema.ldif` file. So, if we click on the top menu and go to **Schema** | **Hide present elements**, we will see that our items will not be empty anymore, as shown in the following screenshot:

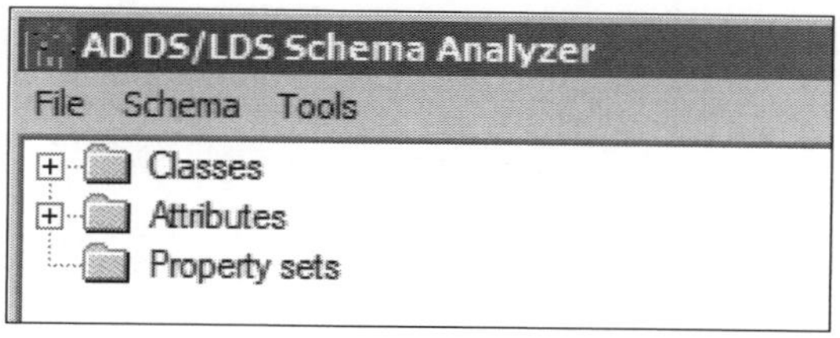

So we know that we have new elements on our new AD DS schema. Expanding all the items in that upper panel, we will have a hierarchy similar to the following screenshot:

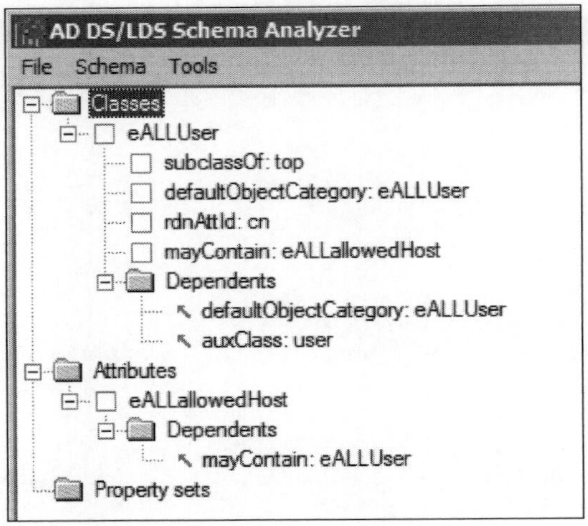

Excellent! We can see exactly which new classes and attributes we have and the relationships between them. This is a very useful tool to analyze changes on the Active Directory schema, and it is a must-have application for system administrators who plan to execute an AD DS schema extension.

Summary

In this chapter, we learned the key consideration points when planning an Active Directory schema extension, how to prepare the tests and validations for the AD DS schema extension procedure, and learned how to export the current AD DS schema configuration.

We could also execute a practical AD DS schema extension procedure using a proper registered OID on top of a real application use case based on a PAM module implemented to solve a real use-case scenario.

At the end of the chapter, we learned how to execute general tests and validations of the health of Active Directory and learned a step-by-step procedure to perform a full comparison between the old AD DS schema and the new extended schema configuration to fully validate the whole process.

In the next chapter, we will learn how to implement a highly available distributed file server using the Samba 4 Server and some auxiliary software such as the GlusterFS distributed filesystem and the **Cluster Trivial Database** (**CTDB**).

8
Implementing a Highly Available Distributed File Server

This chapter, with a more advanced focus, deals with high availability for the file server role in Samba 4 deployments. The objective of this chapter is to show how to implement a highly available file server using Samba 4 and software such as **Clustered Trivial Database** (**CTDB**) and the **GlusterFS** distributed filesystem.

The user will be instructed to implement this solution through step-by-step command-line examples, touching some of the many concepts involved and covering the following topics:

- Preparing the Debian GNU/Linux environment
- Configuring GlusterFS
- Integrating CTDB [43], GlusterFS, and the Samba 4 Server
- Executing some tests and validations on the highly available distributed filesystem server

The chapter will follow the objectives of the book in being practical, hence it should not be an exhaustive source for the technologies referenced here (for example, GlusterFS), and will not cover all the options and possible scenarios. That said, it will provide a great foundation and a solid work example to implement a complete solution to provide highly available file services.

Preparing the Debian GNU/Linux environment

Before we start the configuration of the software involved in the solution, we need to have the proper operating system environment so we can install the software required for our highly available file server. If you have installed the Debian GNU/Distribution 7.2 (Wheezy) or above, the CTDB version that is available to be installed on that environment is ready to use for our requirement. In this case, just make sure to execute the following commands before you proceed to the software installation:

```
root@gluster1:~# apt-get update
Hit http://ftp.br.debian.org wheezy Release.gpg
Hit http://ftp.br.debian.org wheezy-updates Release.gpg
Hit http://ftp.br.debian.org wheezy Release
Hit http://ftp.br.debian.org wheezy-updates Release
Hit http://ftp.br.debian.org wheezy/main Sources
Hit http://ftp.br.debian.org wheezy/main amd64 Packages
...
... SKIPPED FOR BREVITY ...
...
Reading package lists... Done
root@gluster1:~# apt-get upgrade
Reading package lists... Done
Building dependency tree
Reading state information... Done
0 upgraded, 0 newly installed, 0 to remove and 0 not upgraded.
root@gluster1:~#
```

The two preceding commands will update the package list for our distribution and apply any upgrades needed to bring our Debian GNU/Linux installation to the most up-to-date version. For older versions of the Debian GNU/Linux distribution (for example, 6.x Squeeze), the user will need to upgrade the whole distribution with the preceding commands, followed by the `apt-get dist-upgrade` command. The references have a link for the official Debian documentation explaining the distribution upgrade process in detail [`50`].

After the operating system environment is configured and ready (for example, Debian Wheezy 7.2+), we can proceed with the installation of the CTDB software. We will need two packages for our configuration: `ctdb` and `libctdb-dev`. Just issue the following command in a terminal window, for example, as a `root` user or using `sudo`[`73`]:

```
root@gluster1:~# apt-get install ctdb libctdb-dev
Reading package lists... Done
Building dependency tree
Reading state information... Done
The following extra packages will be installed:
    ctdb    libctdb-dev
…
… SKIPPED FOR BREVITY …
…
root@gluster1:~#
```

With the operating system environment configured and ready, we can proceed to the installation of the GlusterFS and XFS filesystem tools. Just log in and use the `su` or `sudo` commands to install the packages as follows:

```
root@gluster1:~# apt-get install glusterfs-server xfsprogs
Reading package lists... Done
Building dependency tree
Reading state information... Done
The following extra packages will be installed:
  fuse fuse-utils glusterfs-client glusterfs-common libibverbs1
libreadline5
Suggested packages:
  glusterfs-examples xfsdump quota
The following NEW packages will be installed:
  fuse fuse-utils glusterfs-client glusterfs-common glusterfs-server
  libibverbs1 libreadline5 xfsprogs
0 upgraded, 8 newly installed, 0 to remove and 0 not upgraded.
Need to get 13.6 MB of archives.
…
… SKIPPED FOR BREVITY …
…
Setting up xfsprogs (3.1.7+b1) ...
Processing triggers for initramfs-tools ...
update-initramfs: Generating /boot/initrd.img-3.2.0-4-amd64
Setting up fuse-utils (2.9.0-2+deb7u1) ...
Setting up glusterfs-client (3.2.7-3+deb7u1) ...
Setting up glusterfs-server (3.2.7-3+deb7u1) ...
[ ok ] Starting glusterd service: glusterd.
root@gluster1:~#
```

In the preceding procedure, we can see the command needed to install the GlusterFS server package, XFS tools, and all their dependencies on the Debian GNU/Linux distribution. Just remember that we need the preceding software on all nodes, and in our specific cluster, we will have two servers (for example, `gluster1` and `gluster2`), so we need to execute the previous procedures on both nodes.

The last step in our preparation phase is to install the Samba 4 software. The reader can refer to the previous chapters, where we executed the Samba 4 installation instructions step-by-step. The only attention point is to add the essential option, `-with-cluster-support`, to the `configure` command so that Samba 4 will be compiled with the needed cluster features.

Configuring GlusterFS for high availability and scalability

In this topic, our first goal is to explain an important distinction when we discuss cluster filesystems. In IT, we have many words that are used out of context many times and start to mean many different things. Here, we will not try to create any definition or concept though, but just explain why we have decided to use the GlusterFS filesystem for our highly available file server and the important difference between GlusterFS and other cluster filesystems, approaches (for example, **Oracle Cluster File System** (**OCFS**) [`41`]).

If there is a word in IT that has the most different meanings for different people, it is the word "cluster". We have many filesystems that are called cluster filesystems, and if we go to the homepage of the GlusterFS project (`http://www.gluster.org/`), we will see that the word cluster is used many times. But the most important word for our use case, and the reason we have selected the GlusterFS project for our solution, is "distributed". The majority of the cluster filesystems and many users that think about it may imagine solutions to be more in accordance with the OCFS [`41`] approach.

OCFS is a type of filesystem where different machines share access to the same storage device (for example, disks). OCFS has a mechanism to control simultaneous access to the underlying storage between the different servers, but it still provides a consistent filesystem view for the clients, independent of which server a client is connected to. This is a legitimate solution, and OCFS is a very robust production filesystem. The issue in this design for the purposes of our use case is the fact that to use it we need to have access to a shared-disk infrastructure [for example, **Storage Area Network** (**SAN**)] and rely on the high availability of the disk arrays underneath. Beside this, the scalability of our solution will be dependent on the scalability of the backend disks for performance and space requirements.

Now enters the distributed filesystem approach (where we have GlusterFS [42] as an example), which does not rely on a shared-disk infrastructure but combines storage from different machines/servers together as building blocks to present to the clients a single global namespace. This model is much better in our experience for scalable, highly available, high-performance file server solutions, as there isn't a single point of failure and performance and space requirements scale horizontally as well.

It's important to note that the OCFS used here as an example of a shared-disk cluster filesystem has its requirements and use cases very well defined on the Oracle OCFS page [41]. OCFS has great features and a specific use case for Oracle Real Application Clusters [41]. It is used in many other solutions as it can be used as the base for a Samba 4 highly available file server too. We have just explained the reasons behind choosing to use a distributed filesystem (GlusterFS), so feel free to utilize whatever is more adequate for your environment or you feel more comfortable with (the procedure presented here should help you in a big way even if you decide to use a different filesytem).

> Our file server is for a small/medium network with moderate performance requirements. The scale-out nature of GlusterFS provides us the ability to add more nodes and enhance performance as we need, but every filesystem and solution has its own trade-offs, and you need to evaluate what better fits your use case (for example, small files, big files, random access, and so on).

One last but important point to note is that GlusterFS is not a "full" filesystem per se, but it concatenates filesystems into one big single namespace, so data on those filesystems get distributed, replicated, or both on the GlusterFS nodes [44]. We will use the XFS as the underlying filesystem for the GlusterFS filesystem as it is a very robust filesystem and offers a good general performance (for different use cases).

Now let's begin the real work and start the configuration of the GlusterFS part of our solution. Our highly available distributed file server will be composed of two file servers, three distinct network interfaces, and two **Virtual IPs** (**VIPs**).

One network will be used for our CIFS/SMB clients (`192.168.1.0`), and the VIPs will be on this network too, as follows:

- Node 0 (gluster1/eth0) = 192.168.1.1
- Node 1 (gluster2/eth0) = 192.168.1.2
- VIPs: 192.168.1.20 and 192.168.1.30

The second network will be used for the GlusterFS heartbeat (`10.10.10.0/24`) as follows:

- Node 0 (gluster1/eth1) = 10.10.10.21
- Node 1 (gluster2/eth1) = 10.10.10.22

The third one will be used for the CTDB heartbeat (`10.11.11.0/24`) as follows:

- Node 0 (gluster1/eth1) = 10.11.11.21
- Node 1 (gluster1/eth1) = 10.11.11.22

Every cluster solution that I have worked with needed specific interconnection interfaces for exclusive communication between the machines integrating the cluster. Some clusters needed as much as three different exclusive interfaces for this role (for redundancy) or required the use of a quorum network component (for example, a server), a quorum device (for example, a shared disk), or even both. This is because clusters need to handle different failure scenarios, and specifically two-node clusters have even more specific issues (for example, a communication failure between nodes is a total partition/split-brain).

So, we will use one dedicated interface for each heartbeat communication instance [`46`] (GlusterFS and CTDB) and the data network (for example, client-facing interface). Setting the latter to be a dedicated interface is important for performance and isolation/troubleshooting purposes (for example, NAS Network). Besides that, each server (for example, a cluster node) will have one dedicated disk to be used in the GlusterFS configuration as a data disk (for example, "brick" in GlusterFS terms).

> It's very important to have a dedicated network for the client's data.

The first thing we need to make sure is configured and working properly are our network connections, so that we can start configuring all the interfaces on both nodes. The following commands are an example of the three interfaces for the first node:

```
root@gluster1:~# ifconfig -a | grep -A2 "eth0\|eth1\|eth2"
eth0    Link encap:Ethernet  HWaddr fa:ce:27:ed:bf:39
        inet addr:192.168.1.1  Bcast:192.168.1.255  Mask:255.255.255.0
        inet6 addr: fe80::a00:27ff:feed:bf39/64 Scope:Link
--
eth1    Link encap:Ethernet  HWaddr fa:ca:27:f9:cc:a4
        inet addr:10.10.10.21  Bcast:10.10.10.255  Mask:255.255.255.0
```

```
        inet6 addr: fe80::a00:27ff:fef9:cca4/64 Scope:Link
--
eth2    Link encap:Ethernet  HWaddr ce:fa:27:3e:72:d4
        inet addr:10.11.11.21  Bcast:10.11.11.255  Mask:255.255.255.0
        inet6 addr: fe80::a00:27ff:fe3e:72d4/64 Scope:Link
root@gluster1:~#
```

Now let's take a look at the disks that we have available on our nodes (for example, node 1) as follows:

```
root@gluster2:~# fdisk -l | grep sd
Disk /dev/sdb doesn't contain a valid partition table
Disk /dev/sda: 8589 MB, 8589934592 bytes
/dev/sda1   *        2048    16254975    8126464   83  Linux
/dev/sda2        16257022    16775167     259073    5  Estendida
/dev/sda5        16257024    16775167     259072   82  Linux swap /
Solaris
Disk /dev/sdb: 5368 MB, 5368709120 bytes
root@gluster2:~#
```

> As we start working on disks, it's very important that we make sure on which disks we are working and validate all procedures in a test environment before moving to production. Be aware that some of the commands we will cover hereafter, when executed on improper devices (for example, disks), may lead to data loss.

The script above shows us that we have a disk (`/dev/sda`) that contains the partitions for our OS installation and another (`/dev/sdb`) available and without a partition table (first line in the output above). That is our brand new disk, where our Samba 4 client's data will reside, and thus we can create an XFS filesystem on it (make sure all nodes you are preparing for the cluster have a disk available for our XFS filesystem).

Now we can execute the following script on both servers (for example, `gluster1` and `gluster2`) to create one partition on the `/dev/sdb` disk and list it afterwards to make sure it was created properly:

```
root@gluster1:~# echo -e "n\np\n1\n\n\nw" | fdisk /dev/sdb > /dev/null
2>&1 && fdisk -l /dev/sdb
Disk /dev/sdb: 5368 MB, 5368709120 bytes
181 heads, 40 sectors/track, 1448 cylinders, total 10485760 sectors
Units = sectors of 1 * 512 = 512 bytes
Sector size (logical/physical): 512 bytes / 512 bytes
```

```
I/O size (minimum/optimal): 512 bytes / 512 bytes
Disk identifier: 0xad90d89b
   Device Boot      Start         End      Blocks   Id  System
/dev/sdb1            2048    10485759     5241856   83  Linux
root@gluster1:~#
```

So far so good, let's create the XFS filesystem (execute on both nodes):

```
root@gluster1:~# mkfs.xfs /dev/sdb1 && echo OK
meta-data=/dev/sdb1          isize=256    agcount=4, agsize=327616 blks
         =                   sectsz=512   attr=2, projid32bit=0
data     =                   bsize=4096   blocks=1310464, imaxpct=25
         =                   sunit=0      swidth=0 blks
naming   =version 2          bsize=4096   ascii-ci=0
log      =internal log       bsize=4096   blocks=2560, version=2
         =                   sectsz=512   sunit=0 blks, lazy-count=1
realtime =none               extsz=4096   blocks=0, rtextents=0
OK
root@gluster1:~#
```

The next step is to create the mount point for our brand new XFS filesystem, persist it on our operating system configuration (for example, `/etc/fstab`), and mount it (the procedure to be executed on all cluster nodes) as follows:

```
root@gluster1:~# mkdir -p /var/storage/disk1
root@gluster1:~# cp -pRf /etc/fstab /etc/fstab-`date '+%s%m%d%Y'` &&
echo "/dev/sdb1 /var/storage/disk1 xfs defaults 0 0" >> /etc/fstab &&
echo OK
OK
root@gluster1:~# mount -a && df -h | grep sdb1
/dev/sdb1          5.0G   33M  5.0G   1% /var/storage/disk1
```

The preceding scripts should create a backup of our `/etc/fstab` file before editing it. The last script does mount the XFS filesystem on the mount point we have created (reading it from the `/etc/fstab` directory) and uses the `df` utility to show us the mounted partition information. For the bootstrap of our configuration, let's add the hostname/IP pair of each server on the `/etc/hosts` file for simplicity (execute the same procedure on both nodes) as follows:

```
root@gluster1:~# cp -pRf /etc/hosts /etc/hosts-`date '+%s%m%d%Y'` &&
echo "10.10.10.21 gluster1-gc" >> /etc/hosts && \
```

```
echo "10.10.10.22 gluster2-gc" >> /etc/hosts && \
echo "10.11.11.21 gluster1-cc" >> /etc/hosts && \
echo "10.11.11.22 gluster2-cc" >> /etc/hosts && echo OK
OK
root@gluster1:~#
```

After we have executed these basic procedures successfully (for example, received `OK`, as in the preceding output), we can start the configuration of the GlusterFS distributed filesystem. Make sure you have executed all the previous procedures on both nodes until this point before moving on to the next steps.

Again, we need to execute the following command on both nodes, but just slightly differently. Here, we have one example of running it on the node 2 (`gluster2`) as follows:

```
root@gluster2:~# gluster peer probe gluster1-gc
Probe successful
root@gluster2:~#
```

> The systems should not have previous Samba software versions (for example, Version 3) or old configurations and binaries that can conflict with Samba 4. Remember to remove all configurations and software previously installed (for example, the `apt-get` purge). Test everything in a lab environment and create backups of everything you remove or reconfigure.

The important point in the previous commands is that we need to probe node 0 (`gluster1`) from node 1 (`gluster2`) and vice versa. Note that we are using the Gluster interconnect interface (`gluster1-gc`) because that is the heartbeat interface we have created for the GlusterFS inter-node communication.

Before we do create our volume, let's just clarify two important and distinct configuration options for Gluster: replicate and distribute. We will use the first option, as it replicates data between the nodes of the cluster that gives us redundancy and availability at the Gluster filesystem level (very important as we are using just one disk at each server without RAID [`47`]). The second mode (distribute) will place the files across the nodes (for example, volumes) of the gluster [`45`], which is a good thing for performance and space, but we would need to add a layer of redundancy on our disks or any node failures would result in unavailability for our clients. We can even combine the two modes, but that is out of the scope of this book.

Execute the following commands on just one node. The following is an example of the execution on the `gluster2` node:

```
root@gluster2:~# gluster volume create smb01 replica 2 \
gluster1-gc:/var/storage/disk1 gluster2-gc:/var/storage/disk1
Creation of volume smb01 has been successful. Please start the volume to
access data.
root@gluster2:~# gluster volume start smb01
Starting volume smb01 has been successful
root@gluster2:~#
```

If the two preceding commands were executed successfully, we should have our brand new volume ready to go! As we need to see it to believe it, the following command will show the state of the `glusterfs` volume (executed from any node):

```
root@gluster2:~# gluster volume info
Volume Name: smb01
Type: Replicate
Status: Started
Number of Bricks: 2
Transport-type: tcp
Bricks:
Brick1: gluster1-gc:/var/storage/disk1
Brick2: gluster2-gc:/var/storage/disk1
root@gluster2:~#
```

The preceding command is very informative, as we can see the volume name, the volume type (in our case, `replicate`), the number and nodes/path of the individual bricks, and most importantly, the status (in our execution example, `Started`).

Integrating CTDB, GlusterFS, and the Samba 4 Server

CTDB is the software that implements the clusterization of the **Trivial Database** (**TDB**) [49] used by Samba [43]. As CTDB provides functionalities that are similar to those provided by TDB (for example, the same type of functions), Samba or any other project/software that already uses the Trivial Database can migrate to a clustered version (CTDB) with minimal effort.

CTDB needs a special lock file that is accessible from any node, so we will create it on our `glusterfs` volume (for example, `smb01`) in a specific directory called `ctdb`. The following procedure needs to be run in just one node:

```
root@gluster1:~# mkdir -p /var/lib/samba/glusterfs && echo OK
OK
root@gluster1:~# cp -pRf /etc/fstab /etc/fstab-`date '+%s%m%d%Y'` &&
echo "localhost:/smb01 /var/lib/samba/glusterfs/ glusterfs defaults,_
netdev 0 0" >> /etc/fstab && mount -a && echo OK
OK
root@gluster1:~# mkdir /var/lib/samba/glusterfs/ctdb && echo OK
OK
root@gluster1:~#
```

Now we need to create some files inside that directory, and the first one is the `ctdb` file. Let's copy the default `ctdb` file from the Debian GNU/Linux distribution to use it as a template. For that, just issue the following command in one node (the node you have executed the previous procedure in, as it has the `glusterfs` filesystem already mounted):

```
root@gluster1:~# cp -pRf /etc/default/ctdb /etc/default/ctdb-`date
'+%s%m%d%Y'` && echo OK
OK
root@gluster1:~# rm /etc/default/ctdb && echo OK
OK
root@gluster1:~#
```

In the other nodes of the cluster, just execute the following command:

```
root@gluster2~# rm /etc/default/ctdb && echo OK
OK
root@gluster2:~#
```

The `/var/lib/samba/glusterfs/ctdb/ctdb` file is the main configuration file for the CTDB software (for example, on the Debian GNU/Linux distribution), and we will edit this file in just one node (the one we have the `glusterfs` filesystem mounted in, that is, `gluster1`) and leave it with the following content:

```
root@gluster1:~# cat /etc/default/ctdb
CTDB_RECOVERY_LOCK="/var/lib/samba/glusterfs/ctdb/lock"
CTDB_PUBLIC_INTERFACE=eth0
CTDB_PUBLIC_ADDRESSES="/var/lib/samba/glusterfs/ctdb/public_addresses"
```

```
CTDB_NODES="/var/lib/samba/glusterfs/ctdb/nodes"
CTDB_MANAGES_SAMBA=yes
CTDB_INIT_STYLE=debian
CTDB_SERVICE_SMB=smb4
CTDB_DBDIR=/var/lib/ctdb
CTDB_DBDIR_PERSISTENT=/var/lib/ctdb/persistent
```

The first configuration is for the CTDB lock file, and the second line is the configuration for the file containing the public IP addresses (VIPs). The content for the file pointed in the configuration of `CTDB_NODES` should be the list of the nodes' IP addresses (for example, the nodes' interconnect interfaces). The last lines are configurations for CTDB to be able to manage the initialization of the Samba 4 daemon and CTDB databases' locations.

The following is the content of the `nodes` file; execute the following script on just one node to create the file (in the same node we have executed the previous procedures, as we have the `glusterfs` filesystem already mounted on it):

```
root@gluster1:~# echo -e "10.11.11.21\n10.11.11.22" >
/var/lib/samba/glusterfs/ctdb/nodes
root@gluster1:~# cat !$
cat /var/lib/samba/glusterfs/ctdb/nodes
10.11.11.21
10.11.11.22
root@gluster1:~#
```

> In the official CTDB documentation at `samba.org`, you will find the description of each tunable option [52].

We need virtual IPs (VIPs) for the cluster to use in case of node failures to be able to transfer the services (for example, VIPs) to other nodes. These VIPs need to be on the public interface because they are the point of connection for the Samba 4 client.

Here is the script to be executed just on one node (the same as we executed in the previous steps) to add the content of the `public_addresses` file and show it:

```
root@gluster1:~# echo -e "192.168.1.20/24\n192.168.1.30/24" > /var/lib/
samba/glusterfs/ctdb/public_addresses
root@gluster1:~# cat !$
cat /var/lib/samba/glusterfs/ctdb/public_addresses
192.168.1.20/24
```

```
192.168.1.30/24
root@gluster1:~#
```

The last configuration step is to edit our `smb.conf` file and add the clustering directive and specify our share volume, as highlighted in the following excerpt:

```
root@gluster1:~# cat /usr/local/samba/etc/smb.conf
[global]
        clustering = yes
        workgroup = POA
        netbios name = hafs
        security = ads
        …
…
[share]
        path = /var/lib/samba/glusterfs/data
        comment = Highly Available Share
        read only = No
        valid users = @"POA\Domain Admins"
        browseable = Yes
```

After that, we move the `smb.conf` configuration file for our highly available share (you just need to do the editing in one node—the same way we have executed the previous editing) as shown in the following commands:

```
root@gluster1:~# mkdir /var/lib/samba/glusterfs/data
root@gluster1:~# mv /usr/local/samba/etc/smb.conf \
/var/lib/samba/glusterfs/ctdb/ && echo OK
OK
root@gluster1:~#
```

> You may consider adding the `reset on zero vc = yes` option to your `smb.conf` file. You may have a look into more details about this and other file locking options and considerations [55]. Locking is an important issue in file servers, and so the reader needs to understand all the implications of the different options.

Now we need to create symbolic links for the `ctdb` and `smb.conf` files in every node of the cluster (for example, the `gluster1` and `gluster2` nodes). So, execute the following procedure on all nodes (inclusive of `gluster1`):

```
root@gluster1:~# ln -s /var/lib/samba/glusterfs/ctdb/ctdb /etc/default/
ctdb && echo OK
OK
root@gluster1:~# ln -s /var/lib/samba/glusterfs/ctdb/smb.conf /usr/local/
samba/etc/smb.conf && echo OK
OK
root@gluster1:~#
```

Some utilities will search for files in the default location using default names (for example, `/etc/ctdb/nodes`), so let's create these links as well (on both nodes) as shown in the following commands:

```
root@gluster1:~# ln -s /var/lib/samba/glusterfs/ctdb/nodes /etc/ctdb/
nodes && echo OK
OK
root@gluster1:~# ln -s /var/lib/samba/glusterfs/ctdb/public_addresses  /
etc/ctdb/public_addresses && echo OK
OK
root@gluster1:~#
```

Now we are going to start the services, so let's do it! As we executed the majority of the configuration procedure on the `gluster1` node, we should already have the `glusterfs` volume mounted on that node. Now, we just need to mount it on the second node as shown in the following commands:

```
root@gluster2:~# mkdir -p /var/lib/samba/glusterfs && echo OK
OK
root@gluster2:~# cp -pRf /etc/fstab /etc/fstab-`date '+%s%m%d%Y'` &&
echo "localhost:/smb01 /var/lib/samba/glusterfs/ glusterfs defaults,_
netdev 0 0" >> /etc/fstab && mount -a && echo OK
OK
root@gluster2:~#
```

As we have installed the Samba 4 software by compiling it from the source code directly, we are not using a binary package from the distribution and so we do not have a Samba 4 initialization script. We have made some minor adjustments on a publicly available Samba 4 initialization script referenced here [48] that was based on the script from the Debian GNU distribution for the Samba 3 package, and it is provided as an example initialization script available in the book's repository. So we just need to download it and put it in the `/etc/init.d/` directory and name it `smb4` (on both nodes), as follows:

```
root@gluster1:~# cd /etc/init.d/ && echo OK
OK
root@gluster1:~# wget --quiet https://raw.github.com/packt/bookrepository/
master/smb4-fs && mv smb4-fs smb4 && echo OK
OK
root@gluster1:~# chmod 755 smb4 && cd && echo OK
OK
root@gluster1:~#
```

Execute the following commands to adjust the CTDB script path and create a link for the default Samba configuration file (in all nodes):

```
root@gluster1:~# cp -pRf /etc/ctdb/functions /etc/ctdb/functions-
`date '+%s%m%d%Y'` && sed -e 's/PATH=\/bin:.*$/PATH=\/usr\/local\/
samba\/bin:\/usr\/local\/samba\/sbin:\/bin:\/usr\/bin:\/usr\/sbin:\/
sbin:\$PATH/g'
/etc/ctdb/functions > /etc/ctdb/functions-new && mv
/etc/ctdb/functions-new /etc/ctdb/functions && echo OK
OK
root@gluster1:~# mkdir /etc/samba && ln -s /var/lib/samba/glusterfs/ctdb/
smb.conf /etc/samba/ && echo OK
OK
root@gluster1:~#
```

Ready to start the CTDB software and bring our Samba 4 highly available distributed file server online? Good! Just execute the following commands on both nodes:

```
root@gluster1:~# service ctdb start
[ok]
root@gluster1:~#
```

The CTDB cluster will not be up and running (healthy) right away, as we still need to add our HA file servers into the domain. The `winbindd` daemon will not start unless we do that, and CTDB will identify that error and prevent the system from being fully functional. We can take a look at the `ctdb` logs, as follows, to see the typical error at this configuration stage:

```
root@gluster1:~# tail /var/log/ctdb/log.ctdb
2013/12/12 18:35:35.732508 [18195]: Release freeze handler for prio 3
2013/12/12 18:35:36.031226 [recoverd:18454]: Resetting ban count to 0 for all nodes
2013/12/12 18:35:49.465193 [18195]: 50.samba: ERROR: winbind - wbinfo -p returned error
2013/12/12 18:35:52.046421 [recoverd:18454]: Trigger takeoverrun
2013/12/12 18:35:54.644519 [18195]: 50.samba: ERROR: winbind - wbinfo -p returned error
2013/12/12 18:35:59.863546 [18195]: 50.samba: ERROR: winbind - wbinfo -p returned error
...
root@gluster1:~#
```

In order to fix this error, we need to join the nodes into our domain, but for that we need to execute the `join` procedure in just one node. The CTDB cluster will handle the sync of the `secrets.tdb` file to have consistent credentials between our nodes (a join is made for our `netbios` cluster name, and the same is done for all clusters' members). For our AD DS server, no matter how many gluster, CTDB, and Samba file servers we have in the cluster, they will be like one of these:

```
root@gluster1:~# export PATH=/usr/local/samba/sbin:\
/usr/local/samba/bin:$PATH
root@gluster1:~# net ads join -U administrator
Enter administrator's password:
Using short domain name -- POA
Joined 'HAFS' to dns domain 'poa.msdcbrz.eall.com.br'
Not doing automatic DNS update in a clustered setup.
root@gluster1:~#
```

Now we restart the CTDB services (on both nodes) as follows:

```
root@gluster1:~# service ctdb stop && service ctdb start
[....] Stopping Clustered TDB: ctdb
[ ok ] Starting Clustered TDB : ctdb.
root@gluster1:~#
```

And after a few minutes, we should be able to confirm that the status of the services will be OK, as follows:

```
root@gluster1:~# ctdb status
Number of nodes:2
pnn:0 10.11.11.21      OK (THIS NODE)
pnn:1 10.11.11.22      OK
Generation:225613703
Size:2
hash:0 lmaster:0
hash:1 lmaster:1
Recovery mode:NORMAL (0)
Recovery master:0
root@gluster1:~#
```

The systems need some time to start and verify the services until we get to the `OK` statuses, so just wait a few minutes (for example, `watch ctdb status`). If you face any problems or the system does not come online, the logfile `/var/log/ctdb/log.ctdb` has information about what the problem could be. When debugging the problems with CTDB, we can change the default debug level from `ERR` in the file `/etc/default/ctdb` to a number such as `3` or `5`; for example, I have tested with `5` and it is really verbose, instead of `CTDB_DEBUGLEVEL=5`.

The last point to confirm before going on to more specific tests is to check if the VIPs are online on our nodes, as follows:

```
root@gluster1:~# ctdb ip -v
Public IPs on node 0
192.168.1.20 node[0] active[eth0] available[eth0] configured[eth0]
192.168.1.30 node[1] active[] available[eth0] configured[eth0] root@
gluster1:~#
root@gluster2:~# ctdb ip -v
Public IPs on node 0
192.168.1.20 node[0] active[] available[eth0] configured[eth0]
192.168.1.30 node[1] active[eth0] available[eth0] configured[eth0] root@
gluster2:~#
```

The preceding command is very handy, as we can see information about the IP allocation on the cluster; another important piece of data is the `active` column. From the preceding output, we can see that we have each of our servers with one IP active, so the cluster automatically balances the distribution of IPs evenly on our cluster, which is good for performance and availability. Let's just show the network configuration of each server, so we can see that each node has the IP, as shown in the preceding output:

```
root@gluster1:~# ip add show eth0
3: eth1: <BROADCAST,MULTICAST,UP,LOWER_UP> mtu 1500 qdisc pfifo_fast
state UP qlen 1000
  link/ether fa:ce:27:ed:bf:39 brd ff:ff:ff:ff:ff:ff
  inet 192.168.1.2/24 brd 192.168.1.255 scope global eth0
  inet 192.168.1.20/24 brd 192.168.1.255 scope global secondary eth0
  inet6 fe80::a00:27ff:feac:f0c9/64 scope link
     valid_lft forever preferred_lft forever
root@gluster1:~#
```

Now let's look at the same command execution on node 1, as follows:

```
root@gluster2:~# ip addr show eth0
3: eth1: <BROADCAST,MULTICAST,UP,LOWER_UP> mtu 1500 qdisc pfifo_fast
state UP qlen 1000
  link/ether fa:ce:27:f3:8d:50 brd ff:ff:ff:ff:ff:ff
  inet 192.168.1.3/24 brd 192.168.1.255 scope global eth0
  inet 192.168.1.30/24 brd 192.168.1.255 scope global secondary eth0
  inet6 fe80::a00:27ff:fef3:8d50/64 scope link
     valid_lft forever preferred_lft forever
root@gluster2:~#
```

Everything is up and running and we can go ahead and start our tests on the file server and validate our configuration!

Executing tests and validations on the highly available file server

The first test we need to execute on our highly available file server is to try to access the share directly on the server `localhost` interface. We can perform this test using the `smbclient` tool as follows:

```
root@gluster1:~# smbclient -L localhost -U 'zisala%w1ndow$$'
Domain=[POA] OS=[Unix] Server=[Samba 4.0.9]

        Sharename       Type      Comment
        ---------       ----      -------
        share           Disk      Highly Available Share
...
root@gluster1:~#
```

It's assumed that even if you have specified the interfaces to bind the Samba 4 services, the loopback interface hangs your tests if you have removed this interface from your configuration.

Second, let's try to access using the VIPs as follows:

```
root@gluster1:~# smbclient -L 192.168.1.20 -U 'zisala%w1ndow$$'
Domain=[POA] OS=[Unix] Server=[Samba 4.0.9]

        Sharename       Type      Comment
        ---------       ----      -------
        share           Disk      Highly Available Share
...
root@gluster1:~#
        And...

root@gluster1:~# smbclient -L 192.168.1.30 -U 'zisala%w1ndow$$'
Domain=[POA] OS=[Unix] Server=[Samba 4.0.9]

        Sharename       Type      Comment
        ---------       ----      -------
        share           Disk      Highly Available Share
...
root@gluster1:~#
```

Perfect! It's time to test the access and the high availability of our file server directly from a Microsoft Windows client machine. Let's first create a DNS entry for our VIPs so we can use it instead of the IP addresses to let our cluster handle any failures for us, as it fails over the VIPs transparently between the nodes. Follow these steps:

1. Navigate to **Administrative Tools** | **DNS**, connect to the `addc` AD DS, and expand the DNS server to select our domain as shown in the following screenshot:

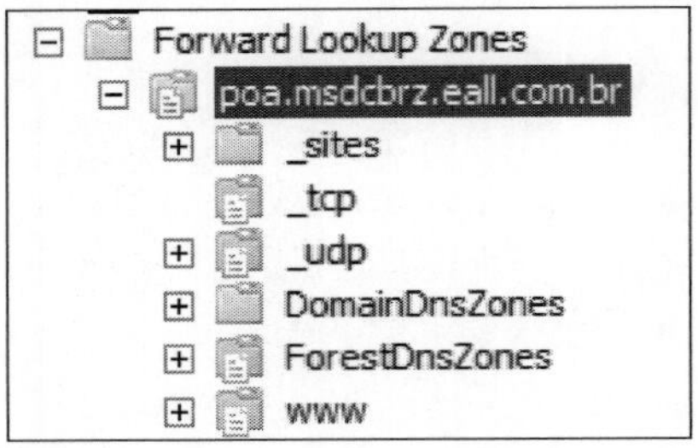

2. In the top menu, select **View** and check the option **Advanced** as shown in the following screenshot:

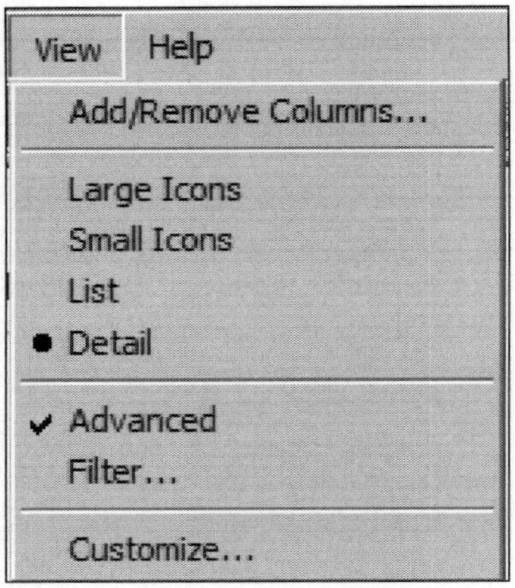

3. The preceding selection is needed to be able to edit the TTL value for our `glusterfs` records [`51`]. We need to edit the TTL to provide a faster recovery time for our file server cluster and some kind of load balancing. Just for our test, we will create `AA` records and set the TTL to `1`. Just right-click on the `poa.msdcbrz.eall.com.br` zone and select **New Host (A or AAAA)...** as shown in the following screenshot:

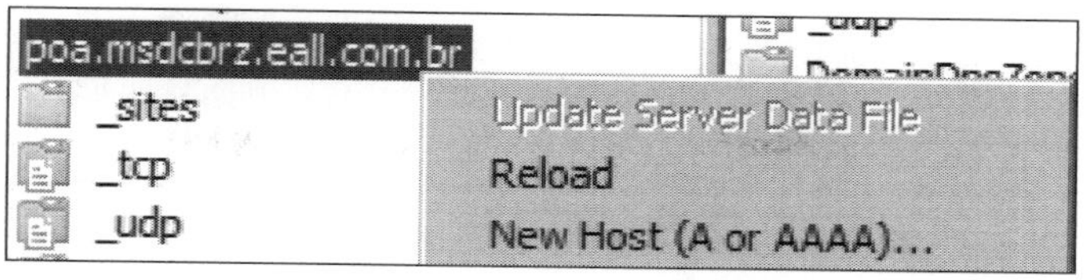

4. In the **New Host** screen next, fill the first box with the name `glusterfs`, fill the **IP address** box with `192.168.1.20`, and at the bottom of the screen set the TTL to `1`. The following screenshot has an example for this procedure:

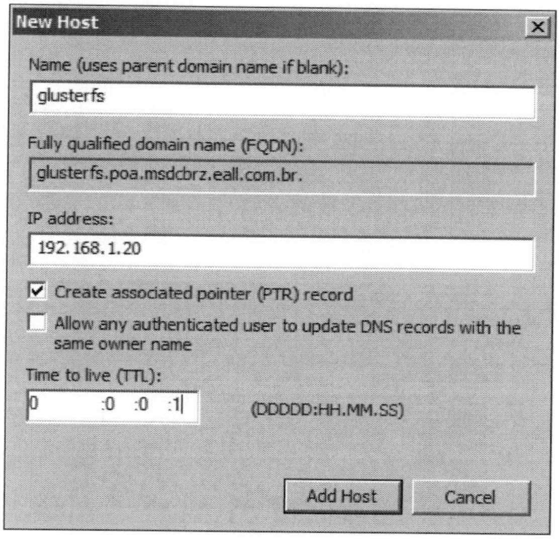

5. After we have clicked on the **Add Host** button in the previous screen, we repeat the process, just changing the IP from `192.168.1.20` to `192.168.1.30`, as shown in the following screenshot. So, at the end, we should have two new `glusterfs` records, each pointing to different IPs and both with TTL `1`. Just click on **Done**.

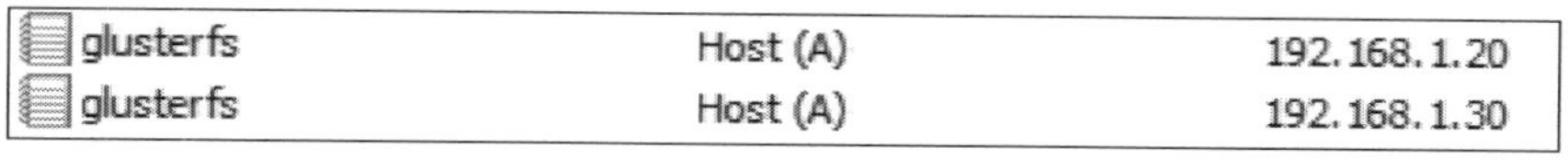

6. As stated in [51], we need to configure the Microsoft Windows client cache time to actually have a consistent configuration and our short TTL effective on our test environment. So, let's open the registry and find the key `HKEY_LOCAL_MACHINE\System\CurrentControlSet\Services\Dnscache\Parameters`, as shown in the following screenshot:

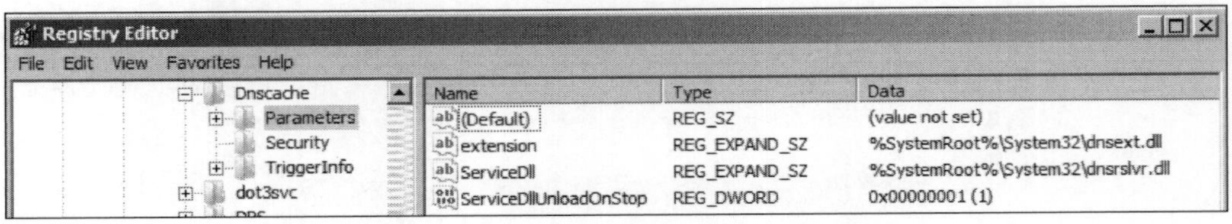

7. We need to add the entry **DWORD (32-bit) Value** with value name `MaxCacheEntryTtlLimit` [51] as shown in the following screenshot:

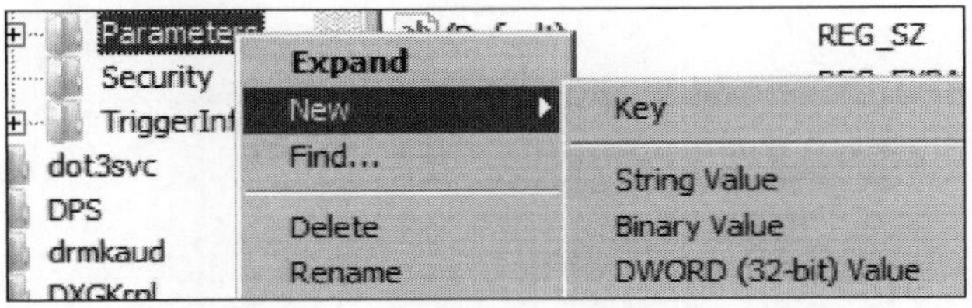

8. The value is in seconds, so let's double-click on it and set it to `1` as shown in the following screenshot:

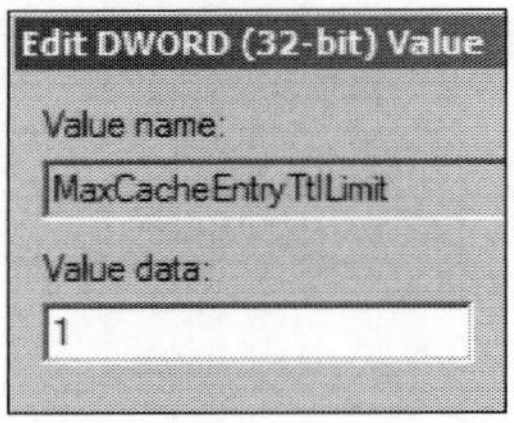

9. In the end, our DNS cache parameters should read like those in the following screenshot:

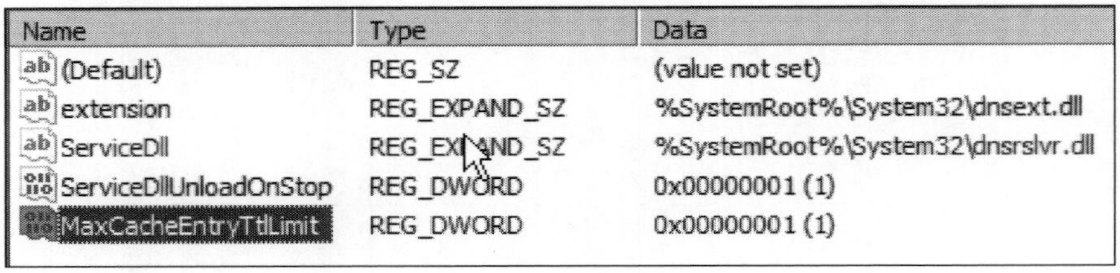
Name
Type
Data
(Default)
REG_SZ
(value not set)
extension
REG_EXPAND_SZ
%SystemRoot%\System32\dnsext.dll
ServiceDll
%SystemRoot%\System32\dnsrslvr.dll
ServiceDllUnloadOnStop
REG_DWORD
0x00000001 (1)
MaxCacheEntryTtlLimit
REG_DWORD
0x00000001 (1)

10. Log in to a Microsoft Windows Server 2008 R2 as a user that has permission to access the share we have created (for example, in Domain Admin group), click on **Start**, enter `\\glusterfs` on the **Search programs and files** input box, as shown in the following screenshot, and press *Enter*:

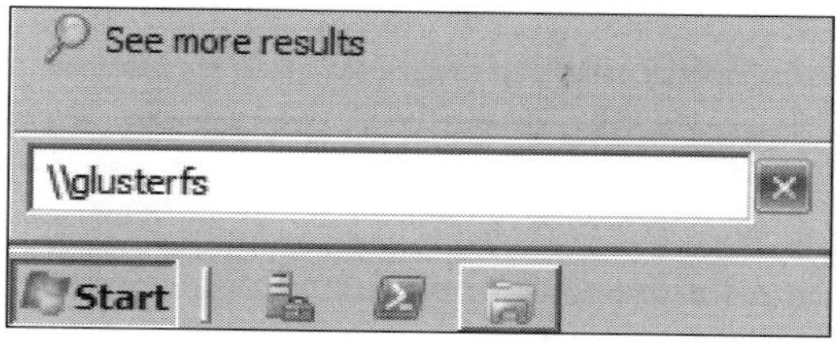

11. We should be presented with an explorer window showing our share. On double-clicking on it, we should see that our share is empty, as shown in the following screenshot:

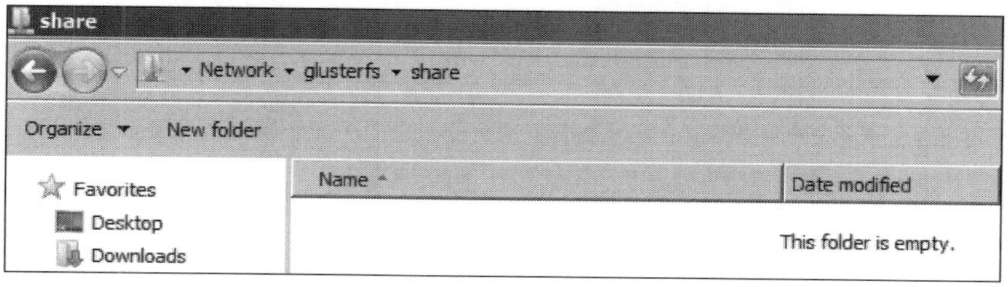

12. Now we can copy some data to our share, and while the copying process is running, we will stop the file server services on our node where we have the preceding Microsoft Windows connection. To identify our connection, let's execute the `ipconfig` command in a command prompt in the Microsoft Windows Server 2008 R2 prompt, as shown in the following screenshot:

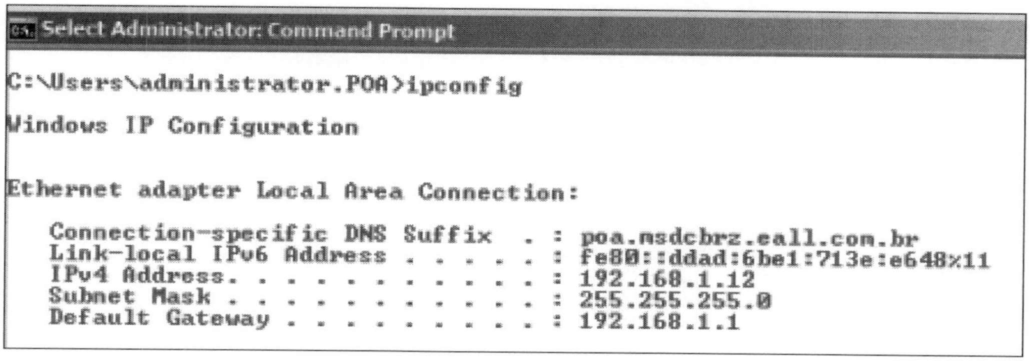

Select Administrator: Command Prompt
C:\Users\administrator.POA>ipconfig
Windows IP Configuration
Ethernet adapter Local Area Connection:
Connection-specific DNS Suffix . : poa.msdcbrz.eall.com.br
Link-local IPv6 Address . . . . . : fe80::ddad:6be1:713e:e648%11
IPv4 Address. . . . . : 192.168.1.12
Subnet Mask . . . . : 255.255.255.0
Default Gateway . . . . : 192.168.1.1

13. From the preceding output, we can see that our client has the IP `192.168.1.12`. Now we can execute the following command in all nodes of our GlusterFS cluster and identify the node that the client is connected to. We can do this using more generic tools from the GNU/Linux world (for example, `netstat` and `grep`) together with the `onnode` utility as a first approach, as follows:

```
root@gluster1:~# onnode all "netstat -anl | grep -w 192.168.1.12"
>> NODE: 10.11.11.21 <<
tcp 0   0 192.168.1.20:445 192.168.1.12:57694  ESTABLISHED
>> NODE: 10.11.11.22 <<
root@gluster1:~#
```

The preceding utility (`onnode`) receives as arguments the nodes where we want to execute commands (for example, `all`) and the script we want to execute (for example, in the preceding example, list the host connections and search for one specific IP).

14. An easier option is to use the `smbstatus` tool to present us with the answer in a well formatted and very clean manner (we will use the `-p` option to show us the processes and `-n` for the numeric data, as seen in the `netstat` command earlier):

```
root@gluster1:~# smbstatus -np

Samba version 4.0.13
PID     Username  Group    Machine
---------------------------------------------------------------
--
0:12624 1500      1513    192.168.1.12 (ipv4:192.168.1.12:57694)
root@gluster1:~#
```

We were lucky because the Microsoft client is connected on the same host where SSH is connected (`node 0 = gluster1`), so we can just stop the services on this node and CTDB will migrate the IP to another node, and that should be transparent for clients.

Let's copy something to our share. We have the matrix's logs on our desktop, so we can copy it to the `glusterfs` share and so other architects can inspect it and look for failures in the system. It's important in tests such as these to have the MD5 of the file so that we are able, at the end of the test, to make sure the file was not corrupt and the cluster really did a consistent job on the IP transfer. So, `glusterfs` and everything else worked as expected for the stability of our file server (we will use `xcopy` [53] to copy the file; this utility has a `/v` option for verification of the file after the copy, and you may use it if you need to). The MD5 for our file is `eeaa7d4c17d5c6c86aa7aac57c3594db`. Follow these steps:

1. First let's see the status of the CTDB services as follows:

```
root@gluster1:~# ctdb status
Number of nodes:2
pnn:0 10.11.11.21      OK (THIS NODE)
pnn:1 10.11.11.22      OK
Generation:985025383
Size:2
hash:0 lmaster:0
hash:1 lmaster:1
Recovery mode:NORMAL (0)
Recovery master:0
root@gluster1:~#
```

> For the services startup (for example, operating system boot), one important step is to make sure the mount of the system partitions/disks (for example, the `glusterfs` volumes) will happen after a gluster is online. Another point to note is to organize the dependencies of each service accordingly with the GNU/distribution initialization framework (for example, `ctdb` needs to be the last service to come online, as it will start Samba and all the underlying infrastructure needs to be up and running before that).

2. Just open a command prompt window and issue the command demonstrated in the following screenshot:

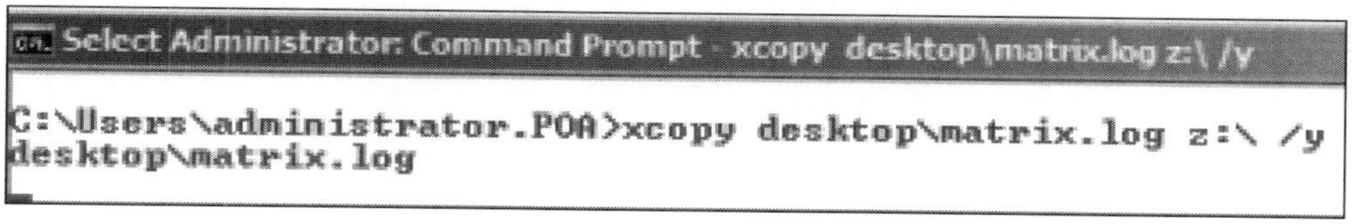
Select Administrator: Command Prompt - xcopy desktop\matrix.log z:\ /y
C:\Users\administrator.POA>xcopy desktop\matrix.log z:\ /y
desktop\matrix.log

3. While our copying process is running, we will use the `smbstatus` command one more time to make sure we will disable only the node where our Microsoft Windows client is connected, as shown in the following command:

```
root@gluster1:~# smbstatus -np

Samba version 4.0.13
PID     Username      Group         Machine
-----------------------------------------------------------------
--
```

```
0:12624   1500          1513          192.168.1.12
(ipv4:192.168.1.12:57694)
root@gluster1:~#
```

4. The Microsoft Windows client is connected on the `gluster1` host (node 0), so we will disable this node, which will make the CTDB software migrate the VIP to `gluster2` (node 1), as follows:

```
root@gluster1:~# ctdb disable -n 0 && echo OK
OK
root@gluster1:~#
```

5. For this example, we have mapped the `\\glusterfs\share` share to `Z:` on our Microsoft Windows client just to facilitate the tests. Z is the first letter offered.
6. Now, we can look at the CTDB's status to confirm that the node 0 is disabled, as follows:

```
root@gluster2:~# ctdb status
Number of nodes:2
pnn:0 10.11.11.21      DISABLED
pnn:1 10.11.11.22      OK (THIS NODE)
Generation:2123322465
Size:2
hash:0 lmaster:0
hash:1 lmaster:1
Recovery mode:NORMAL (0)
Recovery master:1
root@gluster2:~#
```

7. The preceding output is exactly what we were expecting, as it shows the node 0 (`pnn: 0`) disabled, and so we can assume that both the VIPs are on node 1 (`gluster2`). Let's take a look at the following commands:

```
root@gluster2:~# ip addr show eth0
3: eth1: <BROADCAST,MULTICAST,UP,LOWER_UP> mtu 1500 qdisc pfifo_
fast state UP qlen 1000
  link/ether fa:ce:27:f3:8d:50 brd ff:ff:ff:ff:ff:ff
  inet 192.168.1.3/24 brd 192.168.1.255 scope global eth0
  inet 192.168.1.30/24 brd 192.168.1.255 scope global secondary
eth0
  inet 192.168.1.20/24 brd 192.168.1.255 scope global secondary
eth0
```

```
        inet6 fe80::a00:27ff:fef3:8d50/64 scope link
           valid_lft forever preferred_lft forever
    root@gluster2:~#
```

8. Now, looking at `smbstatus` one more time, we should see our Microsoft Windows client connected to `gluster2` (node 1) as follows:

```
root@gluster2:~# smbstatus -np

Samba version 4.0.13
PID     Username    Group    Machine
------------------------------------------------------------------
--
1:26044 1500        1513     192.168.1.12 (ipv4:192.168.1.12:50116)
root@gluster2:~#
```

9. We need to wait until the copying process finishes; the following screenshot shows the end of our example copy:

Select Administrator: Command Prompt
C:\Users\administrator.POA>xcopy desktop\matrix.log z:\ /y
desktop\matrix.log
1 File(s) copied

10. Based on our previously calculated MD5 hash, we can validate if our failover routine had some impact on the consistency of our file/copy. So, we can execute the `md5sum` utility directly on one of our nodes to validate it, as follows:

```
root@gluster2:~# md5sum /var/lib/samba/glusterfs/data/matrix.log
eeaa7d4c17d5c6c86aa7aac57c3594db  /var/lib/samba/glusterfs/data/
matrix.log
root@gluster2:~#
```

[Browse to `samba.org` to watch some cool screencasts. There's even one on a procedure similar to the one presented here. There are some on CTDB and failover scenarios too [54].]

11. Exactly the same! We have a robust solution, which can scale as well, based on the distributed nature of `glusterfs`. This kind of solution leverages administration flexibility and control much better, as well as availability and resilience for the services and all that leads to happier customers. To bring our cluster to the normal operation with all nodes in a healthy state, let's reenable our node 0 (the `gluster1` host) as follows:

```
root@gluster2:~# ctdb enable -n 0 && echo OK
OK
root@gluster2:~# ctdb status
Number of nodes:2
pnn:0 10.11.11.21      OK
pnn:1 10.11.11.22      OK (THIS NODE)
Generation:2123322465
Size:2
hash:0 lmaster:0
hash:1 lmaster:1
Recovery mode:NORMAL (0)
Recovery master:1
root@gluster2:~#
```

Summary

In this chapter, we learned how to create a highly available distributed file server using the Debian GNU/Linux distribution, Samba 4, and other very important components, such as CTDB, XFS, and GlusterFS. We have learned step-by-step procedures from the preparation of the operating system environment, installation of the needed software and dependencies (for example, libraries), to a custom compilation of the Samba 4 application itself.

We have presented the relationship between the different components and how to integrate and implement a proper solution that is robust, highly available, and scalable—all very important characteristics for the highly demanding IT environment. Finally, we executed tests and validations on the high availability and distributed nature of our file server. We even simulated an issue on a node to actually see the behavior of our environment and testify to the resilience of our network file services.

In the next chapter, we will take a look at the Samba's Python binding scripting interface and how we can become familiar with the language and internals of the Samba 4 code. We will also take our first steps into the journey of participation and collaboration in the Samba community.

9

The Samba 4 Python Scripting Interface

This chapter deals with new features of the Samba 4 Server and is focused on the coding of the Samba 4 software. This chapter is the most challenging one in the book as it involves programming and some explorative work as part of our quest and we learn about the Samba 4 code and some existing Python bindings. We will show and explain some excerpts of code as well as a full example of how to use this powerful API on a practical, day-to-day administration script. The following is a list of the topics we will cover in this chapter:

- Open source development and collaborative work
- Exploring and using the Python interface of the Samba 4 Server
- Introducing Samba 4 Python bindings
- Understanding the power of Python and the Samba 4 Server

Open source development and collaborative work

The Samba software and the newest and much-awaited, fully featured Version 4 is the result of a huge project that hides an effortless community and the hard work of hackers from all around the world [71]. No matter how many years I've been involved in open source software initiatives and all the collaborative work and amazing solutions resulting from many different open source projects, I'm still amazed at the dedication and passion these communities employ in building their code and support. Since the beginning of my career [70], I have always been involved in open source projects such as GNU/Linux, FreeBSD, and OpenSolaris. With respect to the last one, I could actually become a contributor for Open Highly Availability Clusters, with my code actually accepted in the mainstream and a book [57] about ZFS [58] published in Brazilian Portuguese. However, I have sent some patches/requests for other open source application software, and even for operating system features (such as the one for FreeBSD [56]).

Open source projects need the collaboration and participation of users, system administrators, developers, and many other individuals who want to be part of it and help with different projects—only that will ensure continuity. It will also help in delivering quality and essential software that today we have running and supporting countless solutions all around the world in different businesses and industries. The Samba project is no exception, and with its scripting interface binding (for example, Python), is a very productive and intelligent move on the part of the project's leaders as the ease-of-use and thus, short learning curve for using a scripting interface such as Python will surely help the project attract more developers quickly.

No software is created by itself; thus, there is a need for collaboration and to have a pulsing community surrounding it that is passionate, always growing, and interacting with users and other developers. The Samba project's leaders know this, and Python bindings as well as some components of the project that are actually written in Python is a clear move towards that objective. I hope this chapter helps the reader embrace this goal and open source ideal, facilitating the adoption, understanding, and participation of new contributors in this amazing project! If we can get at least one new Samba developer or an individual interested in participating in the development of a new feature or helping fix a bug that was incentivized and stimulated, then this book was worth writing!

Exploring and using the Python interface of the Samba 4 Server

Python [59] is a programming language that runs on various platforms and operating systems (for example, Microsoft Windows, GNU/Linux, Illumos [60], FreeBSD [69], Mac OS, and others). Python has some similarities with other interpreted programming languages such as Tcl, Perl, and Ruby, but includes some distinguishing features, such as [61] strong introspection capabilities, intuitive object orientation, full modularity (supporting hierarchical packages), and so on. Based on Wheezy 7.2, a Debian GNU/Linux distribution, we can start playing with Python and the bindings from Samba 4 very quickly. Let's just start looking at the package that already has the python modules ready for installation on Debian Wheezy:

```
root@addc:~# apt-cache show python-samba


Description-en: Python bindings for Samba
    Samba is an implementation of the SMB/CIFS protocol for Unix systems,
    providing support for cross-platform file sharing with Microsoft
Windows, OS X,
    and other Unix systems.  Samba can also function as a domain
controller
    or member server in both NT4-style and Active Directory domains.
  .
    These packages contain snapshot versions of Samba 4, the next-
generation
    version of Samba.
  .
    This package contains Python bindings for most Samba 4 libraries.
...
root@addc:~#
```

To search for packages on Debian GNU/Linux environments, we can use the `apt-cache search` command (for example, `apt-cache search python-samba`). In the command's output in the preceding code, we can see that the `apt-cache show` command is used to describe the `python-samba` package as this is the package that contains the Python bindings for most Samba 4 libraries. The Python programming language should already be installed in our operating system as many parts of the Debian GNU/Linux distribution depend on it (and actually, Samba too). We just need to install the Samba Python bindings package; but, before that, let's take a look at the Python interpreter without installing this extra package. We just need to issue the following command:

```
leal@addc:~$ python
Python 2.7.3 (default, Jan  2 2013, 13:56:14)
[GCC 4.7.2] on linux2
Type "help", "copyright", "credits" or "license" for more information.
```

The last line in the preceding code is the Python interpreter prompt, which tells us that the programming tool is ready. Now let's do some exploration and understand some important commands that will help us with Python programming in a more general sense. By issuing the following `dir()` function, we can find out the modules available on the system:

```
>>> dir()
['__builtins__', '__doc__', '__name__', '__package__']
>>>
```

This is an important command to know when working with Python. As you can see in the preceding output, when we have just the built-in and default modules loaded, the output for the `dir()` command should be similar to the previous output. As we have not installed the `python-samba` package, we do not have any `samba` package available to load in the Python interpreter. So, let's quit the Python interpreter and install the `python-samba` package as follows:

```
>>> quit()
leal@addc:~$ sudo apt-get install python-samba
[sudo] password for leal:
...
Setting up python-samba (4.0.0~beta2+dfsg1-3.2) ...
leal@addc:~$
```

> Modules in Python implement the different functions that are available. For example, the `__builtin__` module implements the `dir()` function that we are using.

Now we can start the interpreter again and look at the modules available one more time:

```
leal@addc:~$ python
Python 2.7.3 (default, Jan  2 2013, 13:56:14)
[GCC 4.7.2] on linux2
Type "help", "copyright", "credits" or "license" for more information.
>>> dir()
['__builtins__', '__doc__', '__name__', '__package__']
>>>
```

Not exactly what we were expecting, as we still do not have anything about Samba on the modules listing. However, that is another important nugget of knowledge about how Python works; as we have just now installed the `python-samba` module, we have only made it available in our operating system environment, but have not loaded it yet. In order to use it, we need to load it on Python and for that, we use the `import` function:

```
>>> import samba
>>> dir()
['__builtins__', '__doc__', '__name__', '__package__', 'samba']
```

We can see that we have used the `import` command to load the `samba` package; after this, we can execute the `dir()` function and finally see our `samba` module listed at the end just after the default loaded modules. We have the module installed and loaded in Python, but now what? How do I know what functions are available? How will I use them? We will answer these questions in the following sections.

Introducing Samba 4 Python bindings

Another use of the `dir()`command is to list the functions and variables available on each module we have loaded on Python. We will issue this command in the Python interpreter as follows:

```
>>> dir(samba)
['Ldb', 'MAX_NETBIOS_NAME_LEN', '_Ldb', '__builtins__', '__doc__', '__
docformat__', '__file__', '__name__', '__package__', '__path__', '_glue',
'_ldb', 'check_all_substituted', 'dn_from_dns_name', 'ensure_external_
module', 'generate_random_password', 'get_debug_level', 'import_bundled_
package', 'in_source_tree', 'interface_ips', 'is_valid_netbios_char',
'ldb', 'nttime2string', 'nttime2unix', 'os', 'param', 'read_and_sub_
file', 'samba', 'set_debug_level', 'setup_file', 'source_tree_topdir',
'strcasecmp_m', 'strstr_m', 'substitute_var', 'sys', 'unix2nttime',
'valid_netbios_name', 'version']
```

So, we used the `dir()` function by passing an argument with it (for example, `samba`), and so the output was different. If we call it without passing arguments, it returns the names in the current scope (best effort [67]); but, with arguments (and depending on the argument), it may return the module's attributes or its class attributes. Thus we can dig deeper and get more information using the `dir()` function on one of the preceding attributes and look deeper into the Samba module. We are making progress, and now let's go one step further. We will continue to use the `dir()` function, but now we will pass one of the names we received in the previous output as an extra argument:

```
>>> dir(samba.MAX_NETBIOS_NAME_LEN)
['__abs__', '__add__', '__and__', '__class__', '__cmp__', '__coerce__',
'__delattr__', '__div__', '__divmod__', '__doc__', '__float__', '__
floordiv__', '__format__', '__getattribute__', '__getnewargs__', '__
hash__', '__hex__', '__index__', '__init__', '__int__', '__invert__',
'__long__', '__lshift__', '__mod__', '__mul__', '__neg__', '__new__',
'__nonzero__', '__oct__', '__or__', '__pos__', '__pow__', '__radd__',
'__rand__', '__rdiv__', '__rdivmod__', '__reduce__', '__reduce_ex__',
'__repr__', '__rfloordiv__', '__rlshift__', '__rmod__', '__rmul__',
'__ror__', '__rpow__', '__rrshift__', '__rshift__', '__rsub__', '__
rtruediv__', '__rxor__', '__setattr__', '__sizeof__', '__str__', '__
sub__', '__subclasshook__', '__truediv__', '__trunc__', '__xor__', 'bit_
length', 'conjugate', 'denominator', 'imag', 'numerator', 'real']
```

We recognize the methods from the preceding output, and so `MAX_NETBIOS_NAME_LEN` should be an `int` object. We can confirm this by just issuing the following command:

```
>>> dir(int)
['__abs__', '__add__', '__and__', '__class__', '__cmp__', '__coerce__',
'__delattr__', '__div__', '__divmod__', '__doc__', '__float__', '__
floordiv__', '__format__', '__getattribute__', '__getnewargs__', '__
hash__', '__hex__', '__index__', '__init__', '__int__', '__invert__',
'__long__', '__lshift__', '__mod__', '__mul__', '__neg__', '__new__',
'__nonzero__', '__oct__', '__or__', '__pos__', '__pow__', '__radd__',
'__rand__', '__rdiv__', '__rdivmod__', '__reduce__', '__reduce_ex__',
'__repr__', '__rfloordiv__', '__rlshift__', '__rmod__', '__rmul__',
'__ror__', '__rpow__', '__rrshift__', '__rshift__', '__rsub__', '__
rtruediv__', '__rxor__', '__setattr__', '__sizeof__', '__str__', '__
sub__', '__subclasshook__', '__truediv__', '__trunc__', '__xor__', 'bit_
length', 'conjugate', 'denominator', 'imag', 'numerator', 'real']
>>>
```

Bingo[62]! Any similarity is not just mere coincidence. Before we continue looking deeper, let's just print the integer number to recognize `MAX_NETBIOS_NAME_LEN`:

```
>>> print samba.MAX_NETBIOS_NAME_LEN
15
>>>
```

That is another beautiful feature of the Python language: we just used `print` and the `int` object, and we got the result (that is not so simple for some other programming languages). It's really intuitive and as you start to play with the language, you will see that it's really simple, and that is one of the reasons we have so many hackers addicted to it. So, in the preceding code, we have the `samba` package defining the maximum name length for NetBIOS[63]. Thus, we can use it just as we implement any program to execute an administrative task and validate the machine's NetBIOS name, for example. As a learning example, let's dig even deeper and use another important built-in function called `help()` on the Python interpreter, following the same utilization pattern of the `dir()` function. Have a look at the following example:

```
>>> help(int)
Help on class int in module __builtin__:


class int(object)
 |  int(x[, base]) -> integer
 |
 |  Convert a string or number to an integer, if possible.  A floating
point
 |  argument will be truncated towards zero (this does not include a
string
 |  representation of a floating point number!)  When converting a
string, use
 |  the optional base.  It is an error to supply a base when converting a
 |  non-string.  If base is zero, the proper base is guessed based on the
 |  string content.  If the argument is outside the integer range a
 |  long object will be returned instead.
 |
 |  Methods defined here:
 |
 |  __abs__(...)
 |      x.__abs__() <==> abs(x)
 |
  ...
```

In the preceding code, we have used the `help` function to show us the documentation for the `Int` class. At the end of the code, we can see that we have listed the methods available for any object of that class, and if we want to, we can use the `help()` method for specific methods to know how we can use it:

```
>>> help(int.__add__)
Help on wrapper_descriptor:
__add__(...)
    x.__add__(y) <==> x+y
(END)
 >>>
```

We can use the methods in a very straightforward way and we can see them in action as follows (for example, `print samba.MAX_NETBIOS_NAME_LEN+5`):

```
>>> print samba.MAX_NETBIOS_NAME_LEN.__add__(5)
20
>>>
```

In our findings, we were expecting a function called `generate_random_password` that can be handy if the name suggests exactly what it does. Let's take a look at the documentation for it as follows:

```
>>> help (samba.generate_random_password)
Help on built-in function generate_random_password in module samba._glue:


generate_random_password(...)
    generate_random_password(min, max) -> string
    Generate random password with a length >= min and <= max.
(END)
>>>
```

It seems really easy to use—actually too easy to be true—so let's try it:

```
>>> print(samba.generate_random_password(15, 20))
ccOy$fxyY[T49k-c
```

That's it! We just call it by passing a minimum and a maximum length for the new generated password, and it's done. The extra aspect of this function is that it will generate a password that satisfies the minimum requirements for the Microsoft Windows OS (for example, special characters). We can create a quick and dirty Python script to use a handy function. First, let's use the `quit()` method in our Python interpreter as follows:

```
>>> quit()
leal@addc:~$
```

> The classes and methods are case sensitive, so we need to pay attention when searching and using specific functions, or we may get the results or information about a subject that is different from the one we are really running a search for.

Now, just type the following command in the shell prompt:

```
leal@addc:~$ python -c "import samba; \
print(samba.generate_random_password(15, 15))"
7LuApNZi4JWx!f-
leal@addc:~$
```

Cool, isn't it? If you have some issues with creating random passwords or want to create a batch of users and one specific password for each one, this function can be a good partner for the job. I'm sure you already have many ideas about how to explore these Samba 4 Python bindings, and in the next section we will take this to a new level!

> The `generate_random_password` function is implemented on the `samba._glue` function where Python bindings for miscellaneous Samba functions reside (for example, `help (samba._glue)`).

Understanding the power of Python and the Samba 4 Server

Now that we already know how to explore the Python interpreter and the Samba 4 Python bindings, we will explore another great feature of the open source community: the source code. I think a general rule for learning programming, and it really works for me, is to actually look at the source code and learn from the examples. The Samba 4 source code has a lot of examples and scripts used to run tests on the compiled server, which we can use to learn many things. The example code combined with our technique to explore the modules and documentation should be sufficient for us to create a full piece of code that we can be proud of.

It seems there was a bug on Debian GNU/Linux-based distributions regarding the `libauth4.so` library [64]. If you face any issues loading some Samba 4 Python bindings, try to install the `libdcerpc-server0` package (for example, `apt-get install libdcerpc-server0`). The idea is to show an approach where we can go from zero to hero. So, the assumption is that we do not know much about Python programming. We just need some understanding of the working of the Samba 4 Server, and some knowledge about operating system and programming languages in general. We want to try our luck with the Samba development for our own utilization and maybe to help the community and make our contribution to the future.

Our objective is to implement a Python script that can be used to query our Samba Server, and for that, we have some idea of the functions we need to use to accomplish our task (for example, connection/authentication and query/search). What I normally do for such tasks is first use the Python interpreter to explore and test the modules and functions and flex the muscles as hard as I can. The point here is to try your best to understand the internals of the language you're learning; because that can give you excellent results if you can actually figure out how it works. Secondly, as it is not possible to fully understand the concepts directly from the documentation or if it is just missing that glue to simply make everything make sense, then it's time to look at some examples and dig into the source code to see how the developers have actually implemented it. We cannot forget that every open source community has discussion mailing lists and IRC channels where many enthusiasts are willing to help everybody [72]. I think that the most important point is that everyone is different, and so I will go through a procedure that has worked for me, but feel free to adapt to your personal preference; the essential point is to be loyal to whatever works for you and makes you feel more comfortable and confident.

Don't be afraid to make mistakes, or being restricted to some programming conventions and all that stuff from the beginning. If you develop something that is useful for others, more experienced programmers will help you with tips on how to conform to any rules or make your code more readable. This comes with practice and time, so take your time and keep going! We already have some idea of the modules and functions available on the `samba` package, but what we have not discussed yet is some underlying implementations of packages, modules, and functions in Python [66]; this is a little over the top for our discussion here, so we will leave that theory for the reader as an exercise for the reader.

> The `dir()` function tries its best to gather information from the object's `__dict__` attribute, if one has been defined, and its `type` object.[67].

So, we cannot always have a complete picture of what is available just by using `dir()`, and if we look at the preceding reference about modules and the `import()` function, we will see that importing one package will not necessarily import all modules. In the references [65], we have a link for the online documentation about the Python API on Samba.

No more talk, let's code! To find our example source codes to learn about specific functions and techniques, we can execute the following script to first find the Python scripts on the Samba 4 source code tree:

```
leal@addc:~$ find workspace/samba-4.0.9/ -type f -name *.py -print
...
workspace/samba-4.0.9/buildtools/wafadmin/Tools/misc.py
workspace/samba-4.0.9/buildtools/wafadmin/Tools/gdc.py
workspace/samba-4.0.9/buildtools/wafadmin/TaskGen.py
workspace/samba-4.0.9/buildtools/wafadmin/ansiterm.py
workspace/samba-4.0.9/buildtools/wafadmin/Logs.py
workspace/samba-4.0.9/buildtools/wafadmin/__init__.py
workspace/samba-4.0.9/buildtools/wafadmin/3rdparty/go.py
workspace/samba-4.0.9/buildtools/wafadmin/3rdparty/boost.py
...
leal@addc:~$ find workspace/samba-4.0.9/ -type f -name *.py -print | wc
-l
478
leal@addc:~$
```

As we can see in the preceding code, we have 478 Python scripts on the Samba 4 source code tree, and that is a good start. Many of them can be good sources of information about utilizing the Samba 4 Python bindings though some may not be of direct use to us at this stage. So, one tip is to actually try to find examples in the source tree, as they are more likely to have the information we need at the moment. A good guess is trying to find exactly these (for instance, `examples`):

```
leal@addc:~$ cd workspace/samba-4.0.9/ && echo OK
OK
leal@addc:~$ find ./ -type f -name *.py -print | grep -i example
./python/examples/winreg.py
./python/examples/netbios.py
./python/examples/dnsserver.py
./python/examples/samr.py
```

```
./lib/dnspython/examples/mx.py
./lib/dnspython/examples/reverse_name.py
./lib/dnspython/examples/ddns.py
./lib/dnspython/examples/e164.py
./lib/dnspython/examples/reverse.py
./lib/dnspython/examples/zonediff.py
./lib/dnspython/examples/xfr.py
./lib/dnspython/examples/name.py
./examples/logon/ntlogon/ntlogon.py
./examples/scripts/vfs/media_harmony/trigger_avid_update.py
./examples/scripts/shares/python/SambaParm.py
./examples/scripts/shares/python/SambaConfig.py
./examples/scripts/shares/python/smbparm.py
./examples/scripts/shares/python/generate_parm_table.py
./examples/scripts/shares/python/modify_samba_config.py
./source3/stf/example.py
leal@addc:~$
```

So, the preceding output has some interesting Python scripts for us to look at when seeking some light to be shed on specific functions. Usually, another good keyword to use when looking for examples is `test`. In the implementation of tests, we need to use the components, so we can try another filter in the first output as follows:

```
leal@addc:~$ cd workspace/samba-4.0.9/ && echo OK
OK
    leal@addc:~$ find ./ -type f -name *.py -print | grep -i test
...
./python/samba/tests/libsmb_samba_internal.py
./python/samba/tests/upgrade.py
./python/samba/tests/dsdb.py
./python/samba/tests/ntacls.py
./python/samba/tests/gensec.py
./python/samba/tests/getopt.py
./python/samba/tests/policy.py
...
leal@addc:~$
```

Well, as we find some `test` folders and our first task before executing queries is to connect/authenticate to the server, let's add another filter:

```
leal@addc:~$ cd workspace/samba-4.0.9/ && echo OK
OK
leal@addc:~$ find ./ -type f -name *.py -print | grep -i test | grep auth
./python/samba/tests/auth.py
./auth/credentials/tests/bind.py
./source3/torture/test_ntlm_auth.py
leal@addc:~$
```

The preceding output is really encouraging as we have just two files: one named `bind` the other named `auth`. Let's start looking at the `bind.py` script, and after going through the script's source code, we can quickly see the following excerpt (the file has just 42 lines):

```
ldb = samba.tests.connect_samdb(host, credentials=creds, lp=lp, ldap_
only=True)
```

The nice part about the preceding line of code is that it is not strange for us as we already know something about the `samba.tests.connect_samdb` construction. This is sufficient, I would say, to know that we need to focus on the `connect_samdb` part and not on `samba.tests`. So, let's look for that definition in the source tree:

```
leal@addc:~$ cd workspace/samba-4.0.9/ && echo OK
OK
leal@addc:~$ find ./ -type f -name *.py -exec grep -q "def connect_samdb"
'{}' \; -print
./python/samba/tests/__init__.py
leal@addc:~$
```

Looking inside the Python script file in the preceding code, we can identify the following relevant lines (inside the `connect_samdb` definition):

```
leal@addc:~$
...
    return SamDB(url=samdb_url,
    lp=lp,
    session_info=session_info,
    credentials=credentials,
    flags=flags,
    options=ldb_options)
...
leal@addc:~$
```

That's it! We have found the function definition that the `bind.py` script was calling and that function is doing the magic. Now that we know the exact method we need to call (for example, `SamDB`), let's look at the beginning of the same Python script file to find out which modules we need to load:

```
...
import samba
from samba import param
from samba.samdb import SamDB
```

Now we have something to start with to write our Python script; for now, just create a file (for example, `ch9.py`) with the following content:

```
#!/usr/bin/python
#byLeal
# Chapter 9 Example Script

# Loading...
import samba
from samba import param
from samba.samdb import SamDB

# Binding...
cx = (url='ldap://localhost',
    lp=lp,
    session_info=session_info,
    credentials=credentials,
    flags=flags,
    options=ldb_options)
```

As we can see in the preceding code, we have just changed the URL variable as it is the only information we know for now and we do not know yet exactly what the others are and how to properly configure them. So, let's continue looking at the `__init__.py` python script and look for the initialization of these variables to understand them and finish the first part of our code. At the beginning of the `connect_samdb` function, we have some interesting information as follows:

```
:param samdb_url: Url for database to connect to.
:param lp: Optional loadparm object
:param session_info: Optional session information
```

```
:param credentials: Optional credentials, defaults to anonymous.
:param flags: Optional LDB flags
:param ldap_only: If set, only remote LDAP connection will be created.
```

The preceding code gives us information about every variable; most of them are optional, so we will take them out of the running for now, except for the `credentials` function as we know that our server needs authentication. We can look at the code for initializing them and as authentication should be our next step, when we look for `credentials` in the code, we find the following:

```
..
    if credentials is None:
        credentials = cmdline_credentials
..
```

When we look for `cmdline_credentials`, we find the following:

```
cmdline_credentials = None
```

This is really not encouraging, so let's take a look at the Python interpreter to see whether or not we can figure out how to set the credentials without command-line parsing at this stage by running the following code:

```
leal@addc:~$ python
>>> from samba.credentials import Credentials
>>> dir(Credentials)
['__class__', '__cmp__', '__delattr__', '__doc__', '__format__', '__
getattribute__', '__hash__', '__init__', '__new__', '__reduce__', '__
reduce_ex__', '__repr__', '__setattr__', '__sizeof__', '__str__', '__
subclasshook__', 'authentication_requested', 'get_bind_dn', 'get_domain',
'get_gensec_features', 'get_named_ccache', 'get_nt_hash', 'get_password',
'get_realm', 'get_username', 'get_workstation', 'guess', 'is_anonymous',
'parse_string', 'set_anonymous', 'set_bind_dn', 'set_cmdline_callbacks',
'set_domain', 'set_gensec_features', 'set_kerberos_state', 'set_krb_
forwardable', 'set_machine_account', 'set_password', 'set_realm', 'set_
username', 'set_workstation', 'wrong_password']
>>>quit()
leal@addc:~$
```

The class has methods to set the username and password, and that should be everything we need. So, with the new things we learned, our updated code would look like the following:

```
#!/usr/bin/python
# Chapter 9 Example Script


# Loading...
import samba
from samba import param
from samba.samdb import SamDB
from samba.credentials import Credentials


badge = Credentials()
badge.set_username('Administrator')
badge.set_password('w1ndow$$!')


# Binding...
cx = SamDB(url='ldap://localhost',
    credentials=badge)
```

Let us now test the preceding code:

```
leal@addc:~$ chmod 755 ch9.py && OK
OK
leal@addc:~$./ch9.py
PANIC: assert failed at ../lib/param/loadparm.c(3790): lp_ctx != NULL
PANIC: assert failed: lp_ctx != NULL
Aborted
leal@addc:~$
```

We are on a mission and the preceding message is pretty interesting because it's related to the `loadparm.c` code and we had a `loadparm` argument (for example, `object`) in `SamDB`, but it was marked as optional. Based on the `PANIC` action in the preceding code (assertion failure, `lp_ctx != NULL`), it looks like one of two options: a *bug* or a *false* statement. If the `lp` object is optional, the Samba code seems to have a bug; on the other hand, if the `lp` object is really needed, the information about it being optional is a false statement. Well, looking for an answer to this situation, I found this reference [68], where developers are discussing it and the bottom line is that the `lp` object seems not to be optional at all as it loads some important definitions of the environment needed for many subsystems (credentials included). In the same link, we know the typical construction for using the `lp` object for the credentials that are mentioned as follows:

```
creds.guess(lp)


    In the file __initi__.py the variable lp is defined at the function
env_loadparm() like this:


def env_loadparm():
    lp = param.LoadParm()
```

Going back to our updated code, initializing the `lp` object (`LoadParm()`), and adding the `lp` object to the credentials and the `SamDB` call, we get the following code:

```
#!/usr/bin/python
# Chapter 9 Example Script

# Loading...
import samba
from samba import param
from samba.samdb import SamDB
from samba.credentials import Credentials

lp = param.LoadParm()
badge = Credentials()
badge.guess(lp)
badge.set_username('Administrator')
badge.set_password('w1ndow$$!')
```

```
# Binding...
cx = SamDB(url='ldap://localhost',
    lp=lp,
    credentials=badge)
```

Upon executing the preceding code, we get:

```
leal@addc:~$ ./ch9.py && echo OK
OK
leal@addc:~$
```

The preceding code is executed without errors, which is a good signal. Now that we have an authenticated connection, we can go to the next phase: performing a query. So, let's take a look at the `SamDB` call using our old friend `dir()` to see whether or not we have a `search` method using the following code:

```
leal@addc:~$ python
>>> from samba.samdb import SamDB
>>> dir(SamDB.search)
['__call__', '__class__', '__delattr__', '__doc__', '__format__', '__
get__', '__getattribute__', '__hash__', '__init__', '__name__', '__
new__', '__objclass__', '__reduce__', '__reduce_ex__', '__repr__', '__
setattr__', '__sizeof__', '__str__', '__subclasshook__']
>>>
```

We have it, so let's take a look at its documentation as follows:

```
>>> help(SamDB.search)
Help on method_descriptor:
search(...)
    S.search(base=None, scope=None, expression=None, attrs=None,
controls=None) -> msgs
    Search in a database.

    :param base: Optional base DN to search
    :param scope: Search scope (SCOPE_BASE, SCOPE_ONELEVEL or SCOPE_
SUBTREE)
    :param expression: Optional search expression
    :param attrs: Attributes to return (defaults to all)
    :param controls: Optional list of controls
    :return: Iterator over Message objects
(END)
>>>
```

We have everything we needed to know! Now let's execute our search, and in order to do so, we just add the following code to our Python script (leaving some optional parameters out of the equation):

```
# Search...
search_result = cx.search('DC=poa,DC=msdcbrz,DC=eall,DC=com,DC=br',
    scope=2,
    expression='(objectClass=user)',
    attrs=["samaccountname"])


    Let's test it to see if everything still executes without error:
```

```
leal@addc:~$ ./ch9.py && echo OK
OK
leal@addc:~$
```

In this case, we use the `dir()` function by just passing `SamDB` as an argument. We will see that it has one method named `domain_dn`. If we call it, we would get the following result: `poa,DC=msdcbrz,DC=eall,DC=com,DC=br`. Well, based on the documentation of the function, we need to iterate our `search_result` function to print all the attribute values we queried (for example, `samaccountname/usernames`). We can accomplish this in Python using a `for` loop, calling the `get` method on our results as follows:

```
# Results...
for username in search_result:
    print("User: %s" % username.get("samaccountname", idx=0))
```

We need to just add the preceding code to our `ch9.py` script and execute it like the following example to see the result:

```
leal@addc:~$ ./ch9.py && echo OK
...
User: djfox
User: joliu
User: kakim
User: lamei
User: root
OK
leal@addc:~$
```

The preceding output is something we are very familiar with, and so we are sure that our first script using the new Samba 4 Python bindings is fully working! How many lines of code were needed? 18 (without blank lines and comments).With 18 lines of code, we could create a useful script, and that just shows how important these Samba 4 Python bindings are. They leverage the participation of new individuals that are just starting with the programming, without them requiring a lot of knowledge, and this is really important to incentivize more and more people to feel capable of helping.

Summary

In this chapter, we learned the importance of the open source community and were introduced to the Samba 4 Python bindings. We used the Python interpreter to explore the Samba 4 Python bindings in a very intuitive way as well as learning some essential Python functions to get insights about packages, modules, and functions/methods. In the end, we learned how to use the source code to help us understand specific functions and implementation details. We used all these components to implement a step-by-step procedure in creating our first Python script that makes use of some Samba 4 Python bindings (for example, to connect to the Samba 4 Server at the local host, authenticate, and execute a simple query listing usernames from the base). We provided users a full, working example that can be useful for anyone who wants to start participating and collaborating, which is a real need for any open source community.

References

The following are the references used in this book:

[1] http://www.samba.org/samba/docs/man/manpages/idmap_rid.8.html

[2] http://www.opengroup.org/rfc/mirror-rfc/rfc86.0.txt

[3] http://wiki.samba.org/index.php/Samba4/FAQ

[4] http://technet.microsoft.com/en-us/library/cc773062(WS.10).aspx

[5] http://technet.microsoft.com/en-us/library/cc731620(v=ws.10).aspx

[6] http://technet.microsoft.com/en-us/library/cc771290(WS.10).aspx

[7] http://msdn.microsoft.com/en-us/library/windows/desktop/aa384649(v=vs.85).aspx

[8] http://technet.microsoft.com/en-us/library/cc753343(v=ws.10).aspx

[9] http://technet.microsoft.com/en-us/library/cc772168(v=ws.10).aspx

[10] http://support.microsoft.com/kb/276382/en-us?fr=1

[11] http://support.microsoft.com/kb/555636/en-us?fr=1

[12] http://blog.frli.se/p/dsct.html

[13] http://technet.microsoft.com/en-us/library/cc759550(v=ws.10).aspx

[14] http://wiki.samba.org/index.php/Samba4/HOWTO/Join_a_domain_as_a_DC

[15] http://wiki.samba.org/index.php/Samba

[16] http://www.samba.org/samba/history/samba-4.0.0.html

[17] http://en.wikipedia.org/wiki/DevOps

[18] https://www.samba.org/samba/news/releases/4.0.0.html

[19] http://technet.microsoft.com/en-us/library/ff625695%28v=ws.10%29.aspx

[20] http://support.microsoft.com/kb/2709568

[21] http://msdn.microsoft.com/en-us/library/windows/hardware/hh706306%28v=vs.85%29.aspx

[22] http://www.cups.org

[23] http://download.microsoft.com/download/5/c/3/5c331f2d-3c1e-40b8-a2ec-0282c047d201/Pointandprint.doc

[24] https://wiki.samba.org/index.php/Samba_as_a_print_server

[25] http://www.cups.org/documentation.php/options.html

[26] http://pen.iana.org/pen/PenApplication.page

[27] http://en.wikipedia.org/wiki/Database_schema

[28] http://technet.microsoft.com/en-us/library/cc759633%28v=ws.10%29.aspx

[29] http://technet.microsoft.com/en-us/library/cc756876%28v=ws.10%29.aspx

[30] http://msdn.microsoft.com/en-US/library/ms675087.aspx

[31] http://technet.microsoft.com/en-us/library/cc756876%28v=ws.10%29.aspx

[32] http://msdn.microsoft.com/en-us/library/cc223360.aspx

[33] http://wiki.samba.org/index.php/Samba4/Schema_extenstions

[34] http://technet.microsoft.com/en-us/library/cc961740.aspx

[35] http://msdn.microsoft.com/en-us/library/windows/desktop/ms676902%28v=vs.85%29.aspx

[36] http://msdn.microsoft.com/en-us/library/windows/desktop/ms677291%28v=vs.85%29.aspx

[37] http://www.oid-info.com/cgi-bin/display?nb=42768&father_oid=1.3.6.1.4.1&action=display

[38] http://technet.microsoft.com/en-us/library/cc731968%28v=ws.10%29.aspx

[39] https://bugzilla.samba.org/show_bug.cgi?id=6714

[40] http://technet.microsoft.com/en-us/library/testing-for-active-directory-schema-extension-conflicts%28v=ws.10%29.aspx

[41] https://oss.oracle.com/projects/ocfs/

[42] http://www.gluster.org/about

[43] http://ctdb.samba.org/

[44] http://www.gluster.org/community/documentation/index.php/Getting_started_common_criteria

[45] http://www.gluster.org/community/documentation/index.php/GlusterFS_Concepts

[46] http://en.wikipedia.org/wiki/Heartbeat_network

[47] http://en.wikipedia.org/wiki/RAID

[48] http://anonscm.debian.org/gitweb/?p=pkg-samba/samba.git;a=blob_plain;f=debian/samba.samba-ad-dc.init;h=3132d2e367675f822342a5b7bc2e50c046aa3b8f;hb=HEAD

[49] http://tdb.samba.org

[50] http://www.debian.org/releases/stable/i386/release-notes/ch-upgrading.html

[51] http://support.microsoft.com/kb/297510

[52] http://ctdb.samba.org/manpages/ctdb-tunables.7.html

[53] http://www.microsoft.com/resources/documentation/windows/xp/all/proddocs/en-us/xcopy.mspx?mfr=true

[54] http://www.samba.org/~tridge/ctdb_movies/

[55] http://www.samba.org/samba/docs/man/Samba-HOWTO-Collection/locking.html

[56] http://www.freebsd.org/cgi/query-pr.cgi?pr=54383

[57] http://www.brasport.com.br/informatica-e-tecnologia/banco-de-dados-br-2/zfs-para-usuarios-opensolaris-windows-mac-e-linux-br.html

[58] http://en.wikipedia.org/wiki/ZFS

[59] http://www.python.org

[60] http://wiki.illumos.org/display/illumos/illumos+Home

[61] http://www.python.org/about/

[62] http://en.wikipedia.org/wiki/Bingo_%28U.S.%29

[63] http://support.microsoft.com/kb/909264

[64] https://bugs.launchpad.net/ubuntu/+source/samba4/+bug/1048338

[65] http://www.samba.org/~jelmer/samba4/pydoctor/

[66] http://docs.python.org/2/tutorial/modules.html

[67] http://docs.python.org/2/library/functions.html#dir

[68] [PATCH] Add LoadParm optional parameter for Py_Credentials at http://marc.info/?l=samba-technical&m=129712320817955

[69] http://www.freebsd.org

[70] http://www.eall.com.br/

[71] http://www.samba.org/samba/team/

[72] https://lists.samba.org/

[73] https://wiki.debian.org/sudo

Index

S

U

V

W

[PACKT] open source
community experience distilled
PUBLISHING

Thank you for buying

Implementing Samba 4

About Packt Publishing

Packt, pronounced 'packed', published its first book "*Mastering phpMyAdmin for Effective MySQL Management*" in April 2004 and subsequently continued to specialize in publishing highly focused books on specific technologies and solutions.

Our books and publications share the experiences of your fellow IT professionals in adapting and customizing today's systems, applications, and frameworks. Our solution based books give you the knowledge and power to customize the software and technologies you're using to get the job done. Packt books are more specific and less general than the IT books you have seen in the past. Our unique business model allows us to bring you more focused information, giving you more of what you need to know, and less of what you don't.

Packt is a modern, yet unique publishing company, which focuses on producing quality, cutting-edge books for communities of developers, administrators, and newbies alike. For more information, please visit our website: `www.packtpub.com`.

About Packt Open Source

In 2010, Packt launched two new brands, Packt Open Source and Packt Enterprise, in order to continue its focus on specialization. This book is part of the Packt Open Source brand, home to books published on software built around Open Source licences, and offering information to anybody from advanced developers to budding web designers. The Open Source brand also runs Packt's Open Source Royalty Scheme, by which Packt gives a royalty to each Open Source project about whose software a book is sold.

Writing for Packt

We welcome all inquiries from people who are interested in authoring. Book proposals should be sent to `author@packtpub.com`. If your book idea is still at an early stage and you would like to discuss it first before writing a formal book proposal, contact us; one of our commissioning editors will get in touch with you.

We're not just looking for published authors; if you have strong technical skills but no writing experience, our experienced editors can help you develop a writing career, or simply get some additional reward for your expertise.

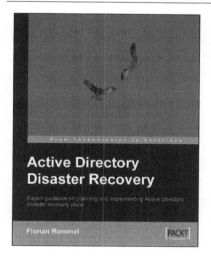

21905423R00158

Printed in Great Britain
by Amazon